The Wealth Paradox

The West is currently in the grip of a perfect storm: a lingering economic recession, a global refugee crisis, declining faith in multiculturalism and the rise of populist anti-immigration parties. These developments seem to confirm the widely held view that hardship and poverty fuel social unrest and, more specifically, scapegoating of minorities. Yet in this provocative new book, Mols and Jetten present compelling evidence to show that prejudice and intergroup hostility can be equally prevalent in times of economic prosperity, and among more affluent sections of the population. Integrating theory and research from social psychology, political science, sociology and history, the authors systematically investigate why positive factors such as gratification, economic prosperity and success may also fuel negative attitudes and behaviours. *The Wealth Paradox* provides a timely and important re-evaluation of the role that economic forces play in shaping prejudice.

FRANK MOLS is a lecturer in Political Science at the University of Queensland. His work, which brings together political science and social psychological theorising, has been published in leading international journals, including the *European Journal of Political Research*, *Political Psychology*, *West European Politics*, the *Journal of Common Market Studies*, *Public Administration*, *Evidence and Policy* and the *Australian Journal of Public Administration*.

JOLANDA JETTEN is Professor of Social Psychology at the University of Queensland. She has served as Chief Editor of the *British Journal of Social Psychology* and as Associate Editor for the *British Journal of Social Psychology*, *Social Psychology* and *Comprehensive Results in Social Psychology*. She was awarded the British Psychological Society's Spearman Medal in 2004 and the European Association of Social Psychology's Kurt Lewin Award in 2014.

The Wealth Paradox

Economic Prosperity and the Hardening of Attitudes

FRANK MOLS
University of Queensland, Australia

JOLANDA JETTEN
University of Queensland, Australia

CAMBRIDGE
UNIVERSITY PRESS

CAMBRIDGE
UNIVERSITY PRESS

University Printing House, Cambridge CB2 8BS, United Kingdom

Cambridge University Press is part of the University of Cambridge.

It furthers the University's mission by disseminating knowledge in the pursuit of education, learning, and research at the highest international levels of excellence.

www.cambridge.org
Information on this title: www.cambridge.org/9781107439139
DOI: 10.1017/9781139942171

First published 2017

Printed in the United Kingdom by Clays, St Ives plc

A catalogue record for this publication is available from the British Library.

ISBN 978-1-107-07980-9 Hardback
ISBN 978-1-107-43913-9 Paperback

Contents

Illustrations

Figures

Tables

Preface

The Western world appears to be in the midst of a perfect storm: the impact of a deep and protracted economic crisis has barely subsided when we are confronted with the largest movement of displaced people since World War II. No wonder there is a declining faith in multiculturalism and a growing concern about free markets, open borders and immigration – all creating the perfect conditions for the rise of far-right parties and populist movements seeking to persuade us, it is time to curb immigration. Similar developments can be witnessed in the United States where the issue of immigration has become politicised by President Donald Trump's election promise to build a wall on the US border to keep Mexican migrants out. Sentiments underlying opposition to Syrian refugees in Europe and Mexican immigrants in the United States appear to be identical: economic hardship and crises provide 'fertile soil' for radical right-wing parties and anti-immigration movements.

What is more, the popularity of parties such as the French Front National, the Belgian Vlaams Blok, the Swiss People's Party, and the Greek 'Golden Dawn' party is typically attributed unreservedly to growing hardship among low-income earners in cities and regions facing economic decline. However, what tends to receive little air-time is (a) that most of these parties rose to prominence in the 1990s, an era of unprecedented growth and prosperity, (b) that far-right parties were able to do exceptionally well in wealthy countries, such as Switzerland, Austria and Australia, and, perhaps most strikingly, (c) that these populist parties tend to attract voters with *above*-average incomes.

At the time of finalising this book in 2016, there were two landmark political events that would underscore the pertinence of our research into the link between affluence and the hardening of attitudes. The first event was the Brexit referendum in the United Kingdom on June 23rd, whereby the winning 'Leave' campaigners were accused of using deceptive populist tactics. The second event was Donald Trump's surprise victory on November 8th, which was seen as yet another triumph for populist politics. Unfortunately, given the timing of these events, it was impossible to include an analysis of them in this book. However, also here, the exit-poll analyses confirmed in both cases that populist parties and leaders can count on support from voters with *above*-average incomes.[1]

Even though these statistics are telling, it appears that rather than to take a broader historical perspective and to examine why populist parties enjoy popularity in times of economic prosperity and among more affluent voters, it has become more common to attribute the successes of successful far-right movements to the Global Financial Crisis (GFC) and its ramifications for ordinary citizens affected by the crisis. The idea that 'harsh times produce harsh attitudes' is of course not new, and can be found under different guises in different literatures. More importantly here, it continues to inform the vast majority of studies into social movements, contentious politics, far-right voting and outgroup hostility.

However, to view post-GFC events exclusively through this economic crisis lens would be to ignore growing empirical evidence that wealth and prosperity can *also* be associated with hostility towards other groups. If one starts to investigate these issues more systematically, there seems to be robust empirical evidence showing that intergroup hostility (and anti-immigration sentiments more specifically) can surge in times of economic prosperity, and among relatively affluent groups. When considering these trends, it becomes clear that the rise in living standards and general wealth, as experienced in most Western countries over the last two or three decades, has not increased tolerance for minorities in society. If anything, there appears to be a growing number of groups, movements and political parties openly advocating

---

[1] We elaborate these points in an online article entitled 'Why Brexit and Trump are NOT working class revolts' (ABC Religion and Ethics, 15 November 2016, www.abc.net.au/religion/articles/2016/11/15/4575585.htm). In this online publication we cite work by Dorling (2016), who analysed Brexit exit polls and found that two-thirds of those turning out to vote were middle-class. Of all those who voted 'Leave' 59% were middle-class (A, B or C1), as opposed to 24% of voters in the lowest two social classes (D, E). Likewise, Jonathan Rothwell and Pablo Diego-Rosell examined Gallup pre-election survey data and found that Trump voters earn *more* than average, not less. They are also less likely than non-voters to have been affected by globalisation and immigration.

anti-immigrant sentiments. Prime ministers and other political leaders have followed suit by openly declaring multiculturalism a failure. But why would prosperity be associated with hostility towards minorities rather than with greater tolerance?

In this book, we provide evidence for a 'wealth paradox'. We show that, ironically, wealth, prosperity and affluence may be associated with scorn for minorities and immigrants. Whereas the vast majority of books and articles examining hardening attitudes focus on material grievances among those at the bottom of society, our focus will be on the psychology of those who feel they are financially and materially *better* off than others. Although most of us will agree that life is easier for wealthier people, as we will show, the well-off have their own anxieties, and, as we will also show, these anxieties can just as easily translate into harsher attitudes towards those who are less well off.

We are aware that this proposition might seem to go against everything we thought we knew about the link between economic conditions and outgroup hostility. However, the empirical research evidence we present (which includes evidence that challenges the standard textbook interpretation of a link between the 1930s Great Depression and the rise of Nazi movement) demands a fundamental rethink: wealth and prosperity can, under some conditions, also be associated with hardening of attitudes and more negativity towards minorities.

In this book, we provide an analysis that offers a first step towards such a fundamental rethink. Drawing from classic social identity theorising, we explain the wealth paradox by focusing on *why* and *when* attitudes among the wealthy can harden. This analysis not only fills a clear gap, it also breaks new theoretical ground. We hope that this will trigger further theoretical innovation in an already well-established literature examining far-right voting, 'contentious politics', political and social attitude formation, anti-minority sentiments, group status and prejudice.

There are a few additional points to make about this book. First, our overview aims to be multidisciplinary and integrative. Even though many social scientists have theorised the relationship between the economic or social standing of a group and their tolerance towards immigrants, it is also fair to say that theoretical insights obtained in one discipline typically have little or no impact in other disciplines. In this book, we bring together and integrate work from across the social sciences (e.g. social psychological, sociological, historical and political sciences theorising). Second, and related to the first point, because we provide an analysis that draws on different fields of social science research, we have been able to study the wealth paradox at the micro, meso and macro levels, using different methods and theoretical concepts. We feel that, by drawing from and building on expertise in all these areas and at different levels, we have achieved real theoretical and empirical progress. As such, we hope that this book will galvanise work in this area and provide direction for future research.

Acknowledgements

Now that we have finished this book, we experience a strange mix of relief, exhaustion and pride. We hope that the latter will stay with us the longest. To indulge in that emotion, though, we also have to be very clear that there are many people who enabled us to feel proud now. This book is not an achievement of two people, but of many. The list of friends, colleagues and family members who were patient enough to listen to our ideas and who encouraged us is long, and it would be impossible to mention all of them by name. We will therefore limit ourselves to the ones that stand out in our memory as having been exceptionally generous with their time and support. We are very grateful for the input and valuable advice from our colleagues Tom Postmes and Russell Spears (both at the University of Groningen), and for the encouragement and feedback we received from our colleagues at home: Alex Haslam, Nik Steffens, Katie Greenaway, Tegan Cruwys and Kim Peters from the Social Identity and Groups Network (the SIGN team) at the University of Queensland. Special thanks go to Christine McCoy for the excellent administrative support she provided, and to our research assistants Coosje Veldkamp, James Schmidt, Michael Thai and Anh Thai (Hannibal) for their help with the research as well as the referencing and organisation of the many reprint permissions. We are grateful to the many honours students who build their research project around ideas presented in this book (Austin Chu, Marcus Goh, Nikita Healy, Rachel Ryan and Andrew Robinson); some of these student projects were essential for us to build our empirical case, and they are proudly presented here. We also would like to thank the editorial team at Cambridge University Press for their valuable feedback and for helping to get the book through production. We are also convinced that there would be no book had it not been for the financial support from the Australian Research Council (ARC,

DP1210053). We are very grateful for this. Last but certainly not least, we would like to thank our teenage daughters, Helen and Sophie, for their patience, and for having to put up with parents who frequently broke their promise not to 'talk shop' over dinner; we will try our best to improve.

What We Know (or Think We Know)

1 | *Recognising the Elephant*

'*Britain could return to racism as recession bites*' (The Telegraph, 19 January 2009)

'*UN chief: Bad economy threatens more racism*' (Fox News, 20 April 2009)

'*Europe: Economic crisis fuels rise in anti-immigration politics*' (Global Voices, 10 May 2010)

'*Economic crisis fueling racism in Europe, report warns*' (EU Observer, 27 May 2010)

'*Racial discrimination in the world of work is on the increase in the aftermath of the global economic downturn*' (International Labor Organization Magazine, August 2011)

'*Hard times lift Greece's anti-immigrant fringe*' (New York Times, 12 April 2012)

As the newspaper headlines opening this chapter illustrate, there was widespread concern in the wake of the 2008 Global Financial Crisis (GFC) that harsh economic times would trigger harsher attitudes towards minorities and immigrants. Such headlines, and the message conveyed in the corresponding articles, appeal to the conventional wisdom that those facing hardship are prone to 'lash out' and 'scapegoat' others. As a result, in times of economic recession, minorities can easily become the target of intergroup violence because they are regarded as a threat and deemed responsible for the misfortunes of the host society. On the one hand, such accounts rely on *relative deprivation* thinking: the notion that when the economy is in crisis or recession, or when there is downturn more generally, people become painfully aware that they are worse off than they were in the past. This reasoning, which relies on what became known as the *frustration–aggression* paradigm, suggests that hostility towards other groups represents the natural response displayed by people facing deteriorating socio-economic conditions and relative deprivation.

It is also possible, and very common, to look at this fear of growing racism and prejudice during times of recession as a *realistic conflict* problem: the shrinking pool of resources during an economic crisis intensifies competition over these scarce resources. In this struggle, and in this highly competitive labour and economic market, newcomers, immigrants and minorities are increasingly unwelcome. People typically rely on this logic to legitimise anti-immigration attitudes. For example, one British commenter, posting on a news website under the name 'James', remarked:

She [Merkel] wanted people from richer nations to embrace and train poorer region folk! It hasn't worked, its cost us all billions and it's getting more expensive year on year! Would you rather have a farmer from Romania working in Britain, claiming to be poor and sending all the money home to build a mansion! That's what's happening.[1]

At times, explanations for the hardening of attitudes towards immigrants focus not so much on relative deprivation or realistic conflict, but on so-called *symbolic threats* posed by immigrant. For example, it has become rather common to hear European leaders (e.g. German Chancellor Angela Merkel, British Prime Minister David Cameron, former Spanish Prime Minister Jose Maria Aznar) argue that multiculturalism has failed, that immigrants have not integrated successfully in their country and that newcomers should make more efforts to assimilate with the host society. For example, former French President Nicolas Sarkozy remarked in 2011:

We have been too concerned about the identity of the person who was arriving and not enough about the identity of the country that was receiving them.

This sentiment has been echoed by leaders elsewhere. For instance, in his 2010 autobiography, Australia's former Prime Minister John Howard reflects on cultural diversity in Australia, arguing that 'Multiculturalism is not our national cement'.

That being said, impactful events such as the GFC appear to have led to slightly different fears and anxieties in different societies. For example, recently, in the United States, Donald Trump's 2016 Presidential election campaign revolved around a powerful narrative focusing on 'making America great again', to be achieved by, among other things,

[1] From 'Europe: Economic crisis fuels rise in anti-immigration politics', translated by Ariane Defreine, Global Voices, 10 May 2012, http://globalvoicesonline.org/2012/05/10/europe-economic-crisis-fuels-rise-in-anti-immigration-politics/.

curbing immigration. This is not all that different from what happened in the immediate aftermath of the GFC. It has been argued that the post-GFC recession increased fear for racism and discrimination against African Americans. As Barbara Ehrenreich and Dedrick Muhammad observed in an article in the *New York Times* in 2009,

What do you get when you combine the worst economic downturn since the Depression with the first black president? A surge of white racial resentment, loosely disguised as a populist revolt. An article on the Fox News Web site has put forth the theory that health reform is a stealth version of reparations for slavery: whites will foot the bill and, by some undisclosed mechanism, blacks will get all the care.[2]

The observation that it is a diverse range of minority groups that become targets of discrimination and prejudice is not unique to the recent GFC. The idea of harsh times (i.e. relative deprivation and realistic conflict) producing harsh attitudes towards minorities and immigrants has been used to explain phenomena as varied as the rise of the Nazi movement in 1930s Weimar Germany, the revival of extreme right-wing parties in Europe in the 1980s, violence against the Roma minority in Hungary, violent attacks against overseas students studying in Australia, and growing support for radical 'white supremacy' movements in the United States. In each of these situations, we find support for the notion that poverty and harsh economic times produce harsh attitudes, resulting in increased intergroup conflict, racial violence and growing support for populist right-wing parties. As we discovered writing this book, this notion is widely accepted and challenged very rarely. The psychological process assumed to be at work in groups and societies facing deteriorating socio-economic conditions can be captured by the following hypothesised relationship between economic downturn and tolerance:

Hypothesis 1a. As societies become less affluent, public opinion should become less permissive and tolerant and, as a result, we should see a rise in anti-immigrant sentiments, xenophobia and prejudice.

It is not just that attitudes against immigrants and minorities will become more negative during a recession; there is also good evidence

---

[2] From 'The recession's racial divide' by Barbara Ehrenreich and Dedrick Muhammad, *The New York Times*, 12 September 2009, www.nytimes.com/20 09/09/13/opinion/13ehrenreich.html?pagewanted=all&_r=0

that the increased discrimination that minorities face during an economic recession is consequential and affects minority members' outcomes. For example, a 2011 study revealed that the recession took a greater financial toll on African Americans and Hispanics than it did on White Americans (Taylor, Kochhar, Fry, Velasco, & Motel, 2011). Of course, not all of these negative outcomes are necessarily the result of discrimination and exclusion. For instance, as these authors showed, part of the reason for these more negative outcomes for racial minorities was due to non-discrimination factors. As an example, their analyses revealed that African Americans and Hispanics were more likely to live in areas where house prices declined more sharply during the GFC and that African Americans and Hispanics had fewer investment savings than White Americans, leaving them more vulnerable to the economic recession (Taylor et al., 2011).

Despite this, there is also evidence that part of the reason that these groups have lost the most in the Great Recession is that exclusion and discrimination of these groups is on the rise during recessions – for example, individuals from minorities are less likely to be hired and they are more likely to be the first to be fired in times of recession, compared to majority members. For example, after analysing data from the Current Population Survey in the United States, economist Marlene Kim concludes that there is a widening gap between the unemployment rates of Asian Americans and Whites when comparing employment rates at the very beginning of the GFC in 2007 and 2008 with statistics in 2009 and 2010 (Kim, 2012). In other words, Asian Americans are more likely to become unemployed than Whites when the negative effects of the recession such as unemployment start to emerge.

Poverty and Harsh Attitudes

A similar rationale (a combination of relative deprivation and realistic conflict) underlies thinking about differences in attitudes towards immigrants among groups in society that differ in affluence. It is often argued, along these lines, that the poor – because they are particularly hard-hit in times of recession – will be most likely to develop anti-immigrant attitudes. For example, in 2013, economist Paul Donovan, cited in the *International Business Times*, argued:

Certainly the data is suggestive of the crisis breeding increased hostility to immigration, perhaps as lower income groups (correctly) perceive both their absolute and relative income levels as falling and seek an external scapegoat to blame for their predicament.[3]

In other words, according to this commonly used logic, the poor will be most dissatisfied during an economic crisis because they are most exposed to the negative effects of a recession, and, so the argument typically goes, xenophobia and prejudice will hence be more pronounced among the relatively poor (i.e. the lower strata of society). This leads to a second hypothesis on the relationship between wealth of a particular group in society and tolerance for minorities:

> **Hypothesis 2a.** Those at the bottom of the economic, social and financial ladder should be least tolerant and generous. This leads to relatively high anti-immigrant sentiments, xenophobia and prejudice among the poor.

The Other Side of the Coin

The benefit of translating received wisdom views into hypotheses is that it becomes much easier to recognise a bias in our thinking about anti-immigration sentiments and outgroup hostility: We tend to focus on the effects of economic decline and poverty (i.e. relative deprivation), not on the effects of economic prosperity and relative wealth (i.e. relative gratification). It thus appears that it is only in times of economic downturn that we start to worry about effects on attitudes towards immigrants and migrants, not in times of economic prosperity. Likewise, when explaining prejudice or support for radical anti-immigration parties, we seem to focus on attitudes of the poor, not on attitudes of the wealthy.

A quick Web of Knowledge search confirms this inkling. A search using the key words 'relative gratification' revealed only nine results, while many more articles were found (884 in total) when entering the search

---

[3] From 'The connection between economics and immigration, poor get poorer, more xenophobic' by Nat Rudarakanchana, 29 October 2013, *International Business Times*, www.ibtimes.com/connection-between-economics-immigration poor-get-poorer-more-xenophobic-1445788.

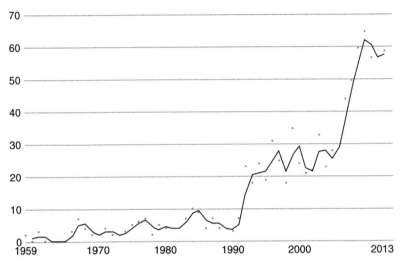

Figure 1.1. Number of articles when entering the search term 'relative deprivation' into a Web of Knowledge search, September 2014.

words 'relative deprivation' (see Figure 1.1), with the oldest papers being published as early as 1959. As Figure 1.1 shows, interest in the effects of economic hardship on outgroup attitudes has grown substantially over the last decade, and in particular in the wake of the 2008 GFC.

Even though the number of articles listed changes somewhat when other search terms are used (e.g. 'privilege'), regardless of the precise term, it is fair to say that the number of articles examining and explaining the effects of economic decline and poverty towards minorities far exceeds the number of papers examining such attitudes in times of economic prosperity or among the wealthy.

Xenophobia and prejudice are topics that have attracted a great deal of scholarly attention, with researchers having developed a keen interest in attitude formation under particular socio-economic conditions (crisis and perceived relative deprivation), and among particular groups in society (low-status groups). The picture that thus emerges is one in which the lower strata of society become regarded as representing a particularly volatile segment of society: as a class with considerable latent aggression, which will manifest itself in times of economic crisis and relative deprivation. The wealthier class, on the other hand is conceived (usually implicitly) as a more tranquil class that can afford to be generous and tolerant even when the economy slows down.

Why would it be the case that concerns about xenophobia and lack of tolerance are only attracting attention in some economic climates and in relation to some wealth groups? Why is it that periods of prosperity and wealthy groups in society have not been a topic of study when attempting to answer these questions? There may be a number of reasons for this. One obvious reason would be that when providing explanations for the rise of anti-immigrant sentiments, the focus is on factors that arouse fear, such as a declining economy. Conversely, because economic prosperity is perceived as a period of stability, the state of the economy is less likely to become the focus of attention to explain negative outcomes such as increased prejudice. Economic prosperity and wealth simply do not seem to spring to mind to the same extent as economic downturn and poverty do to explain rising anti-immigration sentiments or the hardening of attitudes towards minority groups.

However, as we will argue in this book, at best this focus may lead to an impoverished and skewed understanding of the effect of economic performance and wealth on attitudes towards minorities. At worst, the problem we are facing is akin to the one conveyed by the well-known Indian tale of 'the blind men and the elephant'. In this story, a group of blind men are asked to touch a large object and to guess what it is that they are touching. Because the men fail to examine and touch the elephant in its entirety and only touch parts of it, they are unable to correctly identify the object as an elephant. For example, one of the blind men examined the elephant's ear and concluded that he must be touching a rug because he felt something large, flat and leathery.

In line with the lesson conveyed by this old story, we should not focus on examining only *some* forms of economic performance and *some* wealth groups if we aim to develop a complete and accurate understanding of the way that economic performance of societies or groups impacts on attitudes towards minorities. As a first step, then, we need to return to Hypotheses 1a and 2a and articulate two additional hypotheses, ones that expand our horizon and draw attention to the aspect of the relationship that has been explored insufficiently in previous research. Rewording the first hypothesis, and turning the focus to economic prosperity rather than to economic downturn, Hypothesis 1a can be restated as follows (changes in italic):

> **Hypothesis 1b.** As societies become *more* affluent, public opinion should become *more* permissive and tolerant and, as a result, we should see a *drop* in anti-immigrant sentiments, xenophobia and prejudice.

Turning the focus to wealth and those at the top (rather than to those at the bottom of the financial ladder), Hypothesis 2a can be restated as follows (changes again in italics):

> **Hypothesis 2b.** Those at the *top* of the economic, social and financial ladder should be *most* tolerant and generous. This leads to *low* levels of anti-immigrant sentiments, xenophobia and prejudice among the *wealthy*.

The Wealth Paradox

Looking more closely at these hypotheses, it becomes immediately clear that even though Hypotheses 1b and 2b are the logical equivalent of Hypotheses 1a and 2a (assuming linear relationships), they do not have the same immediate appeal as Hypotheses 1a and 2a. Indeed, Hypotheses 1a and 2a appear to *ring true*, while Hypotheses 1b and 2b are less intuitive and more likely to raise eyebrows, especially among people who witnessed first-hand that the well-to-do are not always as generous and welcoming as their wealth affords them to be. By examining the flipside of the coin (wealth and outgroup hostility), this book will contribute to developing a more complete and more accurate understanding of the various forces fuelling anti-immigration sentiments.

The studies and findings presented in this book will enable us to shed new light on the question of when (and under which conditions) more affluent individuals and groups feel they can afford to show a more generous, caring side, and when such attitudes become overshadowed by fear of material losses and/or identity threat. As we will discuss in more detail in the following chapters, at the individual level there is a growing body of work suggesting that increases in wealth do not predict increases in relative giving to others (Giving USA, 2013). At a societal level, historical analyses show that intra-societal tensions are particularly pronounced when the economic tide is rising after a period of economic hardship (see Rudé, 1964; Tilly, Tilly, & Tilly, 1975). There is also robust empirical evidence that shows that intergroup hostility (and anti-immigration sentiments more specifically) can surge in times of economic prosperity, and among relatively affluent groups. Indeed, the rise in living standards and general wealth experienced in most Western countries over the last two or three decades has, paradoxically, not increased tolerance for minorities in society. If anything, there has been a marked increase in groups, movements and political parties openly advocating anti-immigrant sentiments, especially in Europe. This rise started in the 1980s and continued in the 1990s, well before the GFC (Wilson & Hainsworth, 2012), at a time when the economies of many Western countries were booming.

Finally, there are many examples which show that when there is a fertile ground for economic threat and relative deprivation effects to emerge, there is little evidence that attitudes towards immigrants and ethnic minorities become more negative. Let us unpack that a bit further. In the Netherlands, a recent report by the Social and Cultural Planning Bureau (SCP) entitled 'The social state of the Netherlands' mapped out economic developments over the last decade as well as changes in attitudes towards immigrants (Henry, 2013).[4] The findings were startling, and run counter to conventional wisdom views about when attitudes towards immigrants can be expected to harden.

Focusing on CBS unemployment data over the last ten years, it becomes obvious that unemployment declined in the period from 2002 until the GFC hit in 2008, after which unemployment steadily grew until the final measurement point in 2013 (see Table 1.1).

A similar story emerges when studying the responses to the question of what the average Dutch person perceives as the most important problems currently facing Dutch society (data from the European Union Commission). While concerns about the economy and unemployment steadily decline up until the Global Financial Crisis, these

---

[4] 'SCP: negatieve stemming over immigratie en integratie afgenomen' by René Moerland, 11 December 2013, *NRC Handelsblad*, www.nrc.nl/nieuws/2013/12/ 11/scp-negatieve-stemming-over-immigratie-en-integratie-is-afgenomen/

Table 1.1. *Shrinking Dutch economy: Fewer vacancies and paid jobs. Figures representing annual averages, with absolute numbers ×1000 and recalculated in FTE*

	2002	2004	2006	2008	2009	2010	2011	2012	2013
GDP Growth	0.1%	2.2%	3.4%	1.8%	3.7%	1.5%	0.9%	1.2%	
Volume of Work (in years)	5850	5699	5773	6013	5954	5892	5910	5858	5742
Jobs[1] (Employees)	7607	7472	7626	7972	7905	7862	7905	7847	7685
Jobs (Self-Employed)	1244	1250	1293	1315	1317	1328	1354	1399	1444
Unfilled Vacancies	150	119	206	240	143	122	133	112	97

[1] Including small part-time jobs of less than one day per week.

Source: CBS Statistics reported in Social and Cultural Planning Bureau report.

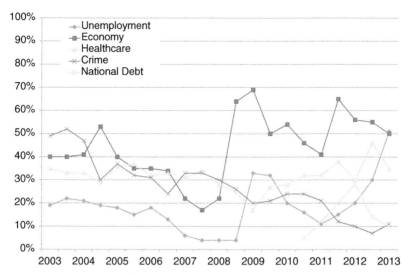

Figure 1.2. The top five most pressing issues according to the Dutch population aged 15 and over. Adapted from the Social and Cultural Planning Bureau showing Eurobarometer Survey findings.

concerns are clearly on the rise after the impact of the 2008 GFC (see Figure 1.2).

In its report, the Social and Cultural Planning Bureau presents additional data, data that are at odds with all hypotheses presented so far: in the Netherlands, over that same period of ten years, attitudes towards immigrants and ethnic minorities become *more positive*. For example, in Table 1.2 it can be seen that while 48% of a representative sample of Dutch people think in 2002 that 'there are too many people of another ethnicity in the Netherlands', only 32% of Dutch respondents agreed with this question in 2013 – a time when the impact of the GFC was particularly felt among ordinary people and when many Dutch people were concerned about the state of the Dutch economy (see Table 1.2).

These studies and data can be regarded as powerful reminders that we still know remarkably little about the attitudes and behaviour of the wealthy, and those in the process of acquiring greater wealth and prosperity. Why would prosperity be associated with hostility towards minorities rather than with greater tolerance? To date, research on the effect of wealth has been one-sided in its outlook, and in this book we

Table 1.2. *Views about non-Western immigrants in the Netherlands between 2002 and 2012, among people aged sixteen years or older. Percentages representing the proportion of participants indicating to agree somewhat or wholeheartedly*

	2002	2004	2006	2008/09	2010/11	2012/13
Ethnic Tensions						
There are too many people of non-Dutch origin living in the Netherlands	48%	47%	41%	39%	39%	32%
I would find it difficult if someone from another ethnic background moved in next door	57%	44%	40%	33%	37%	33%
Would find it difficult if my daughter decided to marry a man with a different ethnic background	–	68%	67%	61%	61%	58%
Residency						
The Government should be lenient when considering residency applications from asylum seekers	77%	81%	82%	85%	86%	85%
The Government should be lenient when considering residency applications from economic refugees	32%	35%	39%	47%	44%	45%
The Government should be lenient when considering residency applications from immigrants marrying a Dutch citizen	33%	32%	40%	44%	44%	48%

Perceptions about Muslims

Most Muslims in the Netherlands respect other cultures	–	32%	32%	41%	45%	52%
The West European and Muslim lifestyle are irreconcilable	–	45%	47%	40%	41%	44%
Muslim men dominate their women	–	82%	82%	75%	74%	75%
Muslims raise their children in an authoritarian way	–	65%	65%	55%	54%	58%

Source: Social and Cultural Planning Bureau (2013).

set ourselves the task rectifying this by examining (as a first step) support for Hypotheses 1b and 2b.

To be sure, we do not dispute that, under some conditions, harsh economic times and affluence can be associated with more hostility towards minorities. Rather, our argument is that wealth and prosperity can *also* engender outgroup hostility. However, as we will argue, the theoretical scope of existing approaches is limited in that they remain wedded to the idea that attitudes towards minorities harden when there is hardship.

In this book, we argue that the one-sided focus on the poor and on economic decline has, by implication, led to a neglect of what we describe as the 'wealth paradox': the notion that it is at times those who are best off who are least generous when it comes to helping others in need or when it comes to welcoming newcomers. The book will not only provide compelling empirical evidence showing that intergroup hostility (such as anti-immigrant sentiments) can be equally prevalent in times of economic prosperity, and among more affluent sections of the population, it will also offer a fresh theoretical look at why this might be the case.

The Structure of This Book

Our approach aims to be multidisciplinary and integrative, and this is reflected in the structure of this book. Many social scientists have theorised the relationship between the economic or social standing of a group and their tolerance of immigrants. However, theoretical insights obtained in one discipline typically have little or no impact in other disciplines. In this book, we bring together and integrate work from across the social sciences (e.g. social psychology, sociology, history and political science) and we examine the wealth paradox at the micro, meso and macro levels. By drawing from, and building on, expertise in all these areas, we hope to have achieved real theoretical and empirical progress. This book is divided into three parts, each consisting of a cluster of chapters. In short, the structure of this book is as follows:

Part I: What We Know (or Think We Know)

The idea that economic hardship fuels negative attitudes towards minorities forms the basis for theorising in social psychology, sociology, history and political science. In Chapter 2, we consider each of these literatures in search of the origins of the now pervasive ideas that (a) the poor are most likely to become frustrated and 'lash out', and (b) this propensity will manifest itself in times of economic crises. In other words, in Chapter 2 we trace the various stages in thinking about human nature, with a view to uncovering the intellectual origins of Hypotheses 1a and 2a.

Building on these insights, we then critically examine the empirical evidence for classic theorising, examining relative deprivation effects in Chapter 3. We expand our analysis by also focusing on economic prosperity and affluent groups in society (i.e. Hypotheses 1b and 2b). We draw two conclusions from reviewing this literature. First, the empirical evidence for Hypotheses 1a and 2a is rather mixed and inconclusive: negative attitudes towards minorities have been observed both in times of economic hardship *and* in times of economic prosperity. Even in contexts where one would expect strong support for Hypotheses 1a and 2a, there are many studies that show no relationship between economic performance and negative attitudes.

Second, and perhaps more interesting for our purposes, the review of the empirical findings leads us to conclude that there is also remarkably little support for Hypotheses 1b and 2b. Specifically, Hypothesis 1b is rarely supported, and negative attitudes towards minorities have often been observed in times of economic prosperity. Indeed, research has shown that those at the top of the social ladder are often less tolerant and generous than those who are less prosperous.

We conclude that while realistic conflict literature accounts well for the finding that economic hardship hardens attitudes, theoretically it cannot account for the finding that, at times, we find harshness towards minorities such as immigrants among people whose economic, financial and social status is relatively high.

Part II: Broadening Our Horizon: The 'Wealth Paradox'

In Part II, we start by examining the relationship between economic performance and attitudes towards immigrants and minorities at the societal level (Chapter 4). Specifically, we focus on the relationship between economic performance in a country on the one hand (using indicators such as GDP per capita and unemployment levels), and voting behaviour, attitudes towards minorities and the popularity of anti-immigrant parties on the other.

In Chapter 5, we examine the relationship between societal and group affluence on another outcome that can inform us about the generosity of those who are relatively prosperous – we examine at the macro-level a country's Overseas Development Aid (ODA) and charitable giving at the group and individual levels. Here too we see that, paradoxically, it is often not the ones who 'have most' who are most generous.

In the recognition that it is often not actual wealth that determines outcomes, but *perceived* wealth and *relative* wealth, in Chapter 6 we explore psychological processes associated with relative deprivation and relative gratification. We will present a series of laboratory studies where participants were made to feel relatively deprived or relatively gratified. Interestingly, this research shows evidence of a so-called v-curve – so named because the highest levels of hostility to minorities are often not just found among the poor, but also among the relatively wealthy (see also Dambrun, Taylor, McDonald, Crush, & Méot, 2006; Jetten, Mols, & Postmes, 2015).

We conclude this part by arguing that we need to examine these effects more closely, and, importantly, that we need to develop theorising to account for these apparently paradoxical findings. The final part of this book will aim to do exactly that.

Part III: Understanding the 'Wealth Paradox'

Once we have corroborated that the relationship between wealth and harsh attitudes is far from straightforward, the final section aims to better understand the processes underlying each of these effects. In Chapter 7 we critically evaluate support for Hypotheses 1b and 2b. The findings presented in this chapter run counter to Hypotheses 1b and 2b (as well as to the more general idea of harsh times producing harsh attitudes) and suggest that, paradoxically, prosperity can *also* harden attitudes. We will then review possible explanations for this wealth paradox and introduce the social identity approach as a theoretical framework that can help us to understand and explain this apparent paradox. We argue that social identity reasoning is particularly suited to help us explain how macro-level perceptions relating to the state of the economy, and how perceptions of the relative wealth and standing of one's group in society, affect attitudes towards other groups.

In Chapter 8 we develop our analysis further, thereby identifying the social identity processes underlying the wealth paradox. What we offer in this chapter is an attempt to pinpoint the conditions under which affluence is most likely to harden attitudes, and, conversely, the conditions under which the affluent will be most likely to display generosity and tolerance. We present a model that predicts that the wealth paradox will be found (a) when boundaries between groups in society are permeable and people (those who are affluent in particular) fear downward mobility, (b) when those who are (relatively) affluent worry that their wealth could vanish rather quickly (instability of wealth due to societal inequality or the fear that financial markets collapse tomorrow), or (c) when the affluent feel greater pressure to justify their wealth. In the latter case, prosperity fuels a sense of entitlement and narratives that justify the exclusion of those less well-off.

Finally, in Chapter 9 we argue that leaders have an important role to play in shaping collective self-definitions as competent, cold and harsh. We argue that leaders interpret socio-economic conditions creatively, and in a way that suits their political agenda. As we will see, leaders may develop powerful narratives to sustain threat perceptions in times of economic prosperity, thereby promoting particular 'us–them' categorisations. In these narratives, immigrants and newcomers are framed as the 'other', and as deviant humans whose values and interests are at odds with those of the host society. At times, leaders can lead us to believe that our wealth is under threat when there is very little evidence suggesting that this is indeed the case. For example, in Australia, the narratives of the country facing a 'tsunami of boat people' took hold in the media and dominated the political debate in the lead-up to the 2013 Federal elections, despite the fact that country-level statistics showed the issue had been grossly exaggerated (Lusher & Haslam, 2007; Mols & Jetten, 2016).

In sum, there is still much to learn, and we might be forgiven for not seeing the elephant up until now. However, it is clear we need to get to know this elephant better, and we hope that this book will help us to achieve that theoretical aspiration.

2 | *Tracing the Origins of 'Harsh Times' Assumptions*

We started the previous chapter with a series of news headlines which all conveyed a warning that tensions between groups in society can be expected to rise as a result of economic decline. What these warnings have in common is that they perpetuate the widespread assumption of a direct and causal link between economic decline and more negative attitudes towards minorities such as immigrants and ethnic minorities. In the previous chapter, we unpacked this assumption and formulated four hypotheses that flow from this reasoning. The following diagram provides a visual representation of the underlying assumptions.

The idea that intergroup tolerance erodes in times of economic crisis (H1a), and in particular among working class people (H2a) is often presented in news stories and public statements as 'self-evident' and no longer requiring further explanation. This is, so the reasoning goes, because poverty and economic crises form 'fertile soil' for frustration and dissatisfaction. According to classic frustration–aggression thinking (Dollard, Doob, Miller, Mowrer, & Sears, 1939), this then triggers a simple causal chain whereby deprivation causes frustration, which, in turn, causes aggression and hostility towards other groups.

The roots for such thinking can be traced back to a large body of historical research into revolutions and uprisings. According to these accounts, it is in times of economic crisis and among the poor that we should find that relative deprivation and realistic conflict will be felt most strongly. From here, it is a small step to also assume that it is therefore poverty and deprivation that triggers hostility towards vulnerable groups and minorities such as immigrants: the poor not only take their aggression out on the group that is oppressing them, but also on other groups that compete with them for scarce resources.

In this chapter we aim to stimulate debate about these assumptions by critically examining the support for them. We propose that although there is abundant historical evidence suggesting that events *can* follow

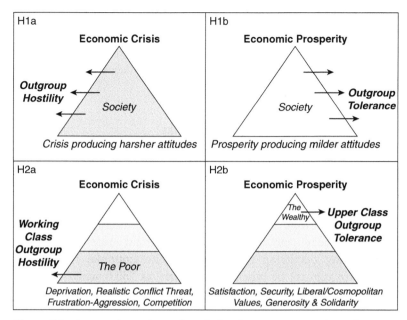

Figure 2.1. Assumptions about the relation between economic performance and attitudes towards minorities; four hypotheses.

this course, to accept this as the rule is to overlook interesting counterfactuals, such as evidence that popular uprisings were often less 'grassroots' than popular accounts would have us believe. What is more, people from relatively well-to-do circles often played a prominent leadership role during revolutions and uprisings. In other words, and undermining simple frustration–aggression accounts, it is not always poor individuals and groups who appear to be at the forefront of popular uprisings that are characterised by hostility and aggression towards outgroups. Instead, at times, it is people who are least likely to experience deprivation who are leading revolutions or are instigating unrests.

If we decouple the proposed automatic relationship between economic decline and poverty on the one hand and frustration and aggression on the other, then we must also reconsider the notion that hostility towards minority groups (such as immigrants) is predominantly a deprivation problem and a working class affair, with material deprivation being considered the root-cause. However, before we get ahead of ourselves, to be able to do the latter with some confidence, we first need to critically review the evidence for the origins of this thinking. It is only after such a review that we can strengthen our call for a thorough re-examination of the empirical evidence on which these pervasive assumptions rest.

Hardship and Early Workers Uprisings

The Industrial Revolution, which is said to have begun in England in the 1760s, had a profound impact on society, and in particular on industrial cities, which became home to a rapidly growing urban working class. It is generally accepted that living and working conditions worsened over time, eventually producing a pressure to rebel. However, there is historical evidence of workers' uprising occurring much earlier. For example, in England there were reports of rebellions as early as 1710 when Keelmen went on strike in the port of Tyne and Wear in protest against rising food prices. Likewise, in 1727 there were reports of tin miners plundering the granaries at Falmouth. Or consider the Luddites, a group of English textile artisans, who rebelled against poor living and working conditions by attacking factory owners and sabotaging the production process. The Luddite rebellion, which was eventually crushed with help of the British Army, can be seen as one of many examples showing that (consistent with H1a) harsh economic conditions can indeed produce intergroup hostility and conflict.

The main problem with this assumption, though, is that it reduces the need to explore other factors that contributed to these events. For example, by accepting this explanation, we easily overlook the role of affluent local elites. A case in point here is the 1819 *Peterloo Massacre* in Manchester, which saw a crowd of approximately 60,000 people taking to the streets to voice their grievances. The protests, initiated in 1817 by a group of disgruntled weavers, ended when the Cavalry charged into the crowd, killing 15 protestors and injuring many more. Although grievances about poor working and living conditions certainly played an important part, to label this a *workers'* uprising is to gloss over the fact that those leading the protests (e.g. Samuel Bamford) were rather affluent. Furthermore, the protestors who rallied around

Figure 2.2. A painting of the Peterloo Massacre, published in 1819 by Richard Carlile, one of the invited speakers at the rally, and founder of the radical newspaper *The Republican*.

him pursued *political* aspirations, namely securing greater parliamentary representation (Parssinen, 1973, p. 516).

Even though historians have a good and sophisticated understanding of the role of elite leaders and the material versus ideational factors fuelling uprisings, the nuances of their analyses are easily lost when words like 'revolution', 'insurrection', 'rebellion' or 'uprising' are used to classify or commemorate these events. Take the example of the 1820 Scottish Insurrection in Glasgow (also referred to as the 1820 Radical War). As historians have shown, the financial burden of almost 25 years of war with Napoleonic France resulted in a severe depression in the UK and Scotland, accompanied by high unemployment. The result was a significant decline in wages and rapid deterioration of working- and living conditions. Here too the label 'insurrection' evokes images of a spontaneous outburst of working class aggression, fuelled by frustration about the economic crisis and targeted at those in power. However, once again, what should not be ignored is the importance of political ideals, and the fact that leaders from the higher echelons of society played a crucial role in arousing emotions and in articulating these ideals.[1] To appreciate this, one only needs to consider the official proclamation issued by the leadership of the rebellion on 1 April 1820, which read:

> Friends and Countrymen! Roused from that torpid state in which we have sunk for so many years. We are at length compelled, from the extremity of our sufferings, and the contempt heaped upon our Petitions for redress to assert our Rights, at the hazard of our lives: and proclaim to the world the real motives, which (if not misrepresented by designing men, would have United all ranks), have reduced us to take up arms for the redress of our Common Grievances.
>
> ... Our principles are few, and founded on the basis of our Constitutions, which were purchased with the dearest blood of our ancestors, and which we swear to transmit to posterity unsullied, or perish in the Attempt – Equality of Rights (not of Property,) is the object for which we contend, and which we consider as the only security for our liberties and lives. Let us show the world that we are not that Lawless, Sanguinary Rabble, which our Oppressors would persuade the higher circles we are – but a brave and generous people, determined to be free. (Cited in Pentland, 2015, p. 97)

Historians may have gone to great lengths to explain that a popular uprising was fuelled by a combination of factors, but this is not necessarily how the events in question are being remembered in popular textbooks and television documentaries. A possible contributing factor (apart from misleading terminology) is that famous revolutions, rebellions and uprisings often began with protests by disgruntled manual workers, before escalating into large-scale civil unrest, and before wealthier political activists became involved. For example, in 1830 there was an uprising of angry silk workers in the French city of Lyon, which became known as the *La Révolte des Canuts* (The Silk Workers Rebellion). The conflict started over decreasing wage levels, with silk workers taking to the streets, and riots erupting when

---

[1] Other examples include England's famous 'Glorious Revolution' of 1688, which did not involve a popular uprising, as one might be inclined to think, but an uprising of Parliamentarians seeking to overthrow James II. Likewise, the equally famous 'Irish Rebellion' of 1798 was not an uprising of workers or farmers, as the word rebellion would seem to suggest, but the uprising by liberal sections of the ruling elite, who found inspiration in the American Revolutionary War of 1775–1783 (Kearney, 1997, p. 6).

manufacturers refused to meet their demands. This uprising eventually spread to Paris, where it culminated in the anti-monarchist 1832 'June Rebellion' (Traugott, 2010). Here, Parisian Republicans, inspired by General Jean Lamarque's Republican ideals, took to the streets to protest against Louis Philippe's succession to the throne.

To be sure, between 1828 and 1932, France was in the grip of a severe economic crisis, brought about by, among other things, costly wars and harvest failures (Harsin, 2002). It is clear that it was the poor in particular who suffered the most and that protest was a way to express their frustration. However, to attribute the June Rebellion entirely to these economic conditions is to overlook that the rebellion gradually turned into a contest between two elite groups: Monarchists and Republicans.

Interesting too, the June Rebellion formed the inspiration for Victor Hugo's seminal play *Les Misérables*, in which Hugo defends the Republican cause and takes on the plight of the deprived. It is plausible that this play, with its graphic depiction of deprived city dwellers resorting to violence, strengthened the belief that uprisings and out-group hostility are a working class affair. The same can be said about Emile Zola's famous 1885 novel *Germinal*. The book tells the tale of extreme poverty and deprivation suffered by miners in Northern France and provides a vivid account of how news that working condition were set to get even worse unleashed extreme rage among the miners.

In sum, in romanticised popular accounts of historic events (e.g. Hugo's *Les Misérables*, Zola's *Germinal*), the image of grass-roots working class rebellions is alive and well. They reinforce the notion that violence reflects a natural human response to economic hardship – a response that is to be expected when people are 'doing it tough'. What may also have contributed to the popularity of these accounts is the fact that those working from a Marxist perspective later interpreted (or perhaps misinterpreted) these events retrospectively as early evidence of growing class-consciousness.

Once again, we do not dispute that economic deprivation *can* fuel outgroup violence, and the above-mentioned examples show this. However, elite-level factors often receive little or no air-time in these popular accounts, and it is thus not surprising that there continues to be such widespread belief in a direct link between economic crisis and societal unrest (Hypothesis 1a), and that it will be the working class rather than the middle or upper class that will become most agitated in times of crisis (Hypothesis 2a).

The French Revolution: The Exception That Proves the Rule?

Whereas, in popular accounts, economic hardship is typically presented as the root-cause of early workers' uprisings, this is not at all the case when considering what is arguably the most famous uprising of all times: the 1789–1799 French Revolution. In this instance we see the exact opposite pattern: a tendency to describe these events as propelled almost exclusively by republican political ideals, thereby glossing over the fact that, in this instance, material factors played a *more* important role than popular accounts would lead us to believe.

As several authors have noted, the French Revolution started with poor Parisians taking to the street to protest against growing food shortages and excessive bread prices (Graham, 1977; Hufton, 1971). Rather than pointing to these economic factors, or to the sources examining these economic factors, the prevailing popular narrative about the French Revolution is one that conveys and perpetuates the romantic image of ordinary Parisian citizens taking to the streets en masse to voice *political* grievances.

Why is it that, in this particular instance, the usual 'deprivation–frustration–aggression' link is not being invoked? And why is there such emphasis, in this instance, on elite-level factors? In our view this is because the French Revolution became regarded as an important – if not *the* most important – history-making moment shaping French citizenship and national identity. In other words, the French Revolution became remembered not as yet another popular uprising fuelled by economic hardship, but as the event that marked the birth of the French 'nation' and the breakthrough of enlightenment ideals such as human rights, democracy and popular sovereignty.

Put differently, the French Revolution appears to have become remembered as a unique 'sui-generis' experience of historic significance for France as well as for European civilisation more generally. From that perspective it is not surprising that, in this instance, economic factors hardly feature in popular accounts of these events. After all, to draw attention to economic factors would be to point to material self-interest, to render the event less glorious and more mundane and, ultimately, to challenge the widespread assumption that the uprising was about '*liberté, egalité et fraternité*. In this case, then, although researchers have found evidence that economic grievances *did* play a part, these insights appear to have had little impact on popular accounts of the French Revolution.

What is more worrying, though, is that these insights have not contributed to a more general rethink of factors fuelling uprisings. Instead, the French Revolution continues to be treated in isolation, as prime evidence that social change can be achieved through elite-led mass mobilisation, and not to be compared with the many uprisings that are typically used as evidence that economic hardship breeds social unrest and protest. In our view this distinction is artificial, unnecessary and unhelpful, because it detracts from the fact that uprisings almost always involve political ideals and elite-level leadership influence. Indeed, by treating the French Revolution as the exception that proves the rule, it becomes much easier to remain wedded to the view that 'normal' uprisings are more likely in times of economic crises (H1a) and that it will be working class people who lead the challenge when the economy slows down (H2a).

A rather different, more nuanced picture emerges when we consider the way in which the so-called *Wave of Revolutions* of 1848 is typically remembered. This wave of uprising, also known as the European *Spring of Nations*, is considered as the revival of French Revolutionary ideals, resulting in a European-wide attempt to overthrow Europe's monarchies. Some popular accounts emphasise shared political ideals, portraying the events as a second phase of the French Revolution, a stage in which republican ideals spread across Europe. These accounts tend to downplay or ignore economic factors. For example, in the online edition of the *Encyclopaedia Britannica* the events are described as 'a series of republican revolts against European monarchies, beginning in Sicily and spreading to France, Germany, Italy and the Austrian Empire'.[2] Such accounts are similar to the ones that portray the French Revolution as unique and beyond comparison.

On the whole, though, popular accounts of the 1848 wave of revolutions appear to offer a more nuanced picture, acknowledging both economic and political factors. For example, it is widely acknowledged that social unrest began in February 1848 in Paris, and that unrest

[2] https://www.britannica.com/event/Revolutions-of-1848

subsequently spread rapidly across Europe, in particular to cities which
had experienced rapid industrialisation, such as Turin and Milan in
northern Italy, Liège in northeast Belgium, Vienna in the Austrian
Empire, and Cologne, Mannheim, Karlsruhe and Berlin in the then
German Confederal States of Baden, Rhineland, Palatina and Prussia.
However, the revolutions would eventually spread further north to the
city of Kiel in Schleswig-Holstein, further east to the cities of Poznan,
Krakow, Prague and Bucharest, and further south to the city of
Palermo in Sicily, into areas that were less affected by the Industrial
Revolution.

Although Belgian, German, Polish and Danish protestors may well
have shouted similar slogans and felt similar grievances, as historians
have shown, there were important differences in the motivation, political aspiration and goal attainment between the protestors in these
countries. For example, in France, Belgium and the German Confederal
States, where the growing class of poor urban workers faced considerable hardship, uprisings were inspired by Republican and later Socialist
ideas. However, in the Austrian Empire, the uprisings were inspired in
large part not by hardship, but by ethno-nationalist sentiments and
a desire among the middle classes to reassert old national identities and
to regain national self-determination. Historians have pointed to these
differences when explaining why the 1848 uprising succeeded only in
France, while in other countries conservative reactionary forces eventually prevailed.

When comparing academic and non-academic accounts of the 1848
wave of revolutions, and leaving aside some exceptions, it becomes
clear that there is considerable consistency between the two. More
specifically, both acknowledge that there were important local differences, that powerful elites played an important leadership role and that
the uprisings were inspired by a combination of economic grievances
and political aspirations. However, judging from the number of available sources,[3] there appears to be much less interest in the *1848 Wave
of Revolutions* than in the *1789 French Revolution*. This may explain
why these 'multi-cause' accounts have had limited 'bite' on our beliefs

---

[3] In order to get a sense of this imbalance, one only needs to conduct a simple
Google search for the terms 'French Revolution' and '1848 Revolutions'.
Whereas the term 'French Revolution' will generate around 37,600,000 hits, the
term '1848 Revolutions' will only generate 449,000 hits.

and assumptions, thereby leaving the presumed link between economic hardship and intergroup hostility unchallenged.

The Industrial Revolution, 'Mass Protest' and Classic Social Science Perspectives

The Industrial Revolution, which began in earnest in the late 18th century, brought about rapid technological change and fundamental social changes. It was the era in which Europe, and especially northwest Europe, experienced rapid urbanisation, and – more importantly here – saw the emergence of large urban working-class populations living in poverty. The Industrial Revolution would lead to a surge in thinking and writing about what became known as 'the Social Question', and, not surprisingly given the context at the time, thinkers turned their attention to working-class deprivation and hardship. Before considering the impact of this body of social science research on our thinking, it is useful to first consider the main historical and political developments of that era, and the way they are typically remembered.

As we saw, there were small-scale strikes and insurgencies in England as early as the 1700s. However, it was not until the early 19th century that British workers started to unite and form trade unions. One of the earliest unions was the General Union of Trades, established in Manchester in 1818. At the time, trade unions were illegal and therefore the organisation was initially referred to as the Manchester Philanthropic Society so as to hide its real purpose. However, in 1824 the UK government repealed the 1799 Combination Act banning 'Unlawful Combinations of Workmen', making it possible for unions to operate in broad daylight. The first attempts at establishing nationwide UK trade unions occurred in the 1830s. However, these early attempts failed,[4] and it would not be until the late 1800s that trade unions and labour parties started to become a more permanent feature of the British social and political landscape.

---

[4] The first nation-wide union in the UK was the 'National Association for the Protection of Labor', established in 1830, with headquarters in London. However, the organisation fell victim to internal struggles and disbanded in 1832. In 1834 there was a new attempt to establish a nation-wide organisation, called the Grand National Consolidated Trades Union, which befell the same fate and ceased to exist that same year.

Historians have also examined why the 1848 wave of revolutions did not spread to the United Kingdom. This is arguably rather odd because the UK was the very country where the Industrial Revolution had started: it was among the first to witness the rise of a large and severely deprived urban working class – all representing the 'ideal' conditions for economic grievances and thus for social unrest to take hold. One explanation for this paradox may be the continued faith in 19th century Britain in securing change through petitioning.[5]

Although the 1848 Revolutions failed to materialise in the UK, the country would nonetheless become a major centre for thinking about the Social Question, and about ways in which the working class would and/or should respond to growing hardship and relative deprivation. One of the more famous thinkers to have addressed this question is Karl Marx. His work was inspired by, among other thinkers, Georg Wilhelm Friedrich Hegel, who had criticised faith in capitalist market economies before him, arguing that poverty will be the inevitable outcome of expanding individual freedom. An important difference between the two was Hegel's belief in the modern state as the means to resolve conflict. Marx rejected this idea and saw the modern State as a vehicle for working-class oppression. Marx focused on groups that had been disenfranchised by the Industrial Revolution and who seemed increasingly ready to take to the streets to voice their grievances.

The idea of working-class deprivation and grievances was further reinforced by Friedrich Engels' influential 1845 book *The Condition of the Working Class in England*, which offered an in-depth empirical analysis of the living and working conditions of poor urban workers in Manchester and elsewhere. Karl Marx and Friedrich Engels would later join forces to co-author their famous 1848 book, *The Communist Manifesto*. Although this cannot be ascertained with certainty, it appears plausible that their work, with its causal narrative of working-class 'deprivation' and 'grievances' producing 'frustration', 'aggression' and 'violent uprisings', has come to inform our tacit

---

[5] For example, the fact that the 1848 Revolutions did not take hold in the UK has been attributed to (a) the rise to prominence of the Chartist Movement, a loosely united collection of 'Working Men Associations' established in 1832, which favoured petitioning over rebellion, and (b) to a surge in Irish Catholics fleeing from the Irish Famine and migrating to England, where they became regarded as 'the enemy within' (Merriman, 1996).

understanding of the root causes of contemporary intergroup hostility, contributing to the intuitive appeal of Hypotheses 1a and 2a.

The British labour movements not only benefitted from support by influential thinkers such as Karl Marx and Friedrich Engels, but also from backing from labour movements in other European countries. For example, the 1863 Polish Uprising is believed to have been an important impetus for the rise of the British Labour movement, culminating in the 1st International Workman's Association (IWA), established in London in 1864. The rationale behind the organisation, which at its peak boasted a membership of approximately 5 million, was to unite not only workers across the globe, but also revolutionary thinkers – thinkers who were all concerned with the question of how to end working class exploitation.

Trade Unions would subsequently be established in other industrialising countries such as the United States (1886), France (1887) and Germany (1897), thereby fuelling fears for a global workers' uprising. An additional factor was the Russian 1917 October Revolution, led by Vladimir Lenin, Leon Trotsky and Pavel Dybenko, which ended the Provisional Russian Government, established in March of that same year following the abdication of Tsar Nicholas II. Although Marxist and Communist ideas had played a role in the 1905 Russian Revolution, when workers took to the street to express various (economic and political) grievances, it was not until the 1917 October Revolution and the establishment of a Bolshevik Communist regime that Western leaders started to become truly concerned about a possible global workers' uprising. Fear for a global workers' uprising intensified as a result of the establishment of the 1919 Communist International (or 'third international'), an international organisation of communist parties vowing to overthrow the international bourgeoisie by all available means. It is also likely that the establishment of the Soviet Union in 1922 with its powerful Red Army contributed further to this fear. These factors appear to have played an important role in 'workers' becoming regarded as a particularly volatile segment of the population, with 'economic crises' being the time when workers would most likely become agitated.

Karl Marx was undoubtedly among the more influential thinkers, but certainly not the only one. Equally influential was Emile Durkheim, who wrote extensively about the erosion of social norms and the weakening of social bonds in industrialised societies. The state of normlessness (or 'anomie') that resulted from this was predicted to form a fertile ground for hostility and violence. Those following Durkheim conceived of uprisings as symptomatic of societal 'breakdown'. For them, uprisings reflected the decline of old social bonds in rapidly urbanising and industrialising societies, where workers perform highly specialised routinised tasks. Once again, it was manual workers who were singled out as the group to watch, in this instance as the category of people most likely to regress and become violent. Those following Karl Marx, on the other hand, conceived of uprisings as symptomatic of growing class-consciousness and 'solidarity'. Indeed, for Marx and his followers, uprisings were the beginning rather than the end of a journey, reflecting a growing preparedness to challenge the modern capitalist system.[6]

'Breakdown' and 'Solidarity' became regarded as two competing perspectives, and it is probably fair to say that they have influenced sociological debate about popular uprisings in equal measure. For example, Hannah Arendt took up Durkheim's notion of 'Breakdown' in her work on totalitarian regimes and the ways in which such regimes promote anomie (Arendt, 1951). Nevertheless, and despite the differences, what these two accounts have in common is a preoccupation with those at the bottom of society, and the question of how they will respond to growing hardship in rapidly industrialising societies.

Marx's notion of Solidarity would continue to have appeal among sociologists interested in the link between inequality, relative deprivation and societal instability. More specifically, this Marxian 'solidarity perspective' would become an important – if not *the* most important – source of inspiration for those studying 'contentious politics' and 'protest movements', resulting in a strong emphasis on material living-

---

[6] For Karl Marx, revolutions (defined as the working-class *Proletariat* rising up to challenges the upper and middle class *Bourgeoisie*) occurred spontaneously and relatively frequently. However Leninist-Marxist rejected this view, arguing that proletarian revolutions require leadership and a vanguard of professional revolutionaries. There was also considerable disagreement about whether particular sections of the Proletariat would lead the overthrow of capitalism. Marx differentiated between the *Proletariat* and the *Lumpenproletariat*, arguing that the former would sooner or later gain class-consciousness, while the latter would never gain class-consciousness, and represented a hindrance to the revolutionary struggle. Anarchists such as Mikhail Bukunin rejected this view, arguing that the true revolutionary archetype was found in the peasant milieu, which, so they argued, had an even longer insurrectionary tradition.

and working conditions, relative deprivation and grievances. This Marxist focus also characterises the so-called social movement literature. As several authors have noted, almost all explanations on offer in this literature are based on grievance theory, 'focusing on objective – mostly macro-structurally shaped – conditions that have increased grievances and discontent among the people' (Rydgren, 2007, p.247; see also De Witte & Klandermans, 2000; Koopmans, Statham, Giugni, & Passy, 2005; Rydgren, 2005). In our view this reflects the strong influence of Marxist social theory, an influence which has not only permeated into this particular literature, but also into our more general understanding of the causes of intergroup tension.

The Poor and Their Rebelliousness

What the above-mentioned perspectives have in common is that they focus in particular on grievances *among the lower strata of society.* This notion that working class people are particularly prone to turn violent and lash out was picked up by early criminologists (Lombroso, 1876; Sighele, 1891; Tarde, 1885). This work started from the elitist premise that working class people are more likely to lose their moral compass, and more prone to engage in unethical and/or criminal behaviour. Whereas Marxists would typically glorify the 'working man', criminologists were more likely to pathologise working-class men and women. Regardless of this difference, and although Marxists and criminologists posed very different questions, they both contributed to the working class becoming regarded as a particularly volatile section of the population, albeit for a different reason.

For example, there was lively debate among criminologists and criminal anthropologists in the late 1800s about the personality traits defining 'Criminal Man', and about the need to develop better ways to identify those instigating riots and uprisings (Renneville, 2012). This coincided with a growing interest in the psychology of the 'mob'. For example, at the first International Conference on Criminal Anthropology held in Rome in 1885, there was lively discussion about 'mob behaviour' and 'mob psychology'. This conference was attended by famous social scientists such as the Italian criminologists Scipio Sighele and Cesare Lombroso and the French sociologist Gabriel Tarde. Rather than conceiving of aggression as extreme behaviour displayed by normal people facing extreme

conditions (e.g. hardship), these scholars saw aggression as pathological behaviour, displayed by groups of individuals with low levels
of self-restraint, and thus prone to regress into primitive behaviour.
Such ideas may seem archaic today. However, what should not be
forgotten is that it was an era of important advances in evolutionary
biology and genetics research, which seemed to provide a scientific
basis for Cesare Lombroso's claim that criminality is biologically
determined and inherited.

These rather archaic ideas would also find their way into the field of
social psychology, through the work of the French sociologist and
social psychologist Gustave Le Bon (1896). He too conceived of
'crowd behaviour' as instances in which groups loose self-restraint,
and give in to pernicious primitive instincts. More specifically, Le Bon
saw riots and crowd behaviour not in terms of groups of people
denouncing their working- or living conditions, but as evidence that
individuals who immerse themselves in a crowd risk losing their ability
to make sound rational judgements, and their sense of individual moral
obligation vis-à-vis society at large. What also comes to mind is
Frederick Taylor's (1911) work on human resource management (or
'scientific management', as it was known at the time). This perspective
assumed that, in their 'natural state', workers are reluctant to exert
themselves and prone to lose self-restraint, thus requiring adequate
incentives and supervision.

When considering the many high-profile banking scandals that came
to light in the wake of the 2008 GFC, it would appear that wealthy
business men and women are just as likely to engage in deviant behaviour. Nonetheless, we appear to live in a society in which working
class people continue to be regarded as weak, prone to fall victim to
pernicious peer pressure and more likely to become hostile or violent
towards others. For example, so-called experts, invited to give their
views on current affairs, were quick to attribute the 2011 London riots
to rising normlessness among the working class (Jones, 2012).
In contrast, no such attributions were made when explaining the
Libor banking scandal a year later. Explanations for the rule-
breaking and deviant behaviours that these individuals engaged in
focused on the high-pressure environment and risk-taking culture in
which these bankers found themselves. When contrasting the two, it
becomes clear that we tend to see the poor (rather than the rich) as
a group with latent deviant tendencies, tendencies that remain dormant

when living conditions are satisfactory, but manifest when economic conditions deteriorate.

The Wealthy and Their Rebelliousness

The idea of people with above-average wealth taking part in uprisings and lashing out to certain groups in society may seem strange and counterintuitive. Yet, there is no shortage of historical examples that appear to support this view. A fitting historical example of more general (sociotropic) discontent and frustration boiling over can be found in France in 1852, when Louis-Napoleon (Napoleon III) seized power with help of a coup d'état. Once in power, he dissolved the National Assembly, and restored the French Empire. Although the coup was followed by a decade of relative tranquillity, protestors would eventually return to the streets to express their discontent. For example, in September 1870 angry crowds protested in Paris against Louis-Napoleon's undemocratic regime, and against the deplorable state of the economy. These protests became violent when news reached Paris that Louis-Napoleon had surrendered to Otto von Bismarck following the defeat at the Battle of Sedan in the Franco-Prussian war. The poor state of the economy of that era may well have affected the living- and working conditions of French blue-collar workers in a very direct and personal way. However, it would seem that there was frustration about the nation's economic and political future among the public at large more generally, including among people with above-average wealth, status and income.

The idea of wealthier residents/voters protesting to express their frustration about the economy may seem counterintuitive. Yet, when considering the historical evidence it becomes clear that individuals from relatively well-to-do circles often took the lead in 'workers uprisings'. A case in point here is the short-lived 1871 *Paris Commune*, an uprising that is typically portrayed as a working class uprising, even though the movement had patrons such as Henri Rochefort (also known as Marquis de Rochefort-Luçay) and Georges Pilotell (a political cartoonist and son of a judge) who could hardly be described as working class.[7]

---

[7] Louis-Napoleon's surrender to Bismarck led to the collapse of the government of the Second Empire, and the establishment of a new radical-left government, known as the *Paris Commune*, on 18 March 1871. The Paris Commune was overthrown by government troupes on 28 May, less than three months after its

What is more, there can be little doubt that political sentiments (e.g. the feeling one's nation has been humiliated) often play an important part in fuelling social unrest. This becomes apparent when we consider developments in France towards the end of the 19th century. As Heywood (1995) explains, by 1890 France had largely overcome the economic burden of the Franco-Prussian war. However, this would not stop mass protests by the public at large to voice grievances and discontent. For example, in 1898 violent anti-Semitic protests erupted in Paris and several other French cities, after the acquittal of General Alfred Dreyfus, who had been falsely accused of handing secrets to the German imperial army. Furthermore, it was during these years of relative prosperity that General George Boulanger – famous for his aggressive nationalism aimed at Germany – acquired a considerable following, known as the Boulangist movement (*Le Mouvement Boulangiste*), fuelling fears for a coup d'état and military dictatorship (Irvine, 1988). These developments clearly indicate that intergroup hostility can grow in times of economic prosperity, and that belligerent leaders do not necessarily need a crisis to gain mass followership.

Another case in point, also from France, is Pierre Poujade's Poujadist Movement (*Le Mouvement Poujadiste*), which started in 1953 with the foundation of the Defence Union of Shopkeepers and Craftsmen (*L'Union de Défense des Commerçants et Artisans*). This small traders' revolt gradually evolved into a mass movement with 400,000 official members, and a leader who pitted 'the common man' against 'the elite' and portrayed the National Assembly as the biggest brothel in Paris (Bouclier, 2006).

In sum, it may be tempting to interpret the various uprisings and revolutions witnessed in Europe in the 19th and 20th century – the era described by Tilly, Tilly and Tilly (1975) as the '*Age of Revolutions*' – as providing evidence of growing working-class discontent ('grievances') about material living and working conditions. However, this would be to draw too heavily on Marxist reasoning, and to ignore that political aspirations played an equally if not more important role.

---

inception, during what became known as *La Semaine Sanglante* ('the Bloody Week'), a week in which hundreds of supporters of the Paris Commune (*Communards*) were killed in public.

Nazi Germany and the Holocaust

It should be clear from the above that our thinking about intergroup tensions has been influenced heavily by Marxist social theory and its premise of material working-class deprivation fuelling rebellion. However, the now widely accepted assumption of 'harsh times producing harsh attitudes' appears to be perpetuated in equal measure by the way in which the rise of Hitler's Nazi movement and ensuing Holocaust are typically remembered and explained. The following extract from a website targeting history students and educators illustrates this:

When the stock market collapsed on Wall Street on Tuesday, October 29, 1929, it sent financial markets worldwide into a tailspin with disastrous effects. The German economy was especially vulnerable since it was built upon foreign capital, mostly loans from America and was very dependent on foreign trade. When those loans suddenly came due and when the world market for German exports dried up, the well-oiled German industrial machine quickly ground to a halt. As production levels fell, German workers were laid off. Along with this, banks failed throughout Germany. Savings accounts, the result of years of hard work, were instantly wiped out. Inflation soon followed making it hard for families to purchase expensive necessities with devalued money.

Overnight, the middle class standard of living so many German families enjoyed was ruined by events outside of Germany, beyond their control. The Great Depression began and they were cast into poverty and deep misery and began looking for a solution, any solution ... Adolf Hitler knew his opportunity had arrived. (Source: www.historyplace.com)

As is evident from such popular accounts, the 1930s Great Depression is portrayed as a prerequisite for Hitler's rise to power. Nationalist and anti-minority narratives could take hold so quickly, so the argument typically goes, because the lower and middle classes suffered most from the economic crises. It is without doubt true that the country was in the grip of a severe crisis which led to hyperinflation, mass-unemployment and food shortages, and there can be little doubt that many Germans were experiencing hardship. However, and as we will discuss in greater detail in Chapter 4, more recent research into support for Hitler's NSDAP party has revealed that the role of economic grievances may have been overstated in attempts to explain Hitler's rise to power. This has resulted in the German economic dire situation inadvertently being singled out too readily, at least in non-academic accounts, as the trigger for the poor and the middle classes' hostility and aggression witnessed in the lead-up to World War II.

But why have we remained so focused on economic crises and working-class hardship? And why have we remained so wedded to the idea that economic crises will enable authoritarian leaders to mobilise 'the masses'?[8] As we saw, Marxist social theory appears to have left a lasting legacy, and it has given us a particular understanding of *who* will become agitated (working class citizens), *why* they become agitated (material deprivation) and *when* they become agitated (during economic crises). Ideologically speaking, Communism and Fascism may be each other's opposite; when we are being asked to explain why fanatic Communists and fanatic Fascists are able to gain a mass following, we tend to point to the same underlying cause: economic hardship among the poor.

There have of course been other attempts to theorise Hitler's rise to power that provide a more psychological account. However, rather than questioning tacit assumptions, these attempts often only (implicitly or explicitly) reinforced the idea of a causal link between economic hardship and outgroup aggression. A fitting example is the 'authoritarianism' literature, which began in earnest in the 1930s, when Frankfurt School scholars started to question how ordinary Germans, living in a technologically advanced society, could become receptive to authoritarian leaders such as Adolf Hitler and Benito Mussolini. Their answer was two-fold. On the one hand, these scholars accused fascist regimes of using mass culture as propaganda, with a view to prevent deprived workers from developing class-consciousness.[9] On the other hand – and this is where Marx's focus on material conditions continued to be

---

[8] Here too the use of certain terminology ('the masses') may have inadvertently reinforced the old assumptions of low-status groups as the ones most likely to become aggressive and most prone to 'lash out' to other groups.

[9] From the late 1920s onwards, Theodor Adorno, Max Horkheimer, Erich Fromm and other Frankfurt School neo-Marxist social theorists started questioning why the revolutions predicted by Marx and Engels had not materialised. According to these critics, an important shortcoming of traditional Marxism was a too narrow 'materialist' focus on the means of production, and neglect for the many means of *cultural* production (radio, television, movies) at the disposal of capitalist governments. In contemporary capitalist societies, so they argued, these means of cultural production are deployed not to mobilise the masses, but to socialise citizens into consumer society, and, in so doing, to stop them from developing class-consciousness.

of influence – they pointed to economic hardship as a critical factor shaping ordinary citizens' attitudes towards authoritarian leaders. More specifically, Frankfurt School scholars argued (drawing on Sigmund Freud's insights) that ordinary Germans were suffering from an *authoritarian syndrome*. This syndrome, so they reasoned, originated from the strict parenting style that their parents had adopted during the Great Depression, when conditions were harsh and unforgiving. This manifested itself later in life in a tendency to idealise authority figures and to blame socially sanctioned scapegoats for personal setbacks. This theorising provides perhaps the clearest link between frustration and aggression towards vulnerable groups and minorities. According to this line of thinking, because people feel inhibited to aggress directly against the source of their aggression (i.e. their parents or other authority figures) they instead turn on minorities that have a low standing in society. Frankfurt School scholars developed a scale to measure an individual's authoritarian tendencies, the so-called F-Scale. Psychologists would subsequently propose more refined versions, such as the Right Wing Authoritarianism (RWA) scale, which were used in new theories about attitudes towards authority, and to assess political attitudes more generally.[10]

World War II and the Holocaust would, not surprisingly, form the catalyst for a new wave of psychological research into intolerance. Broadly speaking, two strands of theorising emerged, with one strand focusing on factors fuelling intergroup violence and hate crime (to be explored further in Chapter 3), and the other strand focusing on the electoral appeal of extreme right leaders (to be explored in more depth in Chapter 9). Sociologists and political scientists have historically also been interested in the latter question, and have focused in particular on which *groups* in society are most likely to vote for a far-right political party or join a protest

---

[10]　The idea of an authoritarian personality lost appeal in the 1960s, when researchers started questioning the validity of personality-based models of human behaviour (Mischel, 1968). However, the idea resurfaced in the 1980s, when Altemeyer (1981) advanced the RWA scale to measure people's inclination to support authoritarian leaders. More recently, researchers interested in the remarkable stability of social hierarchies developed a scale to measure Social Dominance Orientation (SDO; Pratto, Sidanius, Stallworth & Malle, 1994), and this scale continues to be used (often alongside RWA) to measure people's propensity to accept and endorse authoritarian leaders.

movement. Drawing on authoritarian personality theorising, this
work once again singled out the working class as the problem
group. A case in point here is work on *working-class* authoritarianism (Dekker & Ester, 1987; Lipset & Raab, 1978; Middendorp &
Meloen, 1990). For example, Lipset and Raab (1978) argued that, all
other things being equal, working class people will have more diffi-
culty grasping complex information and will hence be more likely to
be drawn to extreme political leaders and parties.

Trapped in a Relative Deprivation Mindset

From the 1960s onwards, research into authoritarianism gradually
became overshadowed by the much broader social movement literature. Rather than pursuing a radical break with the past and questioning underlying assumptions, researchers continued to conceive of
deprivation as the main driving force motivating people to become
disgruntled, to join protest movements or to vote for right-wing
parties.

To be sure, there were important advances in relative deprivation
thinking in this literature. For example, in his seminal 1970 book *Why
Men Rebel*, Ted Gurr makes a compelling case for the need to differentiate between (objective) *deprivation* and (subjective) *relative deprivation* (RD), arguing that groups can have grievances when their
economic *expectations* are not fulfilled (see Chapter 6). As Gurr
(1970, p. 58) put it, 'men are quick to aspire beyond their social
means, and quick to anger when those means prove inadequate, but
slow to accept their limitations'. Gurr described such discrepancies
between aspirations and actual fulfilment as *expectation-capability
gaps*, and it is now widely accepted that such gaps can produce grievances and increase the appeal of radical leaders and parties.

In sum, what Gurr showed was that both deprivation and relative
deprivation can produce frustration, and his work serves as an important reminder that it is not necessarily the *objective* economic conditions in which people find themselves that matter for levels of tolerance,
but *perceptions* about one's relative position vis-à-vis others. Although
researchers such as Ted Gurr made valuable contributions, in particular with regards to the need to distinguish between actual and
perceived deprivation and between current and anticipated

deprivation, this literature nonetheless remained trapped in a mindset focusing on (different forms of) 'relative deprivation'.[11]

Time for a Thorough Rethink

In this chapter, we trace the origins of the assumption that crises breed intergroup hostility (H1a) and the assumption that working class people are most likely to become agitated when the economy slows down (H2a). We reflect on the pervasiveness of these two assumptions, and we did so by considering the main historical and intellectual developments that appear to have influenced our thinking about uprisings and intergroup hostility.

Although it is impossible to arrive at firm conclusions, our analysis suggests that two historic eras had a disproportionate impact on our thinking; The first is the rise of Marxism and the ensuing 1917 Bolshevik revolution in Russia, which increased fears for a 'proletarian uprising' once working class deprivation reached a critical tipping point. The second era is the rise of Hitler's NSDAP in Germany during the Great Depression, which became regarded as providing irrefutable evidence that nations undergoing economic hardship are inclined to become less tolerant towards immigrants and ethnic minorities.

We also considered the influence of the 1789–1799 French Revolution, but concluded that these events are remembered in a different light: as an important step towards enlightened modernity. This may be why this event has had so little impact on our thinking about intolerance and hostility towards minorities. Although there is some research evidence that the 1789 French Revolution started with grievances about food prices and more general economic hardship, this is not how the Revolution is typically remembered in popular accounts.

---

[11] The 1990s 'New Social Movements' literature would later take issue with this focus on material factors, pointing to the reduced significance of old socio-economic cleavages, and the increased significance of post-material values (e.g. peace, gender equality, human rights, environmental sustainability) as motivating factors for voting and collective action (Habermas, 1981). However, and this is understandable if we consider the kinds of movements this literature has investigated, this challenge has not diminished belief in the assumptions that crises provide fertile soil for radical leaders (Hypothesis 1a), and that working class people are more likely to vote for radical leaders (Hypothesis 2a).

What has not been questioned (at least not to our knowledge) is the tacit assumption that it was ordinary, working-class people who took to the streets and who stormed the Bastille.

As we saw, early criminology and psychology research would also influence our thinking about who would be most likely to respond with hostility to economic downturn or to relative deprivation. In both literatures, working class people ended up being considered as latent deviants and thus most likely to lose their moral compass and/or to take part in unruly 'mob behaviour'. Although these early contributions have long been dismissed as out-dated, elitist and politically incorrect, the more general underlying idea of deprived working class people being more prone to become agitated and hostile towards minorities survived in the more recent *social movement* literature. Here, this view continues to form the predominant outlook for researchers examining the appeal of anti-immigration movements. What these accounts have in common – and this is not surprising if we consider their (Marxian) focus on grievances about economic conditions – is fascination with groups at the bottom of the social ladder, and little eye for those at the top of the social ladder. It is time to examine the empirical support for these ideas, and this will be the focus of our next chapter.

3 | *Empirical Evidence for the 'Harsh Times Producing Hard Attitudes' Hypothesis*

The popular accounts of historical events that we reviewed in the previous chapter all lead to the same conclusion: relative deprivation should have negative effects on a range of social outcomes – it should enhance intolerance, unrest and intergroup hostility, and trigger revolutions. But what is the empirical evidence for this idea? In this chapter we examine support for the hypotheses identified in Chapter 1. We begin by examining the 'macro-level' effects of societal wealth. To recap, Hypothesis 1a suggested that as societies become less affluent, public opinion should become less permissive and tolerant. Thus, economic downturn should be associated with a rise in anti-immigrant sentiments, xenophobia and prejudice. Hypothesis 1b is concerned with the flipside of this argument: As societies become *more* affluent, public opinion should become *more* permissive and tolerant and, as a result, we should see a *drop* in anti-immigrant sentiments, xenophobia and prejudice.

As we will see below, these hypotheses have been the focus of social science research for decades, and one would expect science to have delivered a clear verdict by now. But as we will also see, the evidence is rather mixed and inconclusive.

A Shortage of Robust Time Series Data

Although the idea that economic downturns and upturns would have a significant impact on human social behaviour is an old one, it has been quite difficult to test this idea. The problem is that in order to do this, one would need to have access to 'time series' data so as to be able to assess population attitudes about immigrants and minorities over several consecutive years. Over time, we might see changes in these attitudes that one could relate to economic change. But ideally we would need to collect this data for several years of economic prosperity, for years of moderate economic performance, and for years characterised by recession. In practice, this means that one would need to conduct research into national attitudes across several decades before one can begin to assess what impact economic developments have on them.

Even though such year-on-year survey data have accumulated in the last decades, for a long time it was particularly difficult for researchers to obtain good quality data on change in national attitudes. In practice, this meant that researchers relied on data that provided an index for hostility, such as the number of hate crimes against members of minority groups in a particular region.

Early Evidence: Does Economic Frustration Lead to Aggression?

One of the earliest studies to examine the long-term impact of the economy on violence was conducted by Hovland and Sears (1940). This study was conducted in the United States, where there was relatively accurate data on the number of per capita lynchings of African Americans. Perhaps because it was the first, and, for a very long time, the only study that examined longitudinal data, this study had a major impact and shaped thinking in the field for more than half a century.

Hovland and Sears's intention was straightforward: their goal was to establish the impact of economic conditions on prejudice against African Americans. More specifically, they wanted to test frustration–aggression theory: the notion that economic downturn causes 'frustration' – a negative pent-up energy. This energy, so this theory suggests, has to be discharged one way or another and takes the form of aggression. In cases where aggression cannot be vented at the source of the frustration (for example, because the person does not know what the source of frustration is or because the source is 'untouchable') there has to be a different outlet for the anger. It is in situations such as these that people search for 'scapegoats' or 'easy targets' to vent their anger and frustration.

Particularly easy targets for such violent discharges, the reasoning went, would be minority groups or individuals perceived as deviant. Thus, likely targets would be people with a different ethnic or religious background, a different sexuality and so on. It is easy to see why, in the early 1940s, this was a particularly appealing idea among social

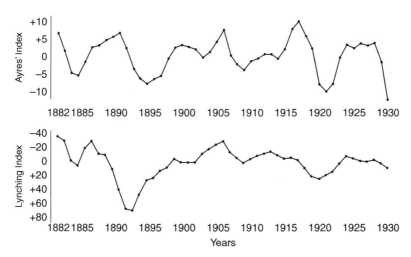

Figure 3.1. The relation between cotton prices (the 'Ayres' index'; see top figure) and lynchings of African Americans (bottom figure) described by Hovland and Sears (1940).

scientists, many of whom fled or had been forced to leave Germany in the course of the 1930s, due to growing intolerance towards minorities. And of course, this intolerance followed close on the heels of the most devastating depression in human history.

In order to test the idea that economic downturn caused ethnic violence, Hovland and Sears (1940) analysed the relationship between cotton prices and the number of lynchings in a particular region. Cotton prices, so they reasoned, were a good indicator of whether life in the Southern States of the USA was good (high prices) or tough (low prices). The number of lynchings of Blacks, so they argued, reflected anti-Black hostility at any given time. Thus, in order to test their theory they assembled annual statistics for both variables, and computed the correlation between the two. The results provided exceptionally strong support for their prediction: in years with when cotton prices were low, many more lynchings were reported (see Figure 3.1).

Even though the effect reported by Hovland and Sears (1940) was unusually strong (thus providing what may seem compelling evidence for Hypothesis 1a), Hovland and Sears were aware of some of the limitations of their analysis. In particular, they highlighted that the cotton price index may affect living conditions for some people, but that it is not a robust indicator of economic conditions for the majority of people living in Southern states. What is more, the number of lynchings is not the best indicator of ethnic tensions (for example, there have also been many lynchings of Whites in the South of the United States). And finally, although the data spanned 48 years, the data spoke to the situation in just one country and may not be generalisable to other contexts and countries. Accordingly, Hovland and Sears warned their readers that this was just a 'minor study of aggression'.

Just a few years after Hovland and Sears (1940) had published their findings, researchers began to question them. For example, Mintz (1946) pointed out that the Hovland and Sears' effect was *abnormally* strong. This, according to Mintz, was because Hovland and Sears had used an exotic statistical method to compute their correlations. If they would have used a more conventional and more appropriate method, the correlation reported by correlation Hovland and Sears of –0.72 (on a scale of –1 to 1) would have shrunk to a much more modest – 0.34. Despite the clear problems associated with Hovland and Sears' analytical technique, Mintz's warnings appeared to fall on deaf ears. It appeared that because Hovland and Sears had found evidence for what people *wanted* to believe – that economic downturns are the cause of ethnic tensions and persecution – Mintz's warning did not diminish the impact of the work. Indeed, Hovland and Sears had provided evidence for 'a thesis too good to be false' (Reed, Doss, & Hulbert, 1987).

Competition

Interest in the relationship between cotton prices and lynchings flared up again during the 1980s. However, this time, researchers wanted to make a different theoretical point. Frustration–aggression theory had long been dismissed on the grounds that it failed to account for tensions and conflict between groups in society. Most prominently, new evidence emerged showing frustration fuelled by economic downturns was unrelated to rioting and civil disturbances (e.g. Tilly, Tilly, & Tilly, 1975). Therefore, in order to account for intergroup violence, researchers began looking for alternative explanations.

The new explanation was that intergroup violence and tensions rise up as a result of competition between groups within society. Because this reasoning could also account for the effect that Hovland and Sears

(1940) had shown, their work was once again in the spotlight. Specifically, the reasoning was that lower cotton prices meant falling wages and more unemployment. In such an economic climate, so the new argument went, Whites and Blacks were competing for the same jobs. Violence was thus no longer considered an emotional outburst targeting scapegoats (i.e.a 'third-party'): it was targeted at direct competitors, and was instrumental in the fight over scarce resources. Interestingly, even though the effect stayed the same, a new theory was used to explain it.

At that time a much more sophisticated arsenal of statistical methods was available to researchers, allowing for more refined analyses than were possible in the 1940s, and many researchers set themselves the task of re-examining the relationship between cotton prices and number of lynchings (Beck & Tolnay, 1990; Hepworth & West, 1988; Olzak, 1990). Unfortunately, however, these new methods were applied to the exact same data that Hovland and Sears had collected some 50 years earlier. That is, researchers in the 1980s used the same economic indicator (cotton prices), the same outcome measure (lynchings of African Americans) and the same historical period (1882–1930). Aside from the above-mentioned methodological problems associated with such an analysis (e.g. there is little evidence that cotton prices caused economic strain for the majority of the population, and lynchings may not be a good indicator of intergroup tensions), the actual contribution of these new research efforts was limited because researchers did not critically re-examine the data set. In particular, the data only ran until 1930 and were incomplete because lynchings continued to happen after 1930. More importantly, the cut-off point is exactly at that time that the mother of all recessions was witnessed: the Great Depression in 1929. Arguably, it would be important to include data from these depression years when testing a hypothesis that is concerned with the effect of economic downturn.

It took until 1998 for researchers to finally start taking account of a longer time period than the one examined by Hovland and Sears in 1940, and this time the results showed a rather different picture. More specifically, research by Green, Glaser and Rich (1998) revealed that the relationship between cotton prices and number of lynchings is relatively small and *only* holds for the period that Hovland and Sears (and all researchers after them) had focused on. Indeed, if Hovland and Sears had stopped collecting data at 1920, they would not have found a relationship between cotton prices and lynchings. Similarly, if they had taken only a few more years into account, including the Great Depression starting in 1929, they would also have failed to find a significant relationship between cotton prices and the number of lynchings. This is because during the Great Depression years, a significant *decline* in the number of lynchings of Blacks was observed – a finding that runs counter to the hypothesis that economic downturn should be associated with increased tension and hostility between groups.

As mentioned, the narrow focus on lynchings is unfortunate for a number of reasons. In an attempt to broaden the examination, Green and colleagues (1998) studied the relationship between economic downturn and hostility towards other groups in other contexts. For instance, they examined the impact of the recession at the end of the 1980s on hate crime in New York. They found that despite sharply increasing unemployment, hate crimes against African Americans, Asians, Jews and GLBTs did not go up.

Other studies confirmed that there was no consistent and clear relationship between economic conditions and hate crime. For example, economists Krueger and Pischke (1997) conducted a study of anti-immigrant violence in Germany in the early 1990s. Controlling for the obvious differences between former East and West Germany, they showed that the incidence of ethnic violence across 543 counties was unrelated to various economic and social indicators such as average manufacturing wage, unemployment rate and education levels. In sum, as soon as researchers began examining other historical periods and other regions of the world in earnest, it became clear that there is simply no support for the idea that economic downturns foster hate crimes.

Looking at the most recent economic recession, often referred to as the 'Great Recession', hate crimes appear to be unrelated to economic conditions. For example, as can be seen from Figure 3.2, which shows how the level of racial or religious hate crime has developed in the UK relative to other crime (Home Office, Office for National Statistics and Ministry of Justice, 2013[1]), hate crime rises more sharply than other crime from 2002–2007. However, as the recession sets in, both crime

---

[1] www.gov.uk/government/uploads/system/uploads/attachment_data/file/266358/hate-crime-2013.pdf

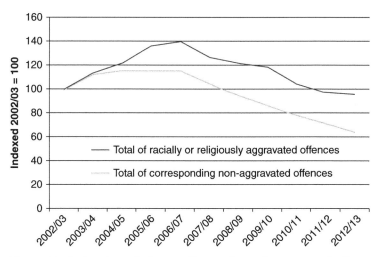

Figure 3.2. Indexed trends for racially or religiously aggravated offences and their corresponding non-aggravated offences. Adopted with permission from the Home Office, Office for National Statistics and Ministry of Justice, 2013.

rates start to drop. Whilst it is unclear what causes the above-average increase of hate crime in the years up to 2007, it is most certainly not the economy: these are exactly the years when the UK's economy was booming. If anything, it appears that the data provide here show evidence for the opposite effect: the economic downturn of 2008 is accompanied by a fall in crime and hate crime alike. This result contradicts the prediction set out in Hypothesis 1a.

Let us review the results of other studies. The relation between economic conditions and hate crime was also examined by economists Jefferson and Pryor (1999), who focused on the presence of hate groups such as the Ku Klux Klan in different counties within the United States. Specifically, they assessed whether, relatively speaking, there were more hate groups in economically deprived counties. Jefferson and Pryor found that 316 counties contained one or more hate groups or White supremacy groups. But these counties did not differ from the other 2774 counties that did not have such groups in their midst in terms of any of the economic indicators examined. The two types of counties did not differ, on average, in terms of their unemployment rate, divorce rate, percentage of Blacks in the county or the income gap between Whites

and Blacks. The only significant difference between the two counties was that the average level of education in counties with hate
groups was slightly *higher*.

In sum, there is simply no evidence to support the suggestion that
macro-economic fluctuations cause significant shifts in hate crime.
Although there might well be historical junctures at which hate crimes
are committed for macro-economic reasons, our review of research
findings suggests that levels of hate crimes fluctuate more or less inde-
pendently of the economy.

Anti-immigrant Attitudes and Competition

One of the problems with hate crime numbers is that they are a rather
crude indicator of intergroup conflict and prejudice. After World War
II, social scientists began taking a much closer look at attitudes towards
minority groups, and thanks to these efforts we are now able to draw
on a very large literature on this topic. That said, summarising this
literature is not easy because so many of the findings appear to contradict each other, making it impossible to draw more general
conclusions.

But why are there are so many contradictions in this literature?
A possible reason is that a large proportion of this research was
conducted in the USA, and focused almost exclusively on prejudice
against African Americans. However, there are good reasons to
believe that anti-Black prejudice is determined by factors other than
ethnocentric exclusion of immigrants (Dixon & Rosenbaum, 2004;
Hood & Morris, 1997). Another possible reason why there are so
many contradictions in the literature is that studies arrive at very
different conclusions depending on which year or historical period
they focus on. With those caveats in mind, let us take a closer look at
some of the evidence.

Towards the end of the 20th century, social scientists gained access to
large multi-year studies that tracked indicators of social and political
attitudes for longer periods of time. This was crucial to better assess the
impact of economic performance on hostility towards minority groups.
The research in question was based on very large datasets containing
some indicators of hostility towards immigrants, prejudice towards
minority groups, xenophobia and ethnocentrism. Sometimes, these variables were taken from national polls, but they were also increasingly

included in large international surveys with multiple waves, enabling the comparison of attitudes across time and across countries.

Although the data, instruments and methods became increasingly sophisticated and more refined, the hypothesis that was tested remained the same. The underlying idea was that competition between groups drives anti-immigrant sentiments, prejudice and ethnocentrism. One prime indicator of competition was economic downturns and decline. Early studies focused mainly on within-country data that tracked changes over time (as mentioned, this data is most useful when a longer time period is included).

However, here too the evidence for a relationship between economic downturn and increased anti-immigrant attitudes is mixed. Semyonov and colleagues (2006), when reviewing the research on this relationship in Canada, conclude that whereas findings of some studies suggest that unemployment levels are related to opposition to immigration (Tienhaara, 1974), other research finds only a very weak effect of unemployment rate on attitudes towards immigrants (Schissel, Wanner, & Frideres, 1989).

There is also cross-sectional data for Europe, where, over a period of many years, national-level statistics were compiled by the European Union. This research has typically recorded attitudes towards immigrants in a given year, and examined how these attitudes relate to economic performance indicators such as the number of unemployed in that year, or the change in unemployment compared to previous years. Even though this method does not allow inferences of causality (i.e. whereby one can assess whether economic performance *causes* anti-immigrant sentiments), such data can still shed light on causality in some respects: a zero relationship makes it likely that there is *no* causal relationship between the two.

What, then, does this cross-sectional research show? In a nutshell, this work shows that the relationship between GDP and prejudice towards immigrants is elusive. Across the board, effects appear to be quite small or non-existent. Early research even suggested that the effect of GDP was in the *opposite direction* to what was expected when both GDP and the size of the foreign population were simultaneously taken into account (Quillian, 1995; 2006). However, using a later data set from the same Eurobarometer data, Scheepers, Gijsberts and Coenders (2002) found *no effect* of unemployment rate, or of change in unemployment, in European countries on a particular

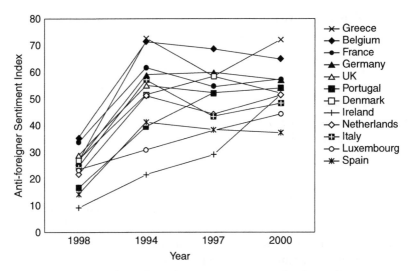

Figure 3.3. Mean values of anti-foreigner sentiment index for twelve European countries at four time points: 1988, 1994, 1997 and 2000. Adapted from Semyonov et al. (2006) with permission.

measure of threat due to immigrants. By contrast, Coenders, Gijsberts and Scheepers (2004), using a dataset from 1995, and with some carefully conducted analyses, showed that economic conditions did predict discriminatory attitudes in the expected way, but only once they had controlled for the change in the number of asylum seekers over time. Also here, even though the relationships were significant, it has to be noted that effects sizes were quite small.

Later, researchers began to use multiple-year datasets to investigate the change in anti-immigrant attitudes in conjunction with between-country differences in several countries at the same time. In Europe in particular, data that kept track of these attitudes were collected for a very long time (see Ceobanu & Escandell, 2010, for a review). Important data sources include the Eurobarometer index (compiled by the European Commission) and the European Social Survey.

This research tended to focus in particular on the dramatic rise in anti-immigrant sentiments in several European countries (see Figure 3.3). What could possibly explain this dramatic increase? Again, the main attention was focused on economic performance and immigrant numbers. Semyonov and colleagues (2006) discovered only very weak effects of GDP over the years 1988–2000. Meuleman, Bavidov and Biliet (2009) conducted an analysis over years 2002–2007, and concluded that GDP was unrelated to attitude changes over this period, across 18 European countries. And finally, some studies showed that opposition to immigrants flared up in countries that were economically affluent (Mayda, 2006).

But perhaps one key reason why the relationship between changes in GDP and anti-immigrant attitudes was so elusive was that much of this research focused on data collected during years of economic improvement and even boom. If one is interested in the effects of economic downturn, one really needs to focus on the GFC that hit Western nations in 2008.

In an attempt to capture this, the relationship between anti-immigrant attitudes and percentage change in GDP over the years 2002 to 2012 is graphed in Figure 3.4. Eyeballing the way the graphs on the left-hand side map onto the graphs on the right-hand side for each of the countries makes one thing very clear: there are no straightforward relationships to be observed between anti-immigrant attitudes and percentage change in GDP.

If anything, the mean level of anti-immigrant sentiments per country appears rather stable over the ten-year period. This is found despite the fact that there are quite significant fluctuations in percentage change in GDP in the same period for most of these European countries.

Where does this leave us in terms of support for Hypothesis 1a (and by extension Hypothesis 1b)? More specifically, to what extent is there empirical support for the prediction that *as societies become less affluent, public opinion should become less permissive and tolerant and, as a result, we should see a rise in anti-immigrant sentiments, xenophobia and prejudice?* Summarising the literature review presented in this chapter, we conclude that the empirical evidence for this prediction is rather mixed and inconclusive: negative attitudes towards immigrants, foreigners and minorities have both been observed in times of economic growth *and* in times of economic decline. Other studies show no relationship between economic performance and negative attitudes. The good news, therefore, is that Hypotheses 1a and 1b are true in some cases and in some contexts: crises (booms) can heighten (attenuate) outgroup tension. The bad news is that Hypotheses 1a and 1b are *only true in a limited number of cases*. That is, at times crises and booms do not impact on outgroup attitudes, and at other times they do

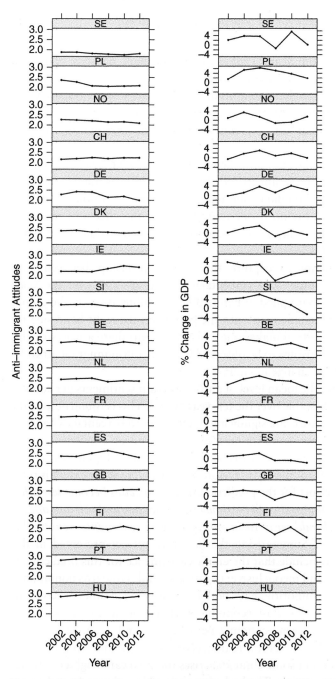

Figure 3.4. Mean values of anti-immigrant attitudes (left-hand graphs) and percentage change in GDP (right-hand graphs) over the years 2002 to 2012. SE = Sweden, PL = Poland, NO = Norway, CH = Switzerland, DE = Germany, DK = Denmark, IE = Ireland, SI = Slovenia, BE = Belgium, NL = Netherlands, FR = France, ES =, GB = Great Britain, FI = Finland, PT = Portugal, HU = Hungary. Eurobarometer data.

have an effect but an effect in the exact opposite direction of what one would expect (i.e. softening attitudes in times of crises, hardening attitudes in times of economic growth and prosperity).

Let us now turn our attention to Hypotheses 2a and 2b. To what extent is there empirical support for these hypotheses?

Does Poverty Lead to Hostility towards Minorities?

Whereas there is a large body of work examining the relationship between economic performance and attitudes towards minorities at the macro-level of society (Hypotheses 1a and b), there are only a handful of studies that directly examine the extent to which differences in economic performance at the group level affect these attitudes (Hypotheses 2a and 2b). That said, the assumption appears to be that processes similar to those that operate at the macro-level affect meso-level and micro-level outcomes: this is because of greater scarcity among the poorer segments of society, enhancing competition over resources, and dissatisfaction resulting from relative deprivation that underlie poor people's more negative attitudes towards minorities.

To recap, then, to what extent do we find support for Hypothesis 2a that those at the bottom of the economic, social and financial ladder should be least tolerant and generous. This leads to relatively high anti-immigrant sentiments, xenophobia and prejudice among the poor, and its mirror prediction that it is the wealthy (and not the poor) who are more tolerant of and generous towards minorities (Hypothesis 2b)? Before exploring the empirical support for these predictions, it is important to highlight that researchers interested in this question have defined those 'at the bottom of the economic, social and financial ladder' in many different ways. Whereas some have focused on direct indicators of economic wealth such as income, others have focused on more indirect indicators such as social class as defined by profession or education level. We will include all these indicators in our review.

Consistent with Hypothesis 2b, there does appear to be a consistent finding that, at least in contemporary society, highly educated and higher SES people tend to be more tolerant towards minorities such as immigrants. Indeed, there is a considerable body of literature showing that manual workers and the less educated are one category of voters to be drawn to populist right-wing parties (Falter & Klein, 1994;

Lubbers & Scheepers, 2000), and more likely to oppose immigration (Lubbers, Gijsberts, & Scheepers, 2002).

In itself, the finding that lower SES social groups (and the professions they occupy) might be less tolerant, more hostile and more aggressive is not all that surprising. One of the most robust findings in the criminological literature is that there is more aggression and violence in lower SES environments (Pratt & Cullen, 2005). These are also the neighbourhoods where immigrants tend to live when they first arrive in their new countries (and where they often remain for a long time). So, if we want to know if lower SES groups are targeting their hostility towards immigrants in particular, we would really need to discount the fact that there is, on average, more hostility and violence in lower SES neighbourhoods. This means that even if we find more hostility towards immigrants and minorities in poorer than in wealthier neighbourhoods, this finding may not be that informative and may not be used as evidence to support Hypothesis 2a and 2b.

Notwithstanding these problems, it is still of interest to examine the characteristics that best predict anti-immigrant attitudes. In Table 3.1, we report the relative strength of a number of predictors of anti-immigrant attitudes in 14 European countries (as measured by the Eurobarometer in the period 2002–2012). Interestingly, the three strongest predictors of anti-immigrant sentiments are age, political orientation and trust in others. It is older people, those who hold more conservative or right-wing views and those who are less trusting of others who are more likely to endorse anti-immigrant statements.

By comparison, economic indicators at the individual level (such as income or education) and economic indicators at the collective level (such as GDP per capita) are weaker predictors of anti-immigrant attitudes. Important for examining support for our hypotheses though, these findings appear to confirm that it is those who are less wealthy and those who are less educated who express stronger anti-immigrant sentiments (Hypothesis 2a). Similarly, lower GDP per capita levels appear to be associated with more negative attitudes towards immigrants (Hypothesis 1a).

There are a few more findings reported in Table 3.1 that are of interest. First, 'year' is not a significant predictor of anti-immigrant attitudes. This suggests that within and across these 14 European counties, anti-immigrant attitudes have not changed between 2002

Table 3.1. *What predicts differences between countries in anti-immigrant attitudes? Looking within and between fourteen European countries, from 2002–2012.*

	Estimate	Std. Error	*t* value	
(Intercept)	−0.69	0.06	−1.13	
Individual-level variables				
Gender	0.12	0.01	1.44	
Age	0.06	0.00	26.30	***
Income	−0.66	0.00	−13.69	***
Unemployed	0.04	0.02	0.24	
Education level	−0.20	0.00	−12.79	***
Year	−0.10	0.01	−1.59	
GDP per capita	0.00	0.00	−3.32	***
Number of foreign migrants	13.06	0.65	2.02	*
Political orientation	0.58	0.00	28.16	***
Trust	−0.71	0.00	−26.91	***
Happiness	−0.08	0.00	−2.47	*
Satisfaction with life	−0.08	0.00	−2.72	**

*p < .05, ** p < .01, *** p < .001.

Source: Eurobarometer data.

and 2012. Even though this does not mean that there may not have been shifts from year to year and shifts within countries, it is an interesting finding in the sense that it disconfirms the general assumption that people have become more intolerant of immigrants in Europe.

A second finding of interest is that happiness and satisfaction with life predict anti-immigrant sentiments: it is those who are happier and more satisfied with life who express more positive attitudes towards immigrants. Even though this is not of direct relevance in relation to the question of whether our hypotheses are supported, this finding does provide indirect support for the notion that it is dissatisfaction that is associated with anti-immigrant attitudes. However, and as we will argue in the following chapters, dissatisfaction is not necessarily lower among the 'haves' than the 'have-nots'.

So far, the evidence for Hypotheses 2a and 2b appears to be quite forthcoming. However, there are also studies that fail to support these hypotheses. The findings of many researchers who examined the societal-level predictors of hostility towards minorities and immigrants are often inconclusive or contradictory: competition and hardship are not always related to hostility towards minorities and immigrants in a straightforward and direct manner (Coenders, Lubbers, Scheepers, & Verkuyten, 2008; Coenders & Scheepers, 2008; Savelkoul, Scheepers, Tolsma, & Hagendoorn, 2011).

Taking Stock

Even though we concluded that there was insufficient support for Hypotheses 1a and 1b, at first sight, it appears that there is more support for Hypothesis 2a and 2b. Specifically, large-scale studies do provide evidence that people with lower incomes and lower levels of education are more negative towards immigrants (Hypothesis 2a). However, it is also clear that these relationships are not that strong (at least not as strong as other predictors of these attitudes). Moreover, evidence for Hypothesis 2a is mostly obtained from cross-sectional data sets – data sets that cannot help us to argue that an individuals' wealth *causes* their attitudes towards immigrants. Notably, it cannot be ruled out that other factors explain the observed relationships. Thus, whilst it appears that overall there are higher levels of anti-immigrant sentiments among groups that *might* be in competition with those immigrants for jobs, there is no evidence that these sentiments are *caused* by increasing competition and increasing immigration.

It is clear that the relationship between competition, hardship and intergroup hostility is tenuous. However, this does not mean that the theoretical concepts themselves are entirely irrelevant. It is clear that populist right-wing politicians in countries such as Austria, Belgium, France, Australia and the Netherlands have found a willing audience with their rhetoric of threats due to competition, hardship and loss of identity. Indeed, it appears that the strongest predictor of support for extreme right-wing parties is 'public opinion' on issues such as democracy and immigration (Lubbers et al., 2002). Thus, the theoretical concepts identified by theories of competition may be important and influential within a *social climate* surrounding specific current affairs.

Immigrant numbers may go up and down, but this only becomes relevant when 'immigration' becomes regarded as a problem. This suggests that if we want to understand when and how *perceptions* of competition, hardship and identity threat become activated and consequential for intergroup behaviour, we need to study public discourse in which these concepts are mobilised. We will explore this issue further in Chapter 9.

Returning to the question of whether our hypotheses are supported, the answer is probably that even though support for Hypotheses 2a and 2b is stronger than support for Hypotheses 1a and 1b, overall support for these hypotheses is rather mixed. More importantly, it appears that research in this area suffers from the problem we identified in Chapter 1: it has narrowly focused on one relationship and has overlooked other ways in which economic performance can affect hostility between groups and attitudes towards minorities. Notably, it has largely overlooked the way in which economic prosperity and wealth can *enhance* negative attitudes and hostility towards minorities such as immigrants. As we will show in the next section, there is considerable empirical evidence challenging Hypotheses 1a–2b.

PART II

Broadening Our Horizon: The 'Wealth Paradox'

4 | Rethinking the Relationship between Wealth and Tolerance: National, Regional and Local Trends

The idea of 'harsh times producing harsh attitudes' also underlies much of the literature on the appeal of political parties that promote an anti-immigration agenda. Although there is a wide variety of perspectives and hypotheses, 'grievances thinking' has continued to dominate this debate (De Witte & Klandermans, 2000; Koopmans et al., 2005; Rydgren, 2007). Voters, so the argument typically goes, will have relaxed attitudes towards immigrants and asylum seekers when the economy is thriving. However, they will become more hostile towards these groups when the economy slows down, when the prospect of unemployment looms, and when immigrants become perceived as competitors in the labour market.

As Rydgren (2007, p. 247) put it, the various explanations on offer in this burgeoning literature are 'almost all based on grievance theory, [focusing on] objective – mostly macro-structurally shaped – conditions that have increased grievances and discontent among the people'. Accordingly, in this body of research, disposable income and employment status are typically predicted to be the main factors shaping voters' receptiveness to populist right-wing messages (Arzheimer, 2009; Arzheimer & Carter, 2006; Golder, 2003; Jackman & Volpert, 1996).

Certainly, it is possible to find examples of populist anti-immigration parties that appear to have benefitted from economic downturn. Consider Greece's Golden Dawn party, which failed to secure seats in parliament in 1996 and 2009, but managed to win 21 seats (6.9% of the vote) in the 2012 elections, when voters felt the full force of the GFC and ensuing Greek Debt Crisis. Likewise, the Sweden Democrats participated in seven consecutive national elections, but without ever reaching the threshold for a seat in parliament. This was to change in the wake of the GFC, with the party securing 20 seats (5.7% of the vote) in the 2010 national elections, and 49 seats (12.9% of the vote) in the 2014 elections. These two examples appear to confirm that far-right parties perform better electorally when the economy slows down.

Providing further support for this notion, a large body of research examining factors fuelling support for populist anti-immigrant parties shows that economic downturn and heightened levels of unemployment *can* increase the appeal of anti-immigration parties (Betz, 1994; Ignazi, 1992; Jackman & Volpert, 1996; Kitschelt, 1995; Kolinsky, 1992; Lipset & Raab, 1978; Stöss, 1991), and that blue-collar workers are more likely to vote for such parties than white-collar workers (Falter & Klein, 1994; Lubbers et al., 2002). Nevertheless, it might be worthwhile to examine these relationships more closely.

In this chapter we will explore the way economic performance (as assessed by GDP per capita and unemployment) affects support for populist anti-immigrant parties at the national, regional and local levels. As we examine the empirical case in greater detail, it will become clear that there is no straightforward support for the widespread assumption of economic crises providing particularly 'fertile soil' for populist anti-immigrant parties (Hypothesis 1a) or for the hypothesis that support for such parties is highest among low-income groups in society (Hypothesis 2a).

The Rise of the Sweden Democrats

Let us start with a closer look at the sudden increase in popularity of the Sweden Democrats after the GFC. It may be tempting to interpret this success as evidence that economic crises (as reflected in high unemployment levels and lower GDP per capita income) provide fertile ground for populist right-wing parties. However, a few observations are noteworthy when examining the popularity of the party over a longer period of time (Figure 4.1). First, even though Sweden Democrats' popularity rose after the 2008 GFC, it did not increase significantly during previous crises (e.g. 1993–1994).

Second, the party was founded in 1988, at a time of relative prosperity in Sweden, with low levels of unemployment and sustained GDP per capita growth – a time when voters should not have had many grievances.[1] Indeed, it appears that the party established itself as

---

[1] Sweden Democrats was formed in 1988 as the successor to the Sweden Party, established in 1986 through the merger of the Keep Sweden Swedish party and

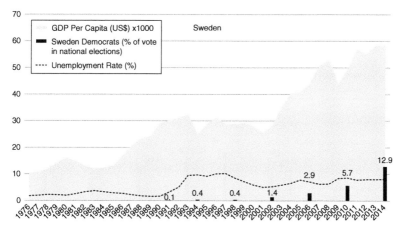

Figure 4.1. Sweden's economy (GDP and unemployment) and Sweden Democrat's electoral performance.
Source: World Bank data.

a player in the political arena at a time when the economy was improving (2002) or even flourishing (2006). More generally, and consistent with this observation, what should not be forgotten is that, as Ignazi (cited in Wilson & Hainsworth, 2012, p. 14) points out, populist right-wing parties began their remarkable comeback in Western Europe in the mid-1980s, well before the GFC, and they continued to gain strength throughout the 1990s, an era in which many European countries experienced unprecedented economic growth and prosperity. In sum, when considering long-term trends, it is not so evident that the Sweden Democrats benefitted from economic crises and rising unemployment levels.

Electoral Success of Anti-immigrant Parties in France and Germany

Even though unemployment and electoral success of popular parties such as the Sweden Democrats appear to be unrelated, it is not too difficult to find examples of populist right-wing electoral successes that

the Progress Party. This too is remarkable if we consider that Sweden had just experienced three consecutive years of GDP per capita growth and falling unemployment levels.

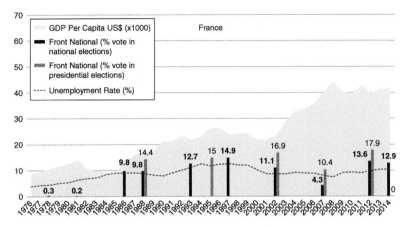

Figure 4.2. France's economy (GDP and unemployment) and Front National's electoral performance.
Source: World Bank.

appear to coincide with peaks in unemployment. Consider, for example, Front National in France. Eyeballing their trajectory over time, whereas this party appears to have achieved electoral success when unemployment is high (e.g. 1986), the party seems to be less popular among voters when unemployment is decreasing (e.g. 2007; see Figure 4.2).

However, it is also possible to find examples of populist right-wing parties that failed to secure strong or stronger support during economic crises and rising levels of unemployment. For example, as shown in Figure 4.3, between 1990 and 2002, support for the German Republikaner declined over the course of four consecutive national Bundestag elections (2.1% of the vote in 1990, 1.9% in 1994, 1.8% in 1998, and 0.6% in 2002). This happened at a time when German reunification was having a negative effect on the country's economic performance, resulting in a considerable decline in GDP per capita across seven consecutive years (1995–2001) and record levels of unemployment (peaking at 11.4% in 1997). Indeed, when considering long-term trends since the mid-1970s, and comparing trends in different national contexts, there is not much support for the predicted link between economic conditions and populist right-wing party appeal (Hypothesis 1a).

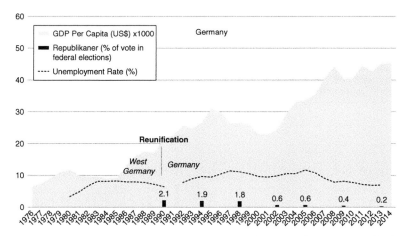

Figure 4.3. Germany's economy (GDP and unemployment) and the Republikaner's electoral performance.
Sources: World Bank (GDP per capita) and Bundesagentur für Arbeit (Unemployment rate).

Electoral Success of Anti-immigrant Parties in Times of Economic Prosperity

It may be tempting to dismiss examples of populist parties failing to capitalise in times of economic downturns as exceptions that confirm the rule. However, this would be to ignore the many examples of populist right-wing parties that secured major electoral victories in times of economic prosperity. One does not have to look very far to find such examples.

Our first example of a populist right-wing party securing significant proportion of the vote in a time of economic prosperity is Pauline Hanson's One Nation party in Australia. The party, established in 1997, took part in Federal elections for the first time in 1998, securing 8.4% of the vote. This sudden rise may be remarkable in and of itself, but is all the more surprising when we consider that Australia had experienced five consecutive years of GDP growth (from US$ 308bn in 1993 to US$ 427bn in 1997), and a steady decline in unemployment (from 10.6% in 1992 to 7.7% in 1998). As can be seen from Figure 4.4, this case not only provides more evidence for the view that there is no simple correlation between crisis and populist right-wing party success

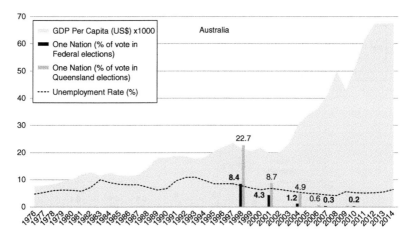

Figure 4.4. Australia's economy (GDP and unemployment) and One Nation's electoral performance.
Source: World Bank data.

(Hypothesis 1a), but also considerable evidence to dismiss the idea that societies experiencing economic prosperity become more tolerant of minorities and immigrants (Hypothesis 1b). What is more, One Nation turned out to have considerable electoral appeal in Hanson's home state of Queensland. Here, Gross State Product had been stable for two consecutive years, followed by two subsequent years of rapid economic growth (from 1998 to 2000).

Also worth noting is One Nation's gradual demise at both the Federal and State levels, which occurred at a time in which Australia and Queensland experienced rapid economic growth. At first glance this pattern appears to support the prediction that economic prosperity leads to more relaxed attitudes towards immigrants and newcomers (H2b). However, this would be to misread the situation, and to ignore that during these years the party in government, the Liberal Party of Australia, managed to increase its appeal significantly by adopting One Nation's rhetoric and harsh stance on immigration and asylum seeking (Wear, 2008). During these years, party-political dynamics weakened electoral support for One Nation, but, nation-wide, support for harsher immigration and asylum policies grew significantly.

There are other examples. For instance, as can be seen from Figure 4.5, the Danish People's Party (DPP) secured two major victories

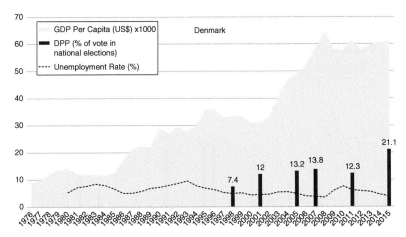

Figure 4.5. Denmark's economy (GDP per capita and unemployment) and the DPP's electoral performance.
Sources: World Bank & IMF data.

in 2005 (13.2% of the vote) and 2007 (13.8% of the vote), this at a time when GDP per capita was rising rapidly, and unemployment dropped to as low as 3.8%. Also noteworthy is that the party slipped back slightly in the subsequent 2011 elections (12.3% of the votes), this at a time when the full scale of the GFC was felt most strongly. During the 2015 elections, the party secured its biggest victory to date (21.1% of the vote), this despite the country's economy showing signs of recovery. For example, GDP per capita grew moderately for two consecutive years (from US$ 57,636 in 2012 to US$ 60,634 in 2014). These trends do not fit traditional thinking, and show that the relationship between economic performance and the popularity of right-wing parties can, and often does, contradict Hypothesis 1a.

Likewise, as can be seen from Figure 4.6, the Austrian Freedom Party secured 33 seats in parliament (16.6% of the vote) in 1990, this despite the fact that the country experienced five consecutive years of GDP per capita growth, and evidence that unemployment levels dropped from 3.8% (1987) to 2.7% (1990).

A similar pattern can be found in Switzerland, where the Swiss Freedom Party (FPS) secured 8 seats (5.1% of the national vote) in the 1991 national elections. Interestingly, this was at a time when

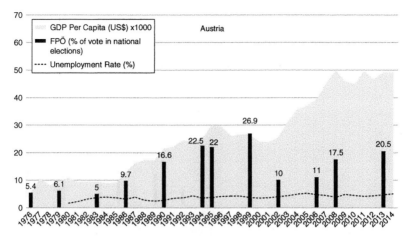

Figure 4.6. Austria's economy (GDP and unemployment) and the Austrian Freedom Party's electoral performance.
Source: World Bank data.

unemployment was as low as 1.1%, and the country's GDP had increased from US$ 179bn in 1987 to US$ 238bn. This is not the only Swiss evidence showing populist anti-immigrant parties can thrive in times of economic boom. For example, due to the growing influence of the more radical Zürich branch of the party in the 1990s, the Swiss People's Party (SVP), once a moderate political party, started promoting a harsher stance on immigration and multiculturalism (Betz, 2009, p. 198). As can be seen from Figure 4.7, the radicalised SVP performed very well in four successive national elections, increasing its share of the vote from 11.9% in 1991 to 28.9% in 2007. Indeed, although the party was successful when the Swiss economy was slowing down (1999), the party secured its greatest victory when the economy was thriving (2007), with the country's GDP per capita level rising for a fifth consecutive year and unemployment dropping to 3.6%.

Another interesting case is the Netherlands. As can be seen from Figure 4.8, populist right-wing parties have been part of the political landscape since the early 1970s. However, even though the country experienced a rather severe economic crisis in the early 1980s (with unemployment rising to 10%), these parties were unable to attract a significant proportion of the votes. This changed dramatically in 2002, when List Pim Fortuyn (LPF) secured a landslide victory (17%

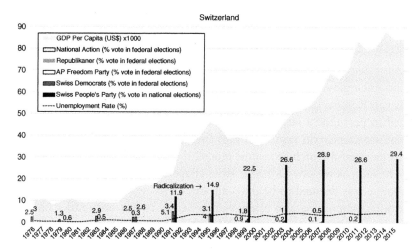

Figure 4.7. Switzerland's economy (GDP and unemployment) and populist right-wing party performance.
Source: World Bank data.

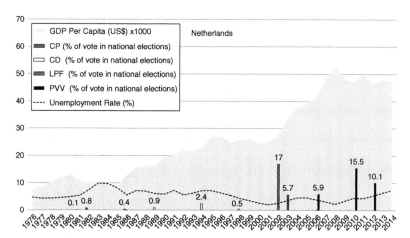

Figure 4.8. The Dutch economy (GDP and unemployment) and performance by various anti-immigration parties.
Source: World Bank data.

of the vote), nine days after the murder of LPFs party leader, Pim Fortuyn. What makes the rapid rise of LPF even more noteworthy is that it occurred at a time at which the Dutch economy was in excellent shape, with per capita GDP on the increase for a third consecutive year, and unemployment levels hovering between 2.1% and 2.7%. Indeed, as van Rossem (2010) observed, it is rather ironic that Fortuyn managed to persuade a large proportion of the electorate that the country was in tatters in the same year that *The Economist* ran a special issue on the successful Dutch economic model, the so-called Polder Model.

In sum, as we saw in the previous chapter, for a long time economic decline was deemed to be the main force driving intolerance for other groups, hate crime and intergroup violence. It was not until scholars took a long-term view that they started to challenge this notion. The same can be said about research into the appeal of populist right-wing parties, which continues to focus heavily on grievances, and in particular grievances about macro-economic conditions (De Witte & Klandermans, 2000; Rydgren, 2007; see also Koopmans et al., 2005). As we saw, when considering the times when such parties have

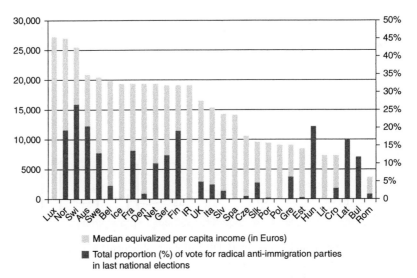

Figure 4.9. Support for anti-immigration parties in affluent and less affluent European countries.
Source: Eurostat and Swiss Bundesambt Für Statistik (median equivalised per capita income)

managed to secure significant election victories, it becomes apparent that although there is some evidence suggesting such parties can benefit from economic crises (e.g. Sweden, Greece) or rising unemployment (e.g. France), there is just as much evidence that such parties can thrive in times of economic prosperity. Moreover, as can be seen from Figure 4.9, anti-immigration parties have done remarkably well in relatively affluent countries, where voters enjoy high levels of disposable per capita income (e.g. Norway, Sweden Switzerland, Austria, Netherlands, Australia).

Unemployment Giving Rise to Realistic Conflict?

There is some evidence that populist anti-immigration parties can benefit from peaks in immigration and asylum seeking. For example, as shown in Figure 4.10, in Sweden the steady growth in support for the Sweden Democrats, which started in the early 2000s, appears to coincide with a steady increase in immigration and asylum applications in that same period. This may help to explain the party's recent historic breakthrough. However, despite the peak in immigration and asylum seeking in the early 1990s, the Sweden Democrats failed to reach the threshold for seats in parliament.

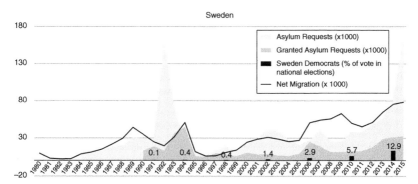

Figure 4.10. Immigration, asylum seeking and Sweden Democrats' electoral performance.
Source: Migrationsverket.

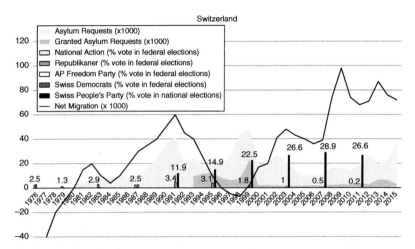

Figure 4.11. Immigration, asylum seeking and the *Swiss People Party*'s electoral performance.
Sources: Bundesambt Für Migration (Net Migration), OECD and UNHCR (Asylum)

Another example of a populist right-wing party appearing to benefit from peaks in asylum and immigration is the Swiss People's Party. As Figure 4.11 shows, the party increased its share of the vote from 2.5% in 1987 to 11.9% in 1991. This was at a time when the number of asylum requests increased sharply from 10,931 in 1987 to 41,629 in 1991. Likewise, the party's share of the vote went up from 14.9% in 1995 to 22.5% in 1999 – a time when the number of asylum requests peaked for a second time, with numbers increasing from 19,502 in 1996 to 48,057 in 1999.

Once again, it may be tempting to attribute these successes to high numbers of asylum seekers. However, as can also be seen from Figure 4.11, the party did not lose electoral appeal when asylum-seeking numbers declined (1995, 2003 and 2007). On the contrary, the party secured its largest victory to date (28.9% of the vote) in 2007, following five consecutive years of declining numbers of asylum seekers and declining net migration. Indeed, when this counterevidence is taken into account, it becomes apparent that although populist right-wing parties may at times benefit from being able to draw attention to peaks in asylum and immigration, on the whole there is no evidence to suggest that these parties perform better electorally when the country faces a sharp increase in immigration.

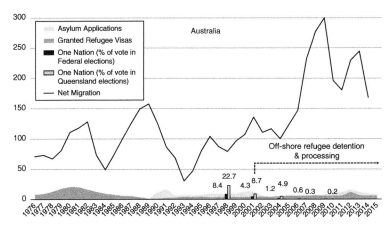

Figure 4.12. Immigration, asylum seeking and One Nation's electoral performance.
Sources: Department of Immigration and Border Protection (Net Migration), Parliament of Australia (Granted Refugee Visas), and UNHCR (Asylum Applications).

Switzerland is not the only country where a populist anti-immigration party performed well despite a significant and prolonged decrease in numbers of immigrants and asylum seekers. Consider the late 1990s electoral successes of One Nation in Australia. As can be seen from Figure 4.12, this party's electoral success did not coincide with a significant increase or peak in immigration. Rather, the opposite appears to be true: these successes occurred at a time of declining humanitarian intake and declining numbers of overseas settlers. What is also worth noting is the absence of a populist right-wing party during times where there were peaks in overseas arrivals (e.g. the mid-1980s and the late 2000s).

Our analysis of the appeal of populist anti-immigration parties in the Netherlands reveals a similar picture. As can be seen from Figure 4.13, the Centrum Democrats secured 0.9% of the vote in 1989, and although the party performed slightly better in 1994, securing 2.4% of the vote, it is fair to say that this is a rather modest gain considering the sharp increase in refugees seeking asylum in the Netherlands (from approximately 13,900 in 1989 to 52,600 in 1994). What is even more

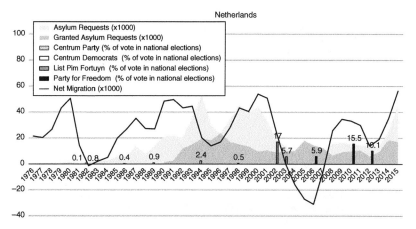

Figure 4.13. Immigration, asylum seeking and anti-immigration party performance. CP = Centrum Party, CD = Centrum Democrats, LPF = List Pim Fortuyn, PVV = Party for Freedom.
Source: CBS Stat Line.

striking is that the sudden rise of Pim Fortuyn's LPF party in 2002 coincided with a decline in net migration and a declining number of refugees seeking asylum in the Netherlands (from approximately 43,600 in 2000 to 18,700 in 2002).

Similar conclusions can be drawn when examining the support for the Austrian Freedom Party more closely. Here, too, it is possible to identify times when the party appears to benefit from a peak in immigration and asylum seeking (e.g. in 1990 and again in 1999). However, we also find evidence that shows an opposite trend (see Figure 4.14.). First, the party lost a significant share of the vote in 2002 (falling from 26.9% of the vote in 2000 to 10% of the vote in 2002), even though the country had seen a sharp rise in asylum seeking and net migration. Second, the party proved able to increase its appeal among voters in 1994 (securing 16.6% of the vote in 1990, and 22% of the vote in 1995) – this despite a rather dramatic decline in immigration and numbers of refugees seeking asylum in Austria.

We can also ask whether the various electoral successes of France's Front National can be attributed to peaks in refugees seeking asylum or to increases in net migration. Front National, founded by Jean-Marie Le Pen in 1972, has taken part in many national elections, allowing for a unique opportunity to examine whether populist right-wing party

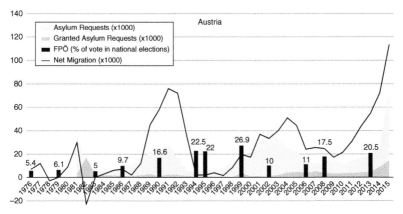

Figure 4.14. Immigration, asylum seeking and Freiheitliche Partei Österreich's (FPO) electoral performance.
Sources: Statistik Austria (Net Migration) and Asylkoordination (Asylum Requests and Admissions).

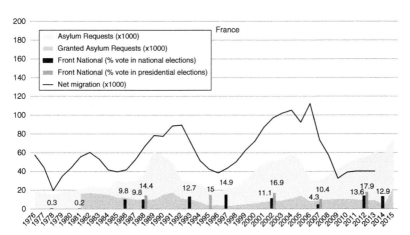

Figure 4.15. Immigration, asylum seeking and Front National's electoral performance.
Sources: INSEE (Net Migration) and OFPRA (Asylum Requests and Admissions).

successes can be attributed to macro-economic and social factors over a longer period of time.

As can be seen from Figure 4.15, Front National has a remarkable track record, with a remarkably consistent level of electoral support, regardless of whether the economy is booming or contracting, and regardless of whether levels of immigration and asylum seeking are up or down. Indeed, France can be regarded as a strong case in and of itself against the presumed causal link between crisis and populist right-wing party appeal (Hypothesis 1a), but also against the presumed causal link between levels of immigration and the appeal of such parties.

It should be clear from the above analysis of long-term trends that there is (a) no straightforward relationship between national economic conditions and support for populist right-wing parties, and (b) no clear relationship between levels of immigration or asylum seeking and support for such parties.

Zooming In: Considering Within-country Differences

Even though it may be tempting to draw conclusions at this point, it might be prudent to look at these electoral patterns once more, and to check whether rises and falls in voter support reflect a *delayed response* to changing economic conditions or changes in the intake of immigrants and asylum seekers. That is, it may well be possible that there is a considerable *delay* between the slowing down of the economy and rises in violence and hate crime (but also populist right-wing voting). Or, it is possible that such rises can be fuelled by concerns about *future* (rather than current) economic conditions. Of particular relevance here is a classic study by James Davies (1962), who analysed famous revolutions and concluded that popular uprisings are most likely to occur when a period of prolonged prosperity comes to an end, and when people begin to fear that their *future* expectations might not be fulfilled.

To examine these two hypotheses, we again considered the data presented so far in this chapter and examined whether – as one would expect, considering Davies' work on uprisings – there are peaks in populist right-wing voting when a prosperous era comes to an end. From the cases reported here, only Australia appears to show some support for Davies' hypothesis. Specifically, One Nation experiences a rather sudden rise in votes in the wake of five consecutive years of GDP growth and falling unemployment levels, and it seems plausible that there were signs on the horizon that the boom was coming to an end. However, in all other cases, there does not appear to be much support for this alternative hypothesis, with many cases showing no greater success of populist right-wing parties when economic booms come to an end.

However, let us dig a bit deeper. It is entirely possible that we do not find evidence for these hypotheses at the national level because the analysis is too coarse. Perhaps we would find more evidence for the hypothesised relationships when examining more confined geographical areas. With help of the rather small but interesting literature examining the appeal of populist right-wing parties in different types of regions, cities and neighbourhoods with different socio-economic characteristics, we can examine this possibility further.

Following H2a, one would expect populist right-wing parties to enjoy greater popularity in rural and industrialised regions suffering relative deprivation, where poor working-class people make up a larger section of the population (and thus of the voters). Here too, however, the evidence reveals a more complex picture. For example, as can be seen from the two maps pictured in Figure 4.16, the United Kingdom Independence Party (UKIP) – a party renowned for its calls to curb immigration from within the EU – tends to enjoy greater popularity in relatively deprived rural peripheral regions (e.g. Cornwall, Wales, East Lincolnshire, Hull and Basildon).

Although this pattern appears to fit with the view that there should be a link between 'the poor' (i.e. those facing relative deprivation) being more likely to be drawn to populist right-wing parties, a number of other oddities emerge when examining this pattern further. For example, as can be seen from Figure 4.17, UKIP appears to draw support in rural regions where there is actually a lower level of immigration and ethnic diversity. In other words, UKIP's anti-immigrant message is popular in areas where immigrants can be expected to pose little immediate symbolic or realistic threat.

Nevertheless, even though the UKIP example can be taken as an example that economic deprivation provides fertile soil for populist parties, there are other cases that appear to run against this notion. Consider Switzerland, a country where a referendum was held enabling the population to have their say about a proposal to introduce stricter immigration regulations. This referendum, referred to as the 'confederal referendum against mass immigration' (*Eidgenössische Volksinitiative Gegen Masseneinwanderung*), was held on 9 February 2014, and the

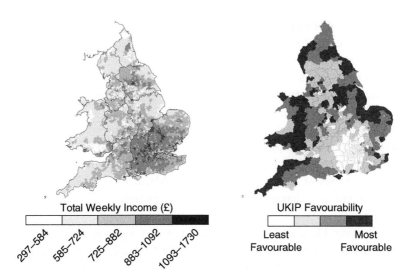

Figure 4.16. UKIP Support in deprived UK regions.
Sources: ONS England and Wales Census 2011 (Total Weekly Income) and House of Commons Library Research Paper 14/32: 2011 Census (UKIP favourability): map featured in Goodwin and Milazzo (2015) UKIP: *Inside the Campaign to Redraw the Map of British Politics*, Oxford, Oxford University Press. Reprinted with permission.

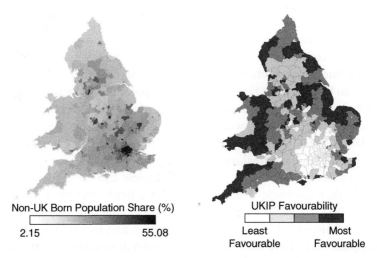

Figure 4.17. UKIP support in regions with low levels of immigration and diversity.
Sources: ONS England and Wales Census 2011 (Non-UK born population share) and House of Commons Library Research Paper 14/32: 2011 Census (UKIP favourability): map featured in Goodwin and Milazzo (2015) UKIP: *Inside the Campaign to Redraw the Map of British Politics*, Oxford, Oxford University Press. Reprinted with permission.

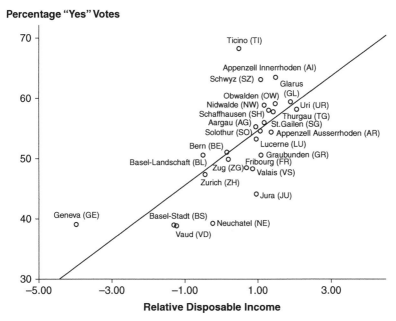

Figure 4.18. The positive linear relationship between percentages 'yes' votes by Kanton in the Swiss referendum (y-axis) and relative disposable income (x-axis).
Source: Credit Suisse Economic Research (Disposable Income).

proposed changes were accepted with a narrow majority (with 50.34% 'yes' votes). This is arguably a remarkable result for a country consistently ranked in the top ten of the world's wealthiest countries, and a country that survived the GFC with minimal harm to its economy. However, this is not the only finding that is surprising.

We analysed the referenda results for each of the 26 Swiss Kantons and found that support for the proposal was strongest in Kantons with *higher* relative disposable income (see Figure 4.18) and *lower* levels of unemployment (see Figure 4.19; see also Jetten et al., 2015).

Interestingly too, in the Netherlands, there is also evidence that it is not necessarily the poor (those who experience relative deprivation) but the more wealthy (those who experience relative gratification) who vote for the Dutch Freedom Party, the PVV. As Figure 4.20 shows, in addition to all the other expected predictors of voting for a populist right-wing party (e.g. education levels, endorsement of right-wing

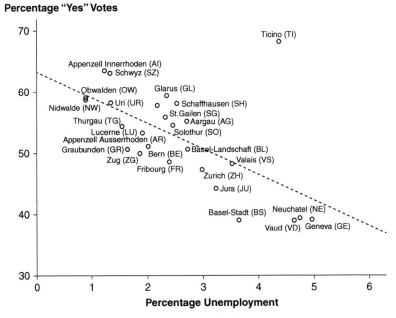

Figure 4.19. The negative linear relationship between percentages 'yes' votes by Kanton in the Swiss referendum (y-axis) and unemployment in percentages (x-axis).
Source: Bundesambt Für Statistik (Unemployment).

beliefs), Dutch PVV voters are likely to earn more rather than less than the national average (21% more than average).

The 2014 Swiss referendum results and the profile of PVV voters in the Netherlands are not the only available empirical evidence suggesting a link between affluence and support for populist, right-wing parties. Scholars examined support for Hitler's NSDAP in Weimar Germany across different German regions. Not surprisingly, and consistent with Hypothesis 2a, it was found that NSDAP support was strong in depressed working-class regions (e.g. Thuringia). However, and contrary to this hypothesis, support was equally strong in affluent protestant rural regions (e.g. Schleswig-Holstein, Mecklenburg, Pomerania and East Prussia), and weaker in industrialised regions (O'Loughlin, Flint, & Shin, 1995; see also Geary, 2002).

The Netherlands - PVV Voter Characteristics

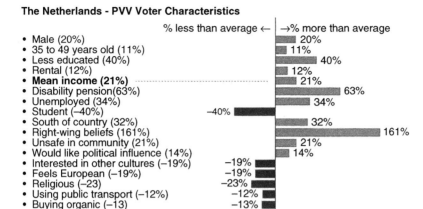

% less than average ← | →% more than average

- Male (20%) — 20%
- 35 to 49 years old (11%) — 11%
- Less educated (40%) — 40%
- Rental (12%) — 12%
- **Mean income (21%)** — 21%
- Disability pension(63%) — 63%
- Unemployed (34%) — 34%
- Student (−40%) — −40%
- South of country (32%) — 32%
- Right-wing beliefs (161%) — 161%
- Unsafe in community (21%) — 21%
- Would like political influence (14%) — 14%
- Interested in other cultures (−19%) — −19%
- Feels European (−19%) — −19%
- Religious (−23) — −23%
- Using public transport (−12%) — −12%
- Buying organic (−13) — −13%

Figure 4.20. Voters' profile of the Dutch Party of Freedom (PVV).
Source: Synovate, 2010.

Equally remarkable were the findings of a study examining the exceptionally high levels of NSDAP support witnessed in the German city of Braunschweig in the early 1930s. Across the city, the NSDAP secured 36% of the vote. However, there were considerable variations in support by precincts. NSDAP support was highest in the seven upper middle-class precincts of the city, with levels of support ranging from 61% to 65.5% (Hamilton, 1984, p. 11).

Equally intriguing is the big-picture question of why fascist movements emerged in the 1930s in some countries in crisis, but not in others. As Hannah Arendt noted in her 1951 book *The Origins of Totalitarianism*, fascist movements took hold in 1930s Germany and Italy, but not in the UK, even though this country was suffering equally from the Great Depression. Arendt attributed this difference to political culture, traditions and institutions, thereby distinguishing between factors hindering and helping the rise of radical far-right movements. What is more, in her book, Arendt describes the attitudes and preferences of the affluent middle-class in Weimar Germany in detail, focusing on the way in which they became attracted to Hitler's radical ideas. Arendt's seminal work can be seen as a useful early reminder that there is no simple 'automatic' link between economic conditions and outgroup attitudes, and that other factors (e.g. political culture, institutions and leadership style) determine this relationship. Consistent with Arendt's thinking, there is now growing recognition that understanding the appeal of populist right-wing parties involves coming to terms with a high level of complexity and acknowledging local contextual differences (Lubbers & Scheepers, 2000).

The Overall Picture

In sum, the evidence presented in this chapter leads us to the modest but nonetheless important conclusion that no firm conclusions can be drawn about the relationship between economic downturn and support for parties with an anti-immigrant agenda (Hypothesis 1a). A smaller body of work examining whether it is the less wealthy who are most attracted to such political parties also provides inconclusive evidence for the proposed relationship (Hypothesis 2a). Indeed, findings reported in this chapter clearly challenge intuitive predictions that support for parties with a populist agenda is a function of crisis and conflict over scarce resources. One other conclusion to draw is that at times there is evidence for the opposite of what Hypotheses 1a and 2a leads us to predict: the possibility of *affluence* engendering hostility towards minorities, and economic *prosperity* providing fertile soil for populist right-wing parties (Lubbers,& Scheepers, 2000; Lubbers et al., 2002; Lucassen & Lubbers, 2012; see also Betz, 1993). Indeed, it is clear from our own research, and from research conducted by others, that populist right-wing parties and leaders can do remarkably well in times of economic prosperity, and among voters with *above*-average incomes.[2] This raises questions about what such parties have to offer to those experiencing economic growth and prosperity. And what theorising can explain the appeal of such populist political parties in times of economic prosperity when economic grievances are not that apparent?

---

[2] As noted in the preface, at the time of finishing this book compelling additional evidence for this counterintuitive proposition started to emerge, with research analysing the UK Brexit referendum results discovering that 'Leave' voters earned *more* than the national average (Dorling, 2016) and researchers analysing support for US presidential candidate Donald Trump discovering that Trump supporters earn *more* than the national average (Rothwell & Diego-Rosell, 2016).

Before addressing these questions, we will first examine support for our hypotheses in the context of development aid and charitable giving. These hypotheses posit that increased wealth and affluence should be associated with tolerance and generosity towards those who are less well off. We focus in particular on generosity as measured by charitable giving and ask whether economic prosperity and wealth is associated with greater generosity.

5 | Development Aid, Charitable Giving and Economic Prosperity

The assumption that harsh times produce harsh attitudes has ramifications for how we think about charitable giving and volunteering. Our analysis starts at the macro-level. Testing H1a and H2a, we examine whether there is a link between a country's macro-economic conditions and preparedness to contribute financially to Overseas Development Aid (ODA). We will then explore the relationship between an individual's wealth and charitable giving (H1b and H2b).

Economic Prosperity and Overseas Development Aid

When thinking of ODA, one would expect governments of wealthier countries ('who can afford it') to be quite generous, and governments with weaker economies ('who can ill afford it') to be more tight-fisted. Likewise, when focusing on individual countries one would expect ODA funding to increase over time when the economy flourishes, and to decline during times when the economy stalls or declines. All this may appear to make perfect sense. After all, citizens of wealthy countries can be expected to worry less about the level of ODA their country donates, while citizens of countries with weaker economies can be expected to be more motivated to scrutinise government contributions to overseas aid programmes, especially at times when the government in question imposes austerity measures and asks citizens to temporarily 'tighten their belts'.

But what empirical evidence is there to suggest that wealthy countries donate more generously than poorer ones? And what evidence is there to suggest that ODA tends to increase in times of economic prosperity and decline in times of economic hardship? As can be seen in Figure 5.1, if we rank EU member-states according to their median equivalised per capita income, and add information about the proportion of Gross National Income (GNI) spent on ODA that same year

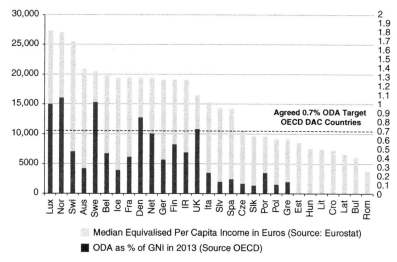

Median Equivalised Per Capita Income in Euros (Source: Eurostat)
ODA as % of GNI in 2013 (Source OECD)

Figure 5.1. European countries and their national ODA spending in 2003. Sources: Eurostat (Equivalised per Capita Income) and OECD (ODA).

(2003), we see that, on the whole, wealthier countries do indeed donate more generously than poorer ones.

At the same time, though, it becomes clear that there are significant differences *between* affluent countries. More specifically, as Figure 5.1 shows, only a small number of EU member-states reach or exceed the agreed OECD-DAC[1] target of 0.7% of GNI. Whereas Luxembourg, Norway, Denmark and the UK all reach or even exceed this target, other wealthy countries, such as Austria and Switzerland, fall well below this agreed target. Such differences are interesting because they can be seen as an initial indication that there is no straightforward link between greater national prosperity and greater preparedness on the part of governments to commit funding to ODA.

A similar pattern emerges when considering longitudinal trends in specific countries' ODA donations. Here too we find clear examples of trends that fit with conventional wisdom, such as governments

---

[1] The Development Assistance Committee (DAC), established in 1962 under the auspices of the OECD, brings together the world's largest aid donor countries. At the time of writing, the DAC group consisted of 29 member-states. Its role is to provide a forum for the world's largest aid donor countries to exchange views and to decide on future strategies. In 1970, the DAC countries agreed on a 7% of GNI target, a target that only a few countries actually meet.

introducing major cuts in ODA in times of economic downturn, presumably justified with the argument that the country can temporarily not afford it. For example, as Roodman (2008) shows, foreign aid from Japan increased steadily between 1985 and 1990, but declined markedly in the wake of the economic crisis, when it became clear that the country's economy was a bubble about to burst. However, when taking a longer-term view, we see a more complex picture emerging. For example, overseas aid from Japan started to increase again in the late 1990s, even though the country was at that time in the grip of a serious banking crisis.

As the above example illustrates, it would be possible to cherry-pick historical examples and to interpret them as evidence of a link between national economic prosperity and ODA. However, as the Japanese example also shows, this would be to ignore times in which the trend runs counter to expectation. Therefore, in order to get a better sense of the complexity of this relationship, and as a mere first step, we examined long-term trends for a randomly selected number of countries. Specifically, we focused on Norway, Switzerland, Austria, Denmark and the Netherlands, and explored whether there is a correlation between economic performance and changes in ODA as a proportion of GNI. As the graphs illustrate, the evidence is rather mixed, and suggests that, on the whole, there is no – or, at least, no straightforward – correlation between national economic performance and levels of ODA spending.

Consider too the UK, where ODA as a percentage of GNI stagnated throughout the 1980s and 1990s (UK House of Commons IDC, 2009). We may be inclined to attribute this decline in ODA directly to the fiscal crisis of the British welfare state, and the government's need to curb public debt levels. However, as can be seen from Figure 5.7, this would be overlooked that, during this era, the country was led by Prime Minister Margaret Thatcher, a staunch advocate of neoliberal free-market ideology who saw increased competition and self-reliance as the way out of the economic crisis. During this era, the political climate changed and harshness became regarded not only a means to an end (e.g. austerity measures to reduce public debt), but also as the new norm for dealing with poorer sections of the population (e.g. welfare cuts to motivate jobseekers).

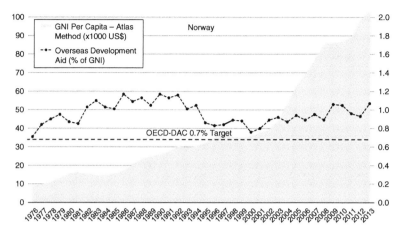

Figure 5.2. Overseas Development Aid as a % of Gross National Income per capita growth in Norway.
Sources: World Bank (GNI per capita) and OECD (ODA as% of GNI).

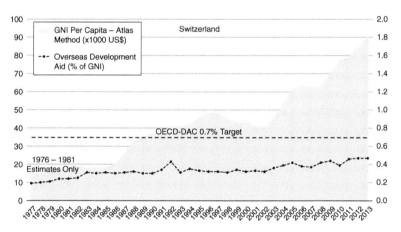

Figure 5.3. Overseas Development Aid as a % of Gross National Income per capita growth in Switzerland.
Sources: World Bank (GNI per capita) and OECD (ODA as% of GNI).

When considering the politics surrounding ODA, it becomes clear that there are limits to what we can learn from tracking and comparing longitudinal macro-level trends. What is more, we know from the literature that ODA trends can be misleading. Depending on what is counted as overseas aid, countries can look more generous than they really are.

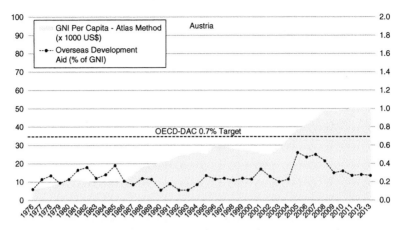

Figure 5.4. Overseas Development Aid as a % of Gross National Income per capita growth in Austria.
Sources: World Bank (GNI per capita) and OECD (ODA as% of GNI).

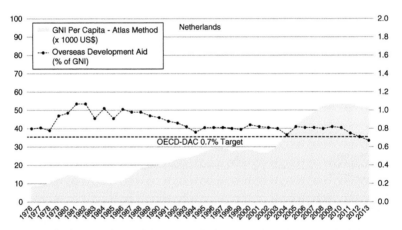

Figure 5.5. Overseas Development Aid as a % of Gross National Income per capita growth in the Netherlands.
Sources: World Bank (GNI per capita) and OECD (ODA as% of GNI).

For example, some countries count waving overseas student fees as aid. It has also been estimated that aid devoted to debt relief and asylum-seeker assistance programmes accounted for 9.3% of ODA from OECD-DAC countries in 2008 (Perroulaz, Fiorini, & Carbonnier,

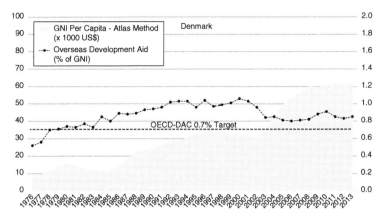

Figure 5.6. Overseas Development Aid as a % of Gross National Income per capita growth in Denmark.
Sources: World Bank (GNI per capita) and OECD (ODA as% of GNI).

2010). Because of inconsistencies in what counts as aid, researchers developed more refined instruments, such as the Commitment to Development Index (CDI). As Barder, Clark, Lépissier, Reynolds and Roodman (2012) show, such measures enable us to better rank and compare countries on aid. However, although some countries appear more generous than first thought (e.g. Austria), the overall picture remains sobering, with many developed countries reneging on their pledges, and many countries remaining well below the agreed 0.7% OECD-DAC target.

Without doubt, it is true that economic crises may limit the amount (and percentage of GNI) governments can spend on ODA. However, they can also use the crisis as an excuse to curb ODA, thereby triggering a race to the bottom. Such concerns were addressed in 2009 in a report by the UK House of Commons International Development Committee entitled *Aid Under Pressure: Support for Development Assistance in a Global Economic Downturn*. In this report, the Committee called upon the UK government to maintain its ODA spending at the level it was at to ensure that the world's poorest were protected from the worst effects of the economic downturn.

Even though Thatcher and many other government leaders found themselves in an actual fiscal crisis that required fixing (hence their reduced ODA spending), what is nonetheless intriguing is the finding

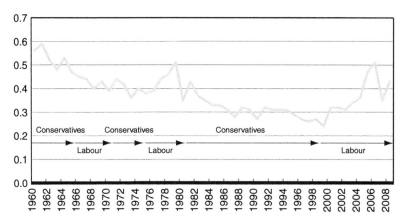

Figure 5.7. UK Overseas Development Aid as a % of Gross National Income under different national governments.
Source: OECD Development Assistance Committee.

that ODA often decreases in times of economic prosperity. For example, there are a number of countries that reduced ODA donations in times of economic growth and prosperity (e.g. Norway 1991–1996, Switzerland 1994–1998, Austria 1985–1993 and the Netherlands 1985–1994). In such cases, it is even more important to consider ideological and party-political influences. After all, why would wealthy countries with strong economies, and that can afford it, seek to reduce their ODA, in some cases to levels well below the agreed 0.7% OEC-DAC target? We will return to this question in Chapter 9, where we analyse the way in which politicians, and especially populist right-wing politicians, justify their calls for a harsher stance on immigration, asylum seeking, multicultur-alism and development aid. Returning to the questions to be addressed in this chapter, we will first briefly consider national trends in charitable giving, and subsequently present the findings of a literature that has studied charitable giving among groups in society that differ in affluence.

Country-level Charitable Giving

According to Hypotheses 1a and 2a, one would expect the total value of charitable donations to rise in times of economic prosperity, and to decline in times of economic recession, when individuals and house-holds become more anxious about their future financial situation.

Figures 5.8 and 5.9 represent longitudinal charitable-giving trends in Canada and the USA. Eyeballing these trends, it appears that the data lend support for the hypothesis that charitable giving should be higher in times of economic prosperity than in times of economic downturns. Specifically, in both Canada and the USA, we see a rather sharp decline in donations in the wake of the GFC. The data for the USA, which cover a longer era, provide good support for the prediction that charitable giving declines during economic recessions.

The above graphs confirm what researchers have known for quite some time: charitable organisations can expect the volume of charitable donations to decline during economic downturns (House of Commons IDC, 2009). This basic insight may be useful for those having to forecast overall trends in charitable giving. However, such figures do not tell us anything about whom in society does most of the heavy lifting. That is, they tell us little about which groups donate most generously, what motivates members of these groups to do so and what motivates others to remain tight-fisted. In order to shed light on these more refined questioned we will need to 'dig deeper' and consider studies that analyse charitable giving within particular groups and social strata.

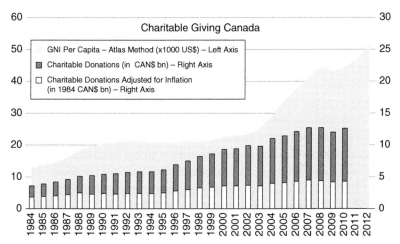

Figure 5.8. Charitable giving in Canada.
Source: Imagine Canada.

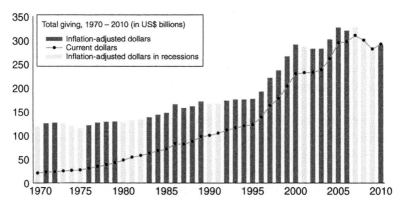

Figure 5.9. Charitable giving in the USA.
Source: Giving USA Foundation.

Individual and Household-level Charitable Giving

One way in which we can dig deeper is by breaking down charitable giving into different income groups in society. As the below graph (Figure 5.10) illustrates, this enables us to recognise that there are clear differences in generosity between the various income groups, at least in terms of the percentage of income donated to charity.

The graph in Figure 5.10 holds an important first clue that levels of generosity can decline as groups become more prosperous. However, in order to recognise this we need to first note that the scale used in this graph is exponential, rather than linear, and that the groups at the top (e.g. those earning in excess of US$ 1,000,000 gross per annum) are much smaller, while the groups at the bottom half (e.g. those earning less than US$ 200,000 gross per annum) are much larger, and represent the vast majority of American income earners. The second issue to keep in mind is that the averages at the top income brackets are inflated by the generosity of a handful of super wealthy philanthropists, who can singlehandedly make this small group look more generous than they would have been without them.[2] In other words, the problem with such graphs is that they invite us to compare the average percentages for two groups that can hardly be

---

[2] Note also that wealthy individuals can set up charitable foundations and donate money into these trusts as a means to avoid paying taxes, a practice which only increases the pertinence of questions about the relationship between affluence and generosity.

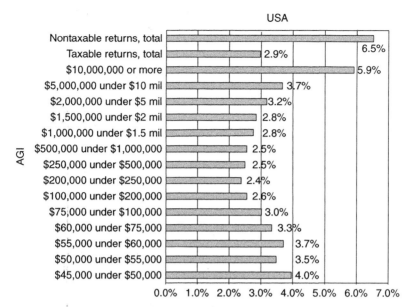

Figure 5.10. Percentage Annual Gross Income (AGI) spent on donations.
Source: National Centre for Charitable Statistics.

compared: relatively small groups of very wealthy people earning in excess of 1,000,000 per annum, and the millions of people earning the mean income of around US$ 50,000.

A more meaningful way to compare generosity across different income groups would be to focus on the lower part of the chart (the area showing the majority of citizens), to divide the categories using a linear scale (so as to avoid stretching categories upwards) and to compare percentages for each of these more common groups. As can be seen from Figure 5.11, in so doing it becomes apparent that even though higher-income households (helped by the efforts of a relatively small number of super rich philanthropists) donate larger sums of money to charity; we also see that, at least percentage-wise, generosity declines as we move from the lowest income groups to more prosperous income groups.

Canada is not an exception. As researchers examining charitable giving in other contexts and jurisdictions have shown, it is indeed typically those who have less who give more (Piff, Kraus, Coté, Cheng, & Keltner, 2010; see also Andreoni, 2001; Greve, 2009;

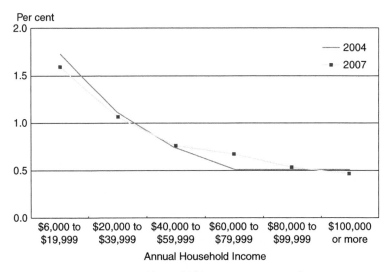

Figure 5.11. Percentage of household income spent on donations (2004 and 2007) by annual household income.
Source: Statistics Canada.

Independent Sector, 2002). For these researchers the question is no longer *whether* this is the case, but *why* this is the case.

The literature on charitable giving, which started in the 1970s and partly overlaps with the literature on helping behaviour, has, at least until more recently, had remarkably little to say about this paradox. As Bekkers and Wiepking (2011) explain in their overview of the charitable giving literature, research has focused on eight mechanisms: 'need awareness', 'solicitation', 'costs and benefits', 'altruism', 'psychological benefits', 'values', 'efficacy' and 'reputation'. Thanks to this literature we now know a great deal about what motivates people to donate to charity. For example, it is clear from experimental and survey studies that people with pro-social values are more inclined to donate money (Bekkers, 2006), and that donating can be a means for people to restore their self-image after harming others (Carlsmith & Gross, 1969) or to overcome feelings of guilt (Basil, Ridgeway, & Basil, 2006).

The charitable giving literature thus provides a wealth of information for charitable organisations about ways in which the effectiveness of fundraising campaigns can be enhanced. For example, we know that people tend to give less generously when exposed to expensive looking campaign materials. This is because such campaigns erode people's trust in the efficacy of the organisation (Schervish & Havens, 2002). We also know that people give more generously when exposed to a campaign that starts with a message that puts people in a positive mood (Aunel & Basil, 1994), or a message which reminds them of their mortality (Jonas, Schimel, Greenberg, & Pyszczynski, 2002).

But why are low-income individuals more generous and pro-social than their higher-income counterparts? Researchers have begun to examine this very question, and we now know that people donate more generously if they know a potential beneficiary (Small & Simonsohn, 2008) or if they themselves have previously benefitted from the service (Schervish & Havens, 2002). One could argue that those at the bottom of the hierarchy are more often exposed to others benefitting from donations, or have benefitted themselves from such donations, than those at the top of the hierarchy. Other researchers have argued that low-income earners donate more generously than their wealthier counterparts because they are on average more religious, and more eager to enact their religious pro-social religious beliefs by donating generously (Andreoni, 2001; Bekkers & Schuyt, 2008; James & Sharpe, 2007). However, recent experimental research showed that religion cannot account for these effects (Piff et al., 2010).

How, then, can we explain the finding that those who have less give more? Piff and colleagues (2010) propose 'interdependence' as a possible explanation, arguing that low-income individuals are more vulnerable and more dependent on others for survival and therefore more inclined to display pro-social attitudes and helping behaviour (see also Oysermans & Lee, 2008; Roberts, 2005; Utz, 2004; Wong & Hong, 2005). This reasoning is not only consistent with cross-cultural research comparing cooperation and sharing behaviour in societies that differed in wealth (Henrich et al., 2001), but also with research examining non-verbal behaviour. The latter studies showed that lower-class individuals are more likely to smile, seek eye-contact and head-nod than their wealthier counterparts (Kraus & Keltner, 2009; Stipek & Ryan, 1997).

These research findings are striking for more than one reason. Aside from the paradoxical nature of the findings, the results are intriguing because in most of these studies, the focus is on the poor, not the wealthy. It is the former and not the latter group that is singled out as the group whose attitudes and behaviours we should seek to understand better. We agree that this would be useful, but argue that it is equally important to study the reason(s) why wealthier people donate less, and display relatively low levels of pro-social behaviour. Interdependence may be a good starting point for such an analysis. After all, from that perspective, compared to the poor, the wealthy can be considered less dependent on others for their survival, and less worried about how others perceive them. They can therefore afford an individualistic stance and they are allowed to focus first and foremost on their own needs. This may seem an entirely plausible explanation for why the wealthy donate a lesser proportion of their income to charity. However, we know from a relatively small body of research focusing on the attitudes towards money that there are two additional psychological factors that shape wealthy people's willingness to donate to charity (Wiepking & Breeze, 2012). These relate to concerns about (a) *retention*, whereby people develop a careful approach to money, and (b) *inadequacy*, whereby they continue to worry about their financial future.

As Wiepking and Breeze (2012) explain in their paper entitled 'Feeling Poor, Acting Stingy', it is not people's actual wealth and income that matter, but people's *perception* about whether their financial future is secure or insecure. It is clear from surveys among wealthy individuals that it is not uncommon for very wealthy individuals to continue to worry about their financial future. For example, a UK survey of 67 individuals holding a net worth of at least £1,000,000 found that 75% of the participants felt their financial future was insecure, with 25% of the participants reporting they would give more to charity if they had more wealth (Lloyd, 2004). Likewise, a study among relatively affluent US households with a net worth of at least US$ 50,000,0000 found that only 21% of the participants felt 'financially extremely secure', with 11% of the participants reporting feeling somewhat insecure financially (Rooney & Frederick, 2007). Other studies have shown that such worries are prevalent among high-income earners more generally. For example, (Brooks, 2006; 2008) examined the attitudes towards money of Americans in the upper income class and found that they too often report being unable to afford to give to charity, due to existing financial commitments, such as mort-gages, car loans and college fees.

It is clear from such studies that people's financial perceptions do not always map onto their actual wealth and income status, and – more importantly – that it is not uncommon for wealthy and relatively affluent people to go through life with what has been described in the literature as a scarcity mentality. As Roux, Goldsmith and Bonezzi (2012) show, a scarcity mentality tends to lead individuals to enter into a competitive mindset and to become harsher and more selfish. To explain this, Aaker and Akutsu (2009) draw attention to the role of identity in charitable giving. These authors argue that our willingness to donate to charity is in large part shaped by our perceptions of who we are, and how we see the world around us. They suggest, in our view rightfully, that those acquiring wealth, and wealthy groups more generally, embrace a new self-understanding or social identity as 'we wealthy people', and this goes together with new norms about 'what we wealthy people do'.

These insights are consistent with social identity theorising (SIT; Tajfel & Turner, 1979), and, from that perspective, charitable giving is not so much determined by ones wealth or personal values, but (as we will outline in more detail in Chapter 8) by the normative content of the wealth group one belongs to (or aspires to belong to). Accordingly, it is possible to find groups of wealthy individuals who donate very gener-ously to charity out of compassion for others, as well as wealthy groups who oppose charitable giving on the grounds that it breeds laziness and creates moral hazards.

Consistent with this, research suggests that allocation of funds to other groups is determined by two factors: (a) the extent to which people identify with the group they belong to, and (b) what people of that group perceive as normative behaviour in that group. At times, those who are highly identified with the group will be harsher towards other groups when they perceive that their group promotes or prescribes hostility towards other groups. However, when group members perceive that their group values generosity, those who are most highly identified with the group will be most generous when allocating money to other groups (see Jetten, Spears, & Manstead, 1997).

Additional Party-political Pressures

As we saw, although levels of ODA do fluctuate in accordance with a country's economic performance (as one would expect when focusing on affordability), the total proportion of ODA as a percentage of GNI is arguably quite small (often around 0.5% of GNI) and much smaller than what most people might think. For example, a survey conducted in 2006 in the UK revealed a tendency to hugely overestimate the proportion of the UK's aid budget as a proportion of total government spending: The actual figure at the time was 1%, but participants estimated that their countries' ODA was 18.5% (Henson, Lindstrom, & Haddad, 2010). Likewise, a survey conducted in 2011 in Australia by the Lowy Institute showed that Australians dramatically overestimated the amount of Australian Federal government spending on ODA. While participants estimated that on average 16% of the budget was spent on aid, the actual proportion was 1.3% (Hanson, 2011).

As Hanson (2011, p. 5) observes, US citizens overestimated their government's contribution to ODA even more dramatically, with the average estimate being 27% of all government spending. On the one hand these results can be dismissed as mere evidence that people are bad at guessing such figures. However, to do so would be to overlook the possibility of such misperceptions potentially being the product of politically motivated exaggeration and scaremongering by politicians who believe they stand to gain electorally from arousing fear and from rendering voters, including relatively wealthy voters, insecure about their financial future.

Populist right-wing parties are renowned for the use of such tactics. These parties tend to offer a 'nativist' perspective on society, arguing that a government's primary duty is to use its power and resources to protect the interest of the autochthonous population. Their calls for harsher treatment of needy immigrants and asylum seekers can be expected to resonate not only among poor working-class voters, who find themselves in a precarious socio-economic condition, but also among wealthy white-collar voters, who have been found to continue to worry about their socio-economic status *despite* the wealth and status they have accrued. These dynamics will be explored in greater depth in Chapter 8, where we identify different kinds of anxieties associated with wealth.

In Conclusion

It should be clear from the above overview of charitable giving statistics and research that there is no clear correlation between financial means and actual charitable giving. Although there is evidence that shows that wealthy people and wealthy countries *can* be extremely generous, there is just as much evidence that these groups and countries can become stingier as their wealth increases. At first sight, this may appear at odds with the image of the wealthy as do-gooders. However, as we will outline in the following chapters, these mixed findings are easier to understand when we take into account research evidence showing that (a) increases in personal wealth can ease but also exacerbate financial worries, and (b) when we have a lot of money, we also want more money (Frank, 1999) and therefore do not want to give much away. As a result of this, we continue to feel concerned about wealth; or, we may feel deprived despite evidence to the contrary.

This has far-reaching consequences for what we thought we knew about the relationship between wealth and generosity. First, it suggests that we humans may well be more like Charles Dickens' fictional character Ebenezer Scrooge than we would like to think: although we are all capable of remarkable occasional generosity, we also do not want to part with our money. Second, and rather paradoxically, money and wealth do not necessarily give us greater security. Often, when we feel wealthy and have a lot of money, we also worry more about losing money. What is more, these anxiety levels will show a marked increase when wealthy people fear that their status or wealth position can change relatively easily. In order to appreciate this, we need to understand both people's natural psychological response to the loss of affluence and wealth (explored in more depth in Chapters 7 and 8), but also the ways in which crafty politicians cultivate and harness these psychological tendencies for political purposes (explored in more detail in Chapter 9).

However, first we need to understand and appreciate that it is not deprivation or gratification per se, but *relative* deprivation and *relative* gratification that predicts harsh attitudes. This issue will be addressed in the next chapter.

6 | *The Relative Nature of Wealth*

In 1835, the Frenchman Alexis De Tocqueville published a book entitled *Democracy in America*, in which he recounts his experiences travelling through America in the early 19th century, studying its political culture. De Tocqueville was intrigued by the American way of life, and in his book he applauds the democracy, liberty and equality he encountered in America, contrasting it with the oppressive hierarchical aristocratic French society he had left behind.

Interesting for our current purposes, though, is that De Tocqueville was not completely blinded by the unlimited opportunities the new world offered and that he noticed a darker side. Despite the fact that Americans were able to afford a lifestyle most Europeans could only dream of, De Tocqueville also detected – in particular among the more affluent – a remarkable level of anxiety and restlessness. The below extract, from a chapter entitled 'Why the Americans are Often so Restless in the Midst of Their Prosperity', illustrates his observations.

In certain remote corners of the Old World you may still sometimes stumble upon a small district that seems to have been forgotten amid the general tumult, and to have remained stationary while everything around it was in motion. The inhabitants, for the most part, are extremely ignorant and poor; they take no part in the business of the country and are frequently oppressed by the government, yet their countenances are generally placid and their spirits light. In America I saw the freest and most enlightened men placed in the happiest circumstances that the world affords; it seemed to me as if a cloud habitually hung upon their brow, and I thought them serious and almost sad, even in their pleasures. The chief reason for this contrast is that the former do not think of the ills they endure, while the latter are forever brooding over advantages they do not possess'. (De Tocqueville, 1834, p. 163)

Here, De Tocqueville touches on an important point that we have so far ignored: the fact that judgements of whether one is wealthy are relative. We can be relatively affluent compared to some, but still feel deprived when our wealth compares negatively to the wealth of others, or to expectations what our wealth ought to be at a particular moment in time. Likewise, we can be poor, but if everyone around us is also poor and expectations for wealth advancement are limited, we can still feel relatively gratified.

In previous chapters, we focused almost exclusively on the relationship between objective indicators of deprivation and gratification and how it affects tolerance of minorities, prejudice and generosity. As we will see in this chapter, it is not always actual wealth, status and power that matter most when judging satisfaction with the current situation, but the *relative* standing compared to other individuals or groups. Often it is the fear that one's own group wealth compares negatively to other relevant groups, or concerns that other groups are climbing the wealth ladder faster than one's own group, or anxiety that one's earlier economic gains might be lost that provoke the kind of displeasure De Tocqueville describes. These (often unrecognised) sentiments matter, and have the potential to feed discontent and hostility towards minorities.

Hirschman and Rothschild (1973) argue that perceived relative deprivation involves not only comparisons with other groups here and now, but also perceptions of *anticipated* gains and losses, and *expected* changes in relative wealth and status. People may therefore be accepting of stagnation so long as others are perceived as equally unable to progress. Hirschman and Rothschild (1973) illustrate this point by using the analogy of a traffic jam on a two-lane motorway:

Suppose that I drive through a two-lane tunnel, both lanes going in the same direction, and run into a serious traffic jam. No car moves in either lane as far as I can see (which is not very far). I am in the left lane and feel dejected. After a while, the cars in the right lane begin to move. Naturally, my spirits lift considerably, for I know that the jam has been broken and that my lane's turn to move will surely come any moment now. Even though I still sit still, I feel much better off than before because of the expectation that I shall soon be on the move. But suppose that the expectation is disappointed and only the right lane keeps moving: in that case I, along with my left lane co-sufferers, shall suspect foul play, and many of us will at some point become quite furious and ready to correct manifest injustice by taking direct action (such a as illegally crossing the double lane separating the two lanes)'. (p. 545).

Even though Hirschman and Rothschild do not provide examples of feeling relatively gratified, one can immediately imagine how drivers would feel if they were the ones in the lane that was moving, passing the motorists who are stuck in the left lane. Even though these drivers will feel elated that they are moving, they may also experience some form of anxiety. This is because, without doubt, those from the lane that is standing still will try to 'jump in' and this will lead to frustration and irritation among those in the right lane. Although some drivers may be kind enough to allow a car to merge, drivers on the fast lane – because they are already on it – are likely to feel a degree of entitlement to the 'good' stretch of the road. What is more, because the lane that is standing still indicates that the traffic jam is not yet resolved, the relatively gratified may realise that their advantage may be short-lived and seek to maximise their advantage while it lasts – for example, by reducing the gap between cars in the fast lane to reduce opportunities for cars from the slow lane to squeeze in. That is, they may know that they will soon not be any different from those that are not moving and that they are about to lose their advantaged and privileged status.

It appears, then, that both relative deprivation and relative gratification can be associated with emotions such as frustration, dissatisfaction and anxiety, this because appraisals of one's own wealth and status involve not only comparisons with others who are better or worse off right now, but also assessments of prospective gains and losses and judgements about the way in which these gains and losses might alter the relative status position between groups. Given this, it seems prudent to take a closer look at research examining relative deprivation and relative gratification from a more dynamic perspective, taking account of the importance of *relative* gratification and *relative* deprivation now and in the future. In particular, and in recognition that relative deprivation or gratification perceptions can be shaped by current perceptions as well as future wealth expectations, we examine two types of relative deprivation/gratification: relative deprivation/gratification resulting from (a) perceptions that one is less or more wealthy compared to other individuals or groups at present, and (b) perceptions that the trajectory of wealth over time for oneself or ones group looks bleaker or brighter than that of relevant comparison groups.

Absolute versus Relative Deprivation or Gratification

Stouffer and colleagues are credited with introducing the term 'relative deprivation' (Stouffer, Suchman, DeVinney, Star, & Williams, 1949). In large-scale research studies examining attitudes of American soldiers during World War II, Stouffer and colleagues noted that in order to explain soldiers' attitudes, it was useful to examine the kinds of inter-group comparisons these soldiers engage in. They describe the concept of relative deprivation as follows:

To help explain ... variations in attitude, by education, age, and marital condition, a general concept would be useful. Such concept may be that of relative deprivation, which we shall see, is to prove quite helpful in ordering a rather disparate collection of data ... The idea is simple, almost obvious, but its utility comes in reconciling data ... where its applicability is not at first too apparent. The idea would seem to have kinship to and, in part, include such well-known sociological concepts as 'social frame of reference', 'patterns of expectation', or 'definitions of the situation'. Being a soldier meant to many men a very real deprivation. But, the felt sacrifice was greater for some than for others, depending on their standards of comparison. (p. 125)

Since then, there have been many attempts to refine our understanding of relative deprivation. For example, in his research, Runciman (1966) distinguishes between egoistical (i.e. intragroup), fraternal (i.e. inter-group) and double deprivation (both intra- and intergroup depriva-tion). Deprivation, so he argued, is a feeling encountered in people who aspire to an object or opportunity that is out of their reach, who feel entitled to that object or opportunity, and who start comparing them-selves with better-off others, including themselves in the past (Runciman, 1966, p. 11).

The conditions for relative deprivation are perhaps most clearly defined in a recent meta-analysis by Smith, Pettigrew, Pippin and Bialosiewicz (2012). They define relative deprivation as 'a judgment that one or one's ingroup is disadvantaged compared to a relevant referent, and that this judgment invokes feelings of anger, resentment, and entitlement'. Importantly too, they argue:

In addition to the fundamental feature that the concept refers to individuals and their reference groups, note that there are four basic components of this definition. Individuals who experience relative deprivation: (1) first make cognitive comparisons, (2) then make cognitive appraisals that they or their ingroup are disadvantaged, (3) perceive these disadvantages as unfair, and finally (4) resent these unfair and undeserved disadvantages. If any one of these four requirements is not met, relative deprivation is not operating. (Smith & Pettigrew, 2015)

It was not until the early 1970s that researchers began to consider the possibility of relative gratification as a possible force 'driving' intergroup hostility. These researchers also emphasised that assessments of wealth aspiration and achievements involve comparisons with *relevant* others (e.g. Grofman & Muller, 1973). At an individual level, this means that expectations and goals are determined by comparisons with others that are relatively similar to the self. At a group or societal level, these expectations and aspirations are determined by comparisons with *relevant* other groups. For example, when asked how well they are doing financially, citizens of wealthy developed countries are likely to compare themselves with fellow citizens and less likely to compare themselves with, say, citizens of developing countries who earn a fraction of their income. They will also be less likely to compare themselves with people who are doing much better financially than they are, such as members of the royal family. Indeed, in such situations people are inclined to compare their position to that of others living and working in similar social, economic and cultural conditions. They focus on marginal differences, differences that would appear negligible when taking into account the huge income disparities between the developed and developing world, or between members of the royal family and average income earners.

Vanneman and Pettigrew (1972) provided evidence for the importance of the relativity of these judgements by showing that relative deprivation and relative gratification perceptions may not map onto actual wealth. These researchers measured relative deprivation by asking workers in Chicago about their economic gains over the past five years and their satisfaction with these gains. They did not find a linear relationship between relative gratification and gains, but a curvilinear relationship whereby perceived deprivation was highest among those at intermediate economic wealth levels.

It thus appears that social comparisons with other individuals or with other groups shape subjective perceptions of wealth and wealth entitlement in important ways. At times these subjective predictors turn out to be better predictors of attitudes and behaviour than more objective indicators of wealth. For example, a classic study by Centers (1949, cited in Vanneman & Pettigrew, 1972) illustrates this point quite nicely. In this study, adult white men in the United States were asked to indicate their economic position. They could choose one out of the following categories: upper class, middle class, lower class and working class. In addition to this subjective class measure, class was also established more objectively by classifying the occupational status of participants.

Interestingly, while for many men, objective and subjective classifications were identical, they were not the same for everyone, with some manual workers referring to their class as 'middle class'. Centers found that objective class predicted political orientation quite well, with higher classes being more conservative than their lower class counterparts. This finding may not be all that surprising. However, information about subjective class did add interesting and important information: manual workers who identified as middle class were more conservative than other manual workers, whereas white-collar workers who saw themselves as working class were less conservative than other white-collar workers. This suggests that to predict attitudinal and behavioural outcomes, one should not only take account of objective demographic information about wealth, but also of subjective perceptions of one's own standing vis-à-vis others.

Relative Gratification, Selfishness and Opposition to Immigration

There is a growing body of social-psychological work examining the effect of feeling relatively poor or wealthy on a range of outcomes, such as self-centredness and anti-social behaviour. For example, Piff (2014) asked participants to indicate their level of income, their highest educational achievement and their occupational prestige relative to others, using a scale from 1 to 10 (where 10 stood for the highest level of prestige and achievement – i.e. relative gratification). His studies showed that higher relative gratification was associated with higher self-reported narcissism and, in part, this relationship could be explained by a higher sense of entitlement among the relatively gratified compared to the relatively deprived (see also Snibbe & Markus, 2005).

Similar findings were observed in China: wealthier Chinese were more likely to score high on measures of narcissistic personality than their poorer counterparts (Cai, Kwan, & Sedikides, 2012). Yet other studies showed that individuals who described themselves as relatively gratified in terms of social class and income behaved in a more selfish fashion in an economic game (Piff, Kraus, Côté, Cheng, & Keltner, 2010) and revealed a stronger tendency to engage in unethical self-serving behaviour (Piff, Stancato, Côte, Mendoza-Denton, & Keltner, 2012).

Whereas this work was mostly concerned with predicting *individuals'* anti-social behaviour towards others in general, other research has shown that expectations that one's *country* will experience future relative gratification or relative deprivation affects the extent to which individuals endorse or oppose immigration. For instance, in an experimental study, Australians were exposed to a newspaper article on the expected state of the Australian economy (Mols & Jetten, 2015, Study 1). Half of the participants read an article entitled 'Stable economic growth for foreseeable future, says Queensland study'. Among other information, readers were told:

Australia's economic situation seems likely to improve significantly in the coming years, according to a report published by economists and business experts at Brisbane's University of Queensland. The report claims that, owing to Australia's prosperity during the resources boom, economic growth is likely to continue strongly into the foreseeable future.

The other half of the participants read an article that was titled 'Economic downturn for foreseeable future, says Queensland study'. Participants randomly allocated to this condition were informed that 'Australia's economic situation seems likely to decline significantly in the coming years'. Furthermore, it was stated that 'The report claims that, despite Australia's prosperity during the resources boom, economic growth is likely to experience decline in the foreseeable future'.

All participants were then presented with a fictitious political speech advocating further restrictions on immigration to Australia. For example, the speaker articulated his position on the topic as follows: 'While I have always believed in the benefits of legal immigration I have also always argued that it needs to be controlled. Immigration is far too high and net migration must be reduced'. After putting forward a number of arguments for this position, the speaker finished by saying 'In sum, immigration must be halted if we want to preserve our economy and to ensure that we are able to thrive economically into the future'. After this, participants were asked to respond to a series of questions assessing their attitudes towards immigration.

The results of this study confirmed our hunch, and showed that participants in the expected future economic *prosperity* condition were more receptive to the anti-immigration speech than those in the economic downturn condition. Specifically, stronger anti-immigrant sentiments were expressed when the national economy was presented as prospering rather than contracting. These findings provide clear evidence that it is possible that economic prosperity, just like economic downturn, provides a 'fertile ground' for parties with an anti-immigrant agenda.

The V-curve Hypothesis: The Shadow-side of Wealth

Research on the so-called 'v-curve' has focused more specifically on the notion that both relative gratification *and* relative deprivation may underlie prejudice and negative attitudes towards minorities. Let us review evidence for the v-curve in greater detail. The term 'v-curve hypothesis' was coined by Grofman and Muller (1973) in a paper entitled 'The strange case of relative gratification and potential for political violence: The v-curve hypothesis'. Among residents of Waterloo in Iowa, the researchers measured the individual's perceived change in relative position over time and their attitudes towards political unrest, political protest and violence more generally. The authors summarised their findings as follows:

Here we report a finding that was unexpected (but not just specific to this sample), namely, that potential for political violence does not vary monotonically with direction and rate of change in discrepancy between achievement optimum and achievement; rather, the greatest potential for political violence is manifested both by individuals who perceive negative change (increasing discrepancy) and by individuals who perceive positive change (decreasing discrepancy), while those who perceive no change manifest the least potential for political violence. In attempting to explicate this finding through the introduction of various control variables, we find that a nonmonotonic 'V' relationship is remarkably persistent. (p. 514)

There is now a large body of work on the v-curve and ample evidence confirming its existence (Dambrun et al., 2006; Guimond & Dambrun, 2002; Moscatelli, Albarello, Prati, & Rubini, 2014; Postmes & Smith, 2009). For example, Dambrun and colleagues (2006) examined the relationship between relative deprivation and gratification among a representative sample in South Africa. In line with the v-curve hypothesis, they found that prejudice towards both African and Western immigrants to South Africa was higher to the extent that participants felt either gratified or deprived. Consistent with our analysis, in explaining the relative gratification effects, these researchers point to a process which takes place in a context where a group perceives to outperform relevant comparison groups into the future, whereby harshness and prejudice is motivated by an attempt to justify and maintain the group's privileged status.

Interestingly too, Dambrun and colleagues noted that the socioeconomic status of the participants themselves affected prejudice levels, and that participants appeared to feel most threatened by immigrants that were seen as potential competitors. More specifically, those higher in socio-economic status perceiving relative gratification reported most prejudice in relation to Western immigrants (those that they were most similar to) than towards African immigrants. Participants lower in socio-economic status who felt relatively gratified did not differ in the prejudice towards Western and African immigrants and derogated both types of immigrant to the same extent.

Even though work by Dambrun and colleagues shows evidence for a v-curve relationship in a real context using a representative sample of South Africans, one potential critique of this work is that such cross-sectional research does not allow us to identify cause and effect. In particular, what remains unclear is whether it is relative deprivation or relative gratification perceptions that *cause* prejudice, or whether it is those people who are prejudiced who are more likely to feel disadvantaged or gratified. In order to show that relative deprivation/gratification perceptions *cause* prejudice, one needs to conduct experiments manipulating such perceptions, and examine the effect of these manipulations on dependent variables that are of interest: hostility towards minorities and attitudes towards immigrants.

Guimond and Dambrun (2002) were the first to assess the relationship between relative deprivation/gratification and attitudes towards immigrants. In a first experiment, they randomly allocated French undergraduate students to one of three conditions. In a relative deprivation condition, they presented participants with a fictitious research report showing that employment opportunities for students in the next four or five years looked rather dire, conveying the message that students should expect high levels of unemployment. In another condition they manipulated relative gratification by informing participants they would be better off in the future than they currently were. In a final control condition, participants were given no information about job opportunities. Rather surprisingly, there was no evidence that participants in the relative deprivation condition showed more prejudice towards a range of minority groups compared to those allocated to the control condition, failing to replicate the often observed relative deprivation effect. Interestingly however, compared to those in the control condition, participants in the relative gratification condition were more prejudiced towards other groups.

In a second experiment, Guimond and Dambrun (2002) examined their predictions in a stronger intergroup context whereby they manipulated relative gratification by providing feedback to psychology students that job opportunities for students in psychology (ingroup) were going to increase sharply in the years ahead, whereas jobs for students in economics/law (outgroup) were going to drop considerably. Results showed that, compared to the control condition, prejudice was higher in both the relative deprivation and relative gratification conditions, confirming the v-curve relationship.

Our own research has also provided experimental evidence for the v-curve hypothesis (Jetten, Mols, & Postmes, 2015). We developed a paradigm with the aim to make participants temporarily feel wealthy or poor. To do this, in the first part of the study, we asked our participants to imagine they had joined a society called Bimboola. Participants read that, just like any other society, Bimboola is a stratified society in which there are clear differences in income between different groups: some are relatively poor and others are relatively wealthy. Participants were informed that Bimboola consists of five income groups, with the poorest group (income group 1) earning less than 5000 Bimboolian Dollars (BD) per year (below the poverty threshold) and the wealthiest group (income group 5) earning more than 1 million BD per year (see Figure 6.1). Participants were then allocated to one of these income groups. We emphasised that allocation was random and that it was not based on merit.

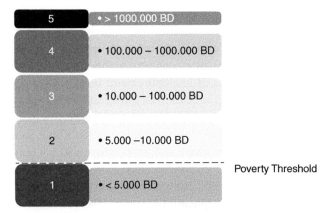

Figure 6.1. Income groups in the hypothetical society of Bimboola.

Once participants were allocated to an income group, they were told that, in order to start their new life, they needed to purchase essential items such as a house and car. We then presented participants with a number of pictures of houses they could choose from, ranging from old and run-down dwellings to luxurious mansions (see Figure 6.2).

Importantly, the houses on offer were listed according to income group, with three houses to choose from per income group. Participants were advised that they could only buy a house within or below their income bracket. If participants selected a house that did not meet this condition (e.g. it was more expensive than their income group could afford), they received a message alerting them to their mistake and they were invited to choose again. The same procedure was used when buying a car (Figure 6.3).

Finally, participants were invited to select a holiday. The first income group was simply told that they could not afford a holiday and they were to skip this question. Whereas the holiday options for income group 2 were quite basic (e.g. camping or a day trip to the beach), participants in income group 3 could choose from options such as a four-wheel-drive adventure, a week-long campervan trip, or a one-week stay in a lakeside cottage. Participants in income group 4 could choose from any of three more luxurious options, such as a shopping trip to Paris. The options for income group 5 were the most extravagant and included a trip to an exclusive upmarket resort, a ski-holiday in

Figure 6.2. Houses by income group. Numbers on the left refer to income groups 1 to 5.

Switzerland or a day trip in the Space Shuttle. Our manipulation checks indicated that our paradigm achieved what we set out to do: in an experimental context, we managed to temporarily evoke the feeling that participants were relatively poor or relatively affluent.

Participants were then informed that a new group (called 'Newcomers') was about to join Bimboola. They were told that these newcomers needed to rebuild their lives in Bimboola, but that in order to do so they would need some assistance from citizens of Bimboola. After this information was provided, participants were asked to indicate their agreement with statements measuring the extent to which immigrants were perceived as a symbolic threat (e.g. 'The cultural

Figure 6.3. Cars by income group. Numbers on the left refer to income groups 1 to 5.

practices of the new group will threaten the Bimboolean way of life') and realistic threat (e.g. 'The presence of people from this new group will increase unemployment in Bimboola') as well as general items assessing resistance to the arrival of these newcomers (e.g. 'I think our group should not allow newcomers to Bimboola').

Our results showed a clear v-curve relationship whereby those in the poor (income group 2) *and* in the above-average wealth income group (income group 4) were most opposed to immigration compared to those in a moderately wealth group (income group 3, see Figure 6.4). These findings are consistent with Guimond and Dambrun's (2002)

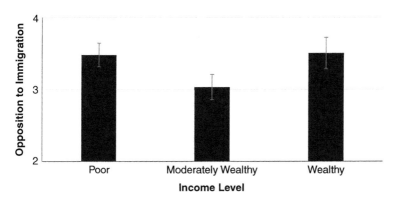

Figure 6.4. Opposition to immigration as a function of income level, means and standard errors. Adapted from Jetten et al. (2015, Study 2).

work, and with other correlational work showing a v-curve relationship, and it complements this work in important ways. More specifically, by manipulating wealth perceptions we were able to show that the own group's wealth perceptions *cause* opposition to immigration.

Relative Wealth: Comparisons with the Past and Future

Of course, perceptions of relative deprivation and relative gratification are not formed in a time vacuum, but often include timelines affecting the extent to which people perceive they are 'on track' to secure what they hope to earn or possess in the future. Runciman (1966) was among the first to draw attention to the importance of perceptions about past and future capabilities. Runciman argued that perceived relative deprivation involves not only social comparisons, but also evaluations of changes in relative opportunity between different groups over time. In other words, it may not be absolute gaps in wealth and status at a particular moment in time that causes attitudes to harden, but the belief that the gap is closing or widening.

This suggests that snapshot assessments of relative deprivation and gratification are somewhat limited in explaining the full range of consequences of these perceptions, and the importance of taking into account expected/prospective gains and losses, and expected gains and losses of comparison groups. Indeed, people may feel happy with what they or their group has right now, but that does not mean that the same achievement will be thought of equally favourable when thinking what one hopes to achieve in future. Consistent with this, Gurr (1970) argued that anticipated future relative deprivation may be a more important source of discontent than perceived current deprivation.

Grofman and Muller (1973) were the first to examine effects of past, present and future relative deprivation versus relative gratification systematically. In contrast to the work presented so far, they were most interested in how these perceptions affected willingness to engage in political violence. These authors examined 14 different ways in which congruence between past, present and future gratification affected willingness to engage in political violence. They summarise their rather complex key findings as follows:

The data provide no support for the Rate-of-Change hypothesis that as degree of relative gratification increases over time, potential for political violence will tend to decrease. However, if we convert the rate-of-change scores into absolute magnitudes, the data consistently support an Absolute Change hypothesis that as absolute magnitude of relative gratification increases over time, potential for political violence will show a tendency to increase. Of the rate-of-change variables, the best predictor of potential for political violence is the absolute magnitude of present to future shift. (p. 536)

Interestingly, even though Grofman and Muller (1973) admit that this was not the finding they expected, it is one that is consistent with De Tocqueville's observations about the antecedents of the French Revolution. As Grofman and Muller put it:

'De Tocqueville noted that the French Revolution occurred after two decades of steady improvement in standard of living and that those parts of France which had experienced the greatest degree of positive change also showed the greatest popular discontent'. (1973, p. 537)

This observation is also consistent with Davies (1962), who argued that a period of economic prosperity followed by an economic hardship and deteriorating living conditions forms the most fertile ground for revolutions (the so-called J-curve). In other words, what Davies showed is that it is not deprivation as such that fuels discontent in times of downturns, but fears associated with the prospect of losing recent gains.

Experimental Evidence

Despite the richness of this work to explain the importance of temporal comparisons to determine the way objective wealth is perceived, much of this work is observational or cross-sectional. There is only a small body of experimental work that has provided evidence for these relationships, thus showing that it is comparisons with the past and present that determine the way that current wealth will be perceived.

In one of our own experimental studies, we investigated the behaviour of participants who started off relatively wealthy and gratified but were made to feel relatively deprived over the course of the study, when another group that started off as relatively poor gained wealth faster than they did (Jetten, Chu, & Mols, 2016). This allowed us to examine situations where people may be relatively gratified objectively, but relatively deprived when others appear to be climbing the ladder faster than they are.

In this study, participants based in the USA took part in an online study in which they were allocated randomly to one of two groups in a virtual society: the blue group (which would turn out to be the poor group) or the red group (which would turn out to be the wealthy group). Participants were told to imagine they lived in the year 2003, that their new life as a citizen had begun, and that they needed to purchase goods that allowed them to start their life in this society. Initially, the wealthy red group members would start with 2.5 million dollars each, whereas the poor blue group members were provided with either (a) 2.5 million dollars, (b) 1.5 million dollars, or (c) only 300,000 dollars. Participants were then provided with opportunities to purchase houses and cars that varied in price. If there was money left after this, they were asked whether they would like to contribute money to charity or buy a luxury boat, paintings or valuable jewellery. The money that they did not spend would automatically go into a savings account.

Next, participants were asked to imagine that ten years had passed and that the year was now 2013. They were provided with an update on their group's wealth: while participants in the wealthy red groups were informed that their income had not changed over these ten years (i.e. remained at 2.5 million dollars), the poor blue group was told that they now had 1.5 million dollars. Note that in all three conditions, the income gap between the poor and the wealthy group was similar in 2013.

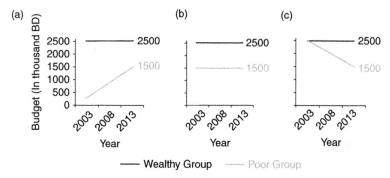

Figure 6.5. Wealth of the wealthy group and poor group over time: a = decreasing wealth gap, b = constant wealth gap, c = increasing wealth gap.

What differed was whether, over time, the poor group had gained or lost wealth *relative* to the wealthy group.

This produced three conditions: a decreasing wealth gap condition (Figure 6.5a), a condition in which the wealth gap between the two groups stayed the same across the course of the study (Figure 6.5b) and a condition in which the gap between the two groups increased over time (Figure 6.5c). Again, participants were provided with an opportunity to shop and to indicate how they wished to spend their money.

After the second spending round, participants learned that a newcomer group (again called the 'Newcomers') would join the game and that the members of this group would also be given an opportunity to purchase goods. Participants were also told that if the Newcomers were unable to purchase essential items, they would be asked to provide them with financial assistance.

Focusing first on the behaviour of the wealthy group whose wealth stayed constant over the course of the study, we found that compared to when the poor group's wealth also stayed stable over time, a decreasing wealth gap (i.e. the poor group gaining wealth over time while the wealthy group stayed stable) led to increased levels of anxiety about the future among those who were relatively gratified. Examining the extent to which members of the wealthy group were opposed to newcomers joining their society, we found that it was also in the decreasing wealth gap condition that opposition to newcomers joining was higher than in the condition where both the poor group's and the wealthy group's relative affluence stayed the same over time.

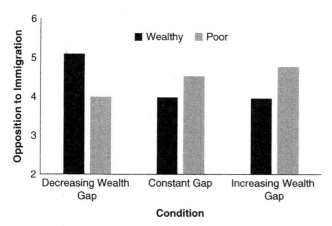

Figure 6.6. Opposition to immigration by newcomers as a function of the extent to which the income gap between the groups decreases, remains constant or increases over time.

Opposition to newcomers was also higher in the decreasing wealth gap condition than in the condition in which there would be an increasing wealth gap because the poor group would become poorer over time (see Figure 6.6).

Closer inspection of the results for the poor group also showed an interesting pattern. Consistent with a relative deprivation hypothesis, the more money the poor group was losing over time, the more opposed they were to newcomers joining their society.

This study provides compelling evidence for the importance of examining *relative* deprivation and *relative* gratification perceptions. The results show that even though the actual wealth of the wealthy group did not change, the mere knowledge that another group was gaining wealth while the own group was standing still led to anxiety and increased opposition towards newcomers to the society. To go back to the analogy used by Hirschman and Rothschild (1973), it appears that those who felt they were in the fast lane and found out that the other group was gaining speed faster than they did ended up quite dissatisfied and anxious. This finding also appears to be associated with rather selfish behaviour and, perhaps because of a fear that the privileged status may be lost in the future, the relatively gratified, who experience relative deprivation compared to expectations, become quite harsh towards minorities.

In Conclusion

There are a number of conclusions to be drawn from the literature. Consistent with our conclusion in previous chapters, it is once again clear that the empirical evidence for a straightforward relationship between *relative* deprivation and harsh attitudes towards minorities is rather mixed and inconclusive. Negative attitudes towards minorities have been observed both in times of relative economic hardship *and* in times of relative economic prosperity. These attitudes have dominated responses among those who are relatively poor *and* those who are relatively wealthy. Other studies show no relationship between perceived relative economic performance and negative attitudes.

Where does this leave us? For one, to get a better understanding of the mixed results so far, it is not only essential to develop theorising that helps us to predict *when* economic deprivation and *when* economic prosperity enhances anti-immigrant sentiments, but also to identify the underlying psychological mechanisms at work in situations where people feel relatively deprived or gratified. Together, these insights will enable us to develop a comprehensive in-depth account of how economic performance affects outgroup attitudes. We will take on this theoretical challenge in the next chapters.

PART III

Understanding the 'Wealth Paradox'

7 | Towards an Explanation of the Wealth Paradox: Introducing Social Identity Theorising

We started this book with a focus on what can be described as the two 'usual suspects' when explaining civil unrest, hate crime and prejudice against minorities: economic downturn, and relatively poor groups at the bottom of society. Indeed, classic theorising would lead us to believe that humans become harsher and more selfish during economic crises, when scarcity and hardship are on the increase, and tolerance and generosity become regarded as a luxury that can no longer be afforded (Hypothesis 1a).

Furthermore, so the argument typically goes, because such economic downturn is felt more strongly by the poor than the wealthy (because they already experience deprivation), those who are at the bottom of the wealth ladder will be most likely to harden their attitudes. When predicting anti-immigrant sentiments, xenophobia and prejudice we would therefore immediately turn our attention to those within a society who are, relatively speaking, less well-off than others, a category of citizens now routinely described as 'losers of globalisation' (Hypothesis 2a).

Although Hypotheses 1a and 2a have been confirmed in some cases, and disconfirmed in others, we noted that there has been remarkably little attention given to attitudes among those who find themselves at the other end of the wealth spectrum (see Figure 7.1). More specifically, and assuming linearity, we asked whether it is therefore also the case that when, relatively speaking, societies become more affluent and when people feel they are doing well financially (in the sense that they are at or near the top of the economic, social and financial ladder), they should be *more* tolerant and display *lower* anti-immigrant sentiments, xenophobia and prejudice. Indeed, in those cases, conventional wisdom would lead us to believe that people should be less fearful about their economic future, and hence more tolerant and generous towards those who are less well off. From that perspective, one would expect the wealthy (i.e. those with the most material means at their

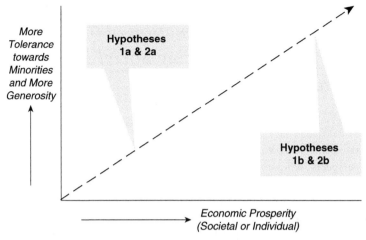

Figure 7.1. The focus of Hypotheses 1a and 2a versus Hypotheses 1b and 2b.

disposal) to be the most tolerant and generous, because they can most easily afford it (Hypotheses 1b and 2b).

As we saw, there is a large body of research examining the relationship between relative deprivation and hostility towards other groups. However, studies examining the link between prosperity and outgroup attitudes are few and far between. In this book – because this side of the coin has so far been relatively neglected – we focus on the empirical evidence for Hypotheses 1b and 2b and focus on the right-hand top corner quadrant of Figure 7.1. It is now time to take stock and to evaluate the support for each of these hypotheses.

Taking Stock: Support for Hypotheses 1b and 2b

Recapping the findings of studies examining the effects of (relative) gratification and assessing the extent to which they buttress our hypotheses, we conclude that there is little support for Hypotheses 1b (milder attitudes in prosperous societies) and 2b (milder attitudes among more affluent people) and that the empirical evidence tells a rather different, more complex story. We started our empirical analysis with a survey of macro-level trends in far-right voting (Chapter 4). Although we only examined correlations (and not causation), our longitudinal analyses of voting patterns in a number of developed countries showed that Populist Right-Wing Parties (PRWPs) advocating harsher policies (in particular with regards to immigrants, asylum seekers and minority groups) have managed to secure significant electoral victories in times of economic growth and prosperity, and in rather affluent jurisdictions.

We subsequently considered longitudinal patterns in government-funded ODA and private charitable giving (Chapter 5), and found that levels of charitable giving do indeed tend to increase in times of economic prosperity, and decline in times of economic recession. However, closer inspection of the literature on charitable giving revealed that absolute levels of ODA and charitable giving are misleading. This is because these statistics do not tell us much about who, relatively speaking, does most of the heavy lifting. More specifically, what tends to go unnoticed, when focusing on long-term trends in ODA and charitable giving, is that, paradoxically, those who have less give more (Piff et al., 2010; see also Greve, 2009; Independent Sector, 2002).

In Chapter 6, we asked whether the lack of evidence for Hypotheses 1b and 2b might be due to the fact that we had mostly considered cases examining *actual* deprivation and gratification, not *relative* deprivation and gratification. We wondered whether perhaps understanding these relative perceptions would increase our ability to predict attitudes and behaviour. However, this was not the case. A review of research on relative gratification and our own work (including experimental work that allows for drawing causal inferences) all suggest that one does not have to look very far to find evidence that clearly contradicts Hypothesis 2b: those who feel (or are made to feel) relatively gratified are at times particularly harsh towards outsiders and newcomers.

Explaining the Relative Gratification–Harshness Relationship

Taken together, the evidence presented in the previous chapters provides compelling evidence for a link between prosperity and the hardening of norms and attitudes. How, then, can we explain this apparent paradox? To understand the link between relative gratification and greater hostility towards minorities, it is instructive to begin with a review of the answers put forward in the past by researchers who asked the very same question.

Starting with classic reasoning, Grofman and Muller (1973) provided three explanations for their 'unexpected' relative gratification
finding. One of them is the 'rising expectations' notion. According to
this account, when a person experiences growth in their wealth, their
expectation for the level of growth quickly exceeds their attained
wealth. As a result, people will become aware of the negative gap
between what they *expected* their wealth to be and the *actual* wealth
they attained. The resulting dissatisfaction and frustration then easily
triggers hostile and violent political behaviour.

This process is well captured by De Tocqueville (1835/2000). In his
chapter entitled 'Why the Americans are Often so Restless in the Midst
of their Prosperity', he speaks about the poor and the wealthy as 'the
former [i.e. the poor] do not think of the ills they endure, while the
latter [i.e. the wealthy] are forever brooding over advantages they do
not possess' (p. 136). The phrase 'keeping up with the Joneses', first
used by cartoonist Arthur Momand in the USA in 1913 and now a well-
known English idiom, captures the same idea. Well-off people often
nervously monitor the spending behaviour of their peers, fearful that
they will not be able to afford the next luxury item their peers purchase,
regarding them as competitors and worrying they may fall behind in the
race for ever greater wealth and status.

A second explanation put forward by Grofman and Muller (1973)
points to the 'present value of the past'. This account focuses on an
assessment of the cost the individual feels they incurred in the past to
achieve good outcomes and the extent to which the cost for their
present wealth is perceived to be 'too high a price to pay'. As a result,
the individual no longer appreciates their current wealth and becomes
dissatisfied because they had to make many sacrifices along the way.
This explanation too accounts for the dissatisfaction among the
relatively gratified, and the ensuing willingness to engage in violent
protest to get what they feel is rightfully theirs.

A third and final explanation from Grofman and Muller (1973) is
labelled the 'more to lose' thesis. According to this explanation, those
who have a lot also become anxious about losing their wealth and
affluence. The willingness to engage in political violence may not so
much be a result of dissatisfaction, but a pre-emptive strike to make
sure that wealth is retained.

In addition to these three explanations, many other processes have
been put forward to clarify the finding that, at times, relative

gratification leads to greater hostility towards minorities. For instance, in addition to the 'fear of losing ingroup advantage' explanation, Moscatelli and colleagues (2014) also reasoned that the relatively gratified are likely to experience feelings of guilt about the advantage they have over relatively deprived groups – feelings that wealthy individuals may seek to suppress subconsciously. The authors found evidence that this in turn justified a 'strike first' attitude, whereby wealthier groups engage in hostility towards other groups because the group in question is expected to be biased against the relatively gratified group (often because they caused their deprived state).

Still other researchers propose that relative gratification enhances the attractiveness of the own group, resulting in stronger intergroup dynamics and increased hostility to other groups (in particular minority groups). Consistent with this, in a study conducted in South Africa, Dambrun and colleagues (2006) found that group identification partially accounted for (i.e. mediated) the relationship between relative gratification and negative attitudes towards other groups.

It has also been argued that relative gratification effects are mediated by collective self-definitions (Jetten, Mols, & Postmes, 2015). Specifically, and in line with the stereotype content model developed by Cuddy, Fiske and Glick (2007; 2008), it is predicted that the stereo-type of the wealthy – because of this group's ability to acquire wealth – tends to revolve around attributes associated with competence. However, wealthy groups are also seen as relatively cold and uncaring. These stereotypes are not just ways in which others perceive the affluent; they are also internalised as ways to understand the group's identity and *self*-understanding, affecting the content of group norms (see also Postmes & Smith, 2009). Thus, one can expect that the more that groups which are relatively prosperous self-stereotype as competent but cold, the more group norms will emerge that condone and justify harsh treat-ment of those who want to become part of society (i.e. immigrants).

Finally, prejudice and exclusion of minority groups may reflect a growing belief in ideologies in which status differences (and the privileged position of one's group) are being portrayed as a 'natural' social order (e.g. White supremacy, sexism, etc.). The cultivation of so-called system justification beliefs (Jost, Banaji, & Nosek, 2004) or legitimising ideologies (Sidanius & Pratto, 1999) allows advantaged groups to preserve the belief that existing status relations are just and fair. Such beliefs and ideologies are appealing for those who are well off because they reduce feelings of guilt and enable the wealthy to sidestep questions pertaining to fairness and equity. In such situations, rather than engaging with the issue at hand, the existing inequality can be justified with simple slogans, such as 'everyone gets the outcomes in life that they deserve'.

It thus appears that there are several processes that we need to take into account when explaining the paradoxical relationship between relative gratification and hostility towards minorities (and the list provided here is certainly not exhaustive). Even though some of these accounts were originally developed to explain the willingness to engage in political violence, it is easy to see how the psychological processes that have been identified could also account for the lack of generosity among the wealthy and negative attitudes and prejudice towards minorities among the affluent.

In particular, relative gratification harshness appears to be associated with a sense of dissatisfaction as well as with a sense of entitlement and a perceived need to protect current wealth. Paradoxically, then, relative gratification is often not perceived as such by those who enjoy it. That

Table 7.1. *Proposed explanations for the relative gratification–harshness relationship*

Explanation	Process
1. Rising expectations	Frustrated upward mobility and status anxiety
2. Present value of the past	Entitlement due to past costs to attain wealth
3. More to lose	Fear of falling and downward mobility
4. Guilt about being advantaged	'Strike first' when dealing with others who are less well off
5. Identification with the advantaged Group	Strong intergroup dynamics with other groups that are less well off
6. Collective self-definition as competent, but cold	Self-definition condones and justifies hostility towards other groups that are less well off
7. Cultivation of system justification beliefs and legitimising ideologies	Justification of harsh stance towards minority groups who 'deserve' negative outcomes

is, the wealthy may be more preoccupied with their *future* wealth and status position, rather than their current wealth and status position. As a result of this preoccupation, they do not notice how their current affluence has affected their norms, values and self-understanding. Or, they may invoke a hierarchy-enhancing ideology and point out that there are good reasons why they have more than others, thereby justifying the existing social order.

Rather than trying to determine which of these seven processes (Table 7.1) is the most important to explain why relative gratification can be associated with harsh attitudes towards minorities, it makes more sense to accept that these processes are not mutually exclusive. Therefore, these explanations are best studied as factors that can *all* contribute simultaneously to the hardening of attitudes among relatively prosperous groups.

A Social Identity Analysis of the Wealth Paradox

Even though all seven processes identified in Table 7.1 provide valid and important reasons why we might see affluence and prosperity going hand-in-hand with diminishing tolerance and generosity, the problem with this analysis is that it is more descriptive than explanatory. More specifically, although Table 7.1 provides a list of processes that might explain this relationship in a particular context at a particular moment in time, it does not necessarily helps us understand *which one* of these processes might be at work *under what conditions*. In other words, to better understand the wealth paradox, it is essential to move beyond a list of processes, and to consider possible triggers in particular contexts. More specifically, in order to be able to predict in advance *when* a particular process is most likely to occur, we need to develop a process model that encompasses all seven processes. Such a model would have the potential to explain when and how negative outgroup attitudes among wealthy people emerge, and helps to predict, a priori, which one would be most likely to be at play in a given setting.

In our view, Social Identity Theory (SIT) provides an ideal overarching theoretical framework to achieve these goals. Indeed, social identity theorising enables us to develop a comprehensive framework within which the various processes can be organised and studied. What makes SIT perfectly suited for this task is that it provides explicit theorising on how individual-level psychological processes are affected and informed by the broader socio-structural context (e.g. economic and political factors affecting status relations between groups).[1]

The social identity approach comprises two closely related theories: *social identity theory* (SIT; Tajfel & Turner, 1979) and *self-categorisation theory* (SCT; Turner, Hogg, Oakes, Reicher, & Wetherell, 1987).[2] A detailed account of the social identity approach is available elsewhere (for a recent overview see Postmes & Branscombe, 2010). Our focus here is on how wealth position is related to beliefs and behaviour. We will outline the origins and main premises of the social identity approach in the remainder of this chapter. In the next chapter, we will outline how SIT can further illuminate the psychological processes contributing to the wealth paradox.

The Origins of the Social Identity Approach

As discussed in previous chapters, early research explains hostility between groups in various ways. Some researchers have focused on personality (e.g. authoritarian personality theory; Adorno, Fenkel-Brunswik, Levinson, & Stanford, 1950), whereas others focused on the way frustration triggers aggression (Dollard et al., 1939). Still others explained prejudice towards minority members in terms of

[1] While both System Justification Theory (SJT; Jost et al., 2004) and Social Dominance Theory (SDT; Sidanius & Pratto, 1999) can help explain why advantaged group members legitimise the status quo, these frameworks are ill-suited to the task of identifying the conditions under which advantaged group members will fail to justify the system and when they instead are likely to be generous and compassionate towards those who are less well-off than they are. That is, because both theories start from the assumption that people want to legitimise the existing system at all costs, the possibility that advantaged group members will challenge the system is insufficiently considered and theorised. Indeed, SJT and SDT are largely silent on this possibility (see Rubin & Hewstone, 2004).

[2] Self-categorisation theory (Turner et al., 1987) has refined some of the ideas of social identity theory and can be seen as a direct development of it. Differences between the two theories are that social identity theory explanations are more motivational and directed at explaining intergroup discrimination, whereas self-categorisation theory focuses more on cognitive processes and represents a general theory of the self. As such it aims to explain a broad range of social behaviour (Turner et al., 1987). To explain the wealth paradox, we focus mainly on classic social identity theorising and will not provide a detailed discussion of self-categorisation theory principles.

assumed dissimilarity in attitudes and beliefs (e.g. Rokeach's belief congruence theory, 1960).

Although some of the above-mentioned theories provided plausible causes for hostility and harsh attitudes towards members of other groups, there are limits to such individualistic accounts, known as 'individual difference' perspectives (Billig, 1976). In such accounts, situational factors, which are often much more powerful determinants of intergroup hostility, tend to be neglected by locating the source of prejudice in the individual's personality. To overcome this particular problem, Sherif and colleagues developed one of the first theories taking account of relations between groups (Sherif, Harvey, White, Hood, & Sherif, 1961). They examined the effect of incompatibility of interests between groups of boys in their 'Robbers Cave summer camp' studies and developed realistic conflict theory. As we outlined in Chapters 2 and 3, in this view, hostility between groups results from competition over scarce resources such as money, power and status.

Like realistic conflict theory, SIT rejects approaches such as the authoritarian personality, frustration–aggression and belief congruence in that it locates the basis of intergroup hostility in intergroup dynamics rather than in individual differences. However, SIT differs from realistic conflict theory in that it argues that identity dynamics and a search for a positive identity are the main drivers of intergroup hostility, rather than realistic conflict over scarce resources. The latter point emerged from the findings of the so-called 'minimal group' studies developed by Henri Tajfel and colleagues (Tajfel, 1970; Tajfel, Billig, Bundy, & Flament, 1971). These minimal group studies were conducted to identify the minimal and sufficient conditions under which intergroup discrimination occurs. What they revealed, with the help of a number of controlled laboratory experiments, was that realistic conflict is not necessary to elicit intergroup discrimination and negative attitudes. Rather, their main finding was that intergroup discrimination can also develop in a context where no interaction takes place between two groups and where there is no conflict of interest or any previously existing hostility. This finding was consistent with an incidental observation by Sherif et al. (1961), namely that just being in one group and becoming aware of another group seems to trigger feelings of competitiveness. However, in contrast to the Sherif et al. studies, these minimal group findings provided clear evidence that additional conflicting goal relationships are not necessary to elicit intergroup hostility (cf. Rabbie & Horowitz, 1969). Let us describe these minimal group studies in a bit more detail.

Minimal Group Studies

A typical minimal group experiment consists of two phases (for detailed descriptions, see Brewer, 1979; Diehl, 1990; Tajfel et al., 1971; Turner, 1975, 1981). In the first phase, participants are brought together and allocated to a group on the basis of a trivial and arbitrary criterion. For instance, participants may be presented with pairs of slides of paintings by Klee or Kandinski, after which they have to provide feedback on the paintings. Next, participants are categorised by providing them with false feedback about their preference. That is, they are told that they had a clear preference for one of the two painters.

In the second part of the experiment, participants are required to allocate small amounts of money to anonymous ingroup and outgroup members. It should be noted that during the whole experiment (a) there is no interaction between group members, (b) group membership of all participants is anonymous, (c) to eliminate self-interest, participants can never allocate money to themselves, and (d) the allocation task is real and allocated goods are meaningful for

---

Booklet for Group Preferring Klee

These numbers are rewards for:

Member no. 74 of Klee group	25	23	(21)	19	17	15	13	11	9	7	5	3	1
Member no. 44 of Kandinsky group	19	18	(17)	16	15	14	13	12	11	10	9	8	7

Please fill in below details of the box you have just chosen:

Reward for member no. 74 of Klee group: **21**
Reward for member no. 44 of Kandinsky group   **17**

Figure 7.2. Example of an allocation matrix used in the Minimal Group Paradigm. Adapted from Tajfel et al., 1971. The page heading reminded the participant which group they were in. In addition to circling the number pair that represented the chosen allocation between an in-group member (Klee) and outgroup member (Kandinsky), the participant was also asked to fill in the blanks to confirm their choice (21 and 17 in this example). The awards were made to persons identified only by number and group.

participants. In short, participants only know which group they themselves belong to, and it is their task to allocate money between ingroup and outgroup members who are only identified by code-numbers. The money is allocated using specially designed matrices that enable the measurement of specific allocation strategies. For example, participants can allocate the same amount of money to ingroup and outgroup members (fairness), maximise the joint profit of ingroup and outgroup members, allocate more money to ingroup members, allocate more money to outgroup members, or maximise the difference between ingroup and outgroup members in favour of the ingroup (maximising difference).

The results of these first minimal group studies were surprising. Even in this meaningless minimal group setting category member-ship made a difference to the way in which money was allocated and intergroup discrimination was exhibited – this despite the entirely arbitrary basis of the categorisation into groups. Although fairness was an influential strategy, some participants also showed a persistent tendency to award more money to ingroup than to outgroup members. Moreover, points were allocated in such a way as to maximise the difference between their ingroup and outgroup, even at the expense of achieving the maximum possible outcome for the ingroup (Billig & Tajfel, 1973; Tajfel & Billig, 1974; Tajfel et al., 1971). Tajfel et al. (1971) summarised these results as follows:

In a situation devoid of the usual trappings of ingroup membership and of all the vagaries of interacting with the outgroup, the participants still act in terms of their ingroup membership and of an intergroup categorization. Their actions are unambiguously directed at favouring the members of their ingroup as against the members of the outgroup. This happens despite the fact that an alternative strategy – acting in terms of the greatest common good – is clearly open to them at a relatively small cost of advantages that would accrue to members of the ingroup. (Tajfel et al., 1971, p. 172)

Intergroup discrimination in this minimal group situation has proved to be a remarkably robust phenomenon (Brewer, 1979; Brewer & Kramer, 1985; Brown, 1988; Tajfel, 1982; Turner, 1981). Numerous experi-ments using different types of allocation matrices, different bases of group categorisation, different cultures and participants of varying ages have replicated the finding that categorisation in and of itself elicits positive differentiation of the own group from other groups (i.e. inter-group discrimination, see Brewer, 1979; Messick & Mackie, 1989; Turner, 1981).

The implications of this finding should not be underestimated. If attitudes towards other groups are not necessarily the result of conflicts over material resources, then it becomes clear that alternative explanations are needed to account for hostility between groups (including hostility between groups that differ in wealth). As we will outline further below, SIT provides such an explanation.

Social Identity Theory

An initial explanation for the results of these minimal group studies was formulated in terms of 'generic norms' (Tajfel et al., 1971). According to this view, being categorised in a group will, in most Western cultures, evoke associations with games and teams, which should in turn make a competitive norm highly salient. However, this explanation was later rejected since there are more predominant socie-tal norms (e.g. fairness) and this explanation cannot predict in advance which norm will become dominant in a specific context. A second and related criticism was that normative accounts are by their nature too general and over-inclusive (Brown, 1988).

Other explanations for intergroup discrimination encountered in minimal groups were that participants displayed such behaviour because of an anticipation of future interaction (Tajfel et al., 1971), because of the unfamiliar situation created in the minimal group paradigm (Tajfel & Billig, 1974) or because of so-called demand char-acteristics (i.e. participants trying to meet the experimenter's expecta-tions) conveyed by the experimenter (Billig, 1973; St. Claire & Turner, 1982). Other explanations included belief congruence theory (Rokeach, 1960), equity theory (Ng, 1981) and category differentia-tion theory (Doise, 1978). Belief congruence theory points to another possible cause of intergroup discrimination, namely the assumption by ingroup members that outgroup members hold attitudes that differ from those of their own group. Equity theory suggests that intergroup discrimination might be a reaction to anticipated discrimination by outgroup members (see also Tajfel et al., 1971). According to cate-gory differentiation theory, intergroup discrimination is caused by the classification into two groups, which increases and exaggerates the perceived difference between these two categories (cf. Tajfel & Wilkes, 1963). Although these theories could account for some aspects of the intergroup discrimination process, they did not offer a complete explanation for the minimal group finding (for an overview, see Diehl, 1990).

Social identity theory offers a comprehensive explanation for the relation between mere categorisation and intergroup discrimination (Tajfel, 1978; Tajfel & Turner, 1979; 1986). Tajfel (1978, p. 63) defines social identity as 'that part of an individual's self-concept which derives from … knowledge of … membership of a social group (or groups) together with the value and emotional significance attached to that membership'. Social identity theory is a general theory about group processes and intergroup relations. The key assumption of the theory is that individuals are motivated to achieve or maintain a positive self-image. Individuals derive their social identity from the groups to which they belong (e.g. student, sports fan, employee, team member), and their positive social identity is to a large extent based on favourable comparisons that can be made between their own group and relevant comparison groups. The result of this comparison is crucial because a positively discrepant comparison between ingroup and outgroup enhances positive identity. In the minimal group setting, money functioned as a relevant dimension of comparison. Since it was the only available dimension of comparison in the experimental setting, participants could only differentiate the ingroup from the outgroup by allocating the money in such a way that a positive difference between ingroup and outgroup was achieved.

Factors Affecting Intergroup Discrimination

One of the more important conclusions to emerge from the minimal group experiments was that categorisation per se is sufficient to elicit intergroup discrimination, and several follow-up studies confirmed this (Brewer, 1979; Diehl, 1990; Messick & Mackie, 1989; Tajfel, 1982; Turner, 1975; 1981). Brewer (1979) concludes that '[o]nce a particular categorization has become salient … the degree of bias obtained is fairly constant' (p. 319). That being said, SIT considers categorisation as a necessary but not a sufficient condition for the occurrence of intergroup discrimination in real-life settings.

Tajfel and Turner (1979) identified a number of aspects of the social-structural context that determine whether intergroup discrimination will be expressed. Structural factors such as group status, permeability of group boundaries and the stability and perceived legitimacy of status relations between groups determine whether other groups will be perceived more or less favourably. We will outline these processes in more detail in the next chapter.

These extensions are crucial because, on the basis of the minimal groups studies, some researchers have long concluded that differentiation is inevitable in an intergroup context (Brown 1988; Messick & Mackie, 1989). In our view, this is an oversimplification of SIT, one that can lead to serious theoretical misunderstandings (for a more detailed discussion, see Mols & Weber, 2013). Indeed, intergroup discrimination is not a universal phenomenon. On the contrary, non-discriminatory interactions between groups are also possible and may even be likely under certain conditions.

A Social Identity Analysis of Status and Wealth

The social identity approach starts from the assumption that of the myriad ways in which social groups differ from one another, perhaps the most consequential differentiator is status (Mullen, Brown, & Smith, 1992; Otten, Mummendey, & Blanz, 1996; Sachdev & Bourhis, 1987; 1991). Status can be defined as the position of a group in the social hierarchy of a given society or culture. More specifically, it can be defined as the prestige or standing associated with the group's position on a valued dimension of comparison, which sets it in relation to relevant other groups (i.e. outgroups). Status can be achieved on different dimensions, and it can be based on a number of different achievements. For example, high status can reflect a group's superior skill set, superior knowledge, physical strength, political power or – of particular relevance here – more wealth and affluence.

As intimated before, a key premise of the social identity approach is that group members will aim to compare positively on a relevant dimension of comparison with other (wealth) groups in order to achieve or maintain a positive identity. Given the different positions in the hierarchy of low- and high-status groups, the strategies these groups will use to achieve positive identity will differ. In a nutshell, members in poor or low-status groups will aim to achieve wealth and status (either individually or as a group). However, members of these groups may feel restricted to achieve this goal because of constraints posed by the social context: because they find themselves at the bottom of the hierarchy (and because there may be pressures within the system to lock the poor into their low-status position), their aim to get ahead may be frustrated. Connecting this with relative deprivation reasoning, it becomes clear how low-status group members who feel thwarted in their wish to advance may become hostile towards others who stand in their way when trying to climb the social ladder – those who are dragging them down or those who they are unable to escape from (e.g. minorities) as well as those who do not allow them to join higher ranks. However, and as we will outline in the next chapter, at times, low-status groups form alliances with other low-status groups, such as minorities, when they challenge the status of higher status groups. That is, in the recognition that collective action is most effective when all those who feel oppressed join forces, under some conditions, lower-status groups such as the poor may open their doors to minority groups and treat them as 'brothers in arms'.

Social identity theorising leads us to predict that wealthy or high-status groups aim to achieve positive identity in different ways. Because they have already achieved a high status and wealth position, their main aim will be to maintain and protect status (Ellemers, Doosje, van Knippenberg, & Wilke, 1990; Harvey & Bourhis, 2011). At times, there will be little need to protect high status because no one is challenging the group's high status position. However, at other times, for many of the reasons outlined in Table 7.1, members of wealthy or high-status groups will feel that their high status position is under threat. As we will outline in the next chapter, it is in such contexts that high status or relative gratification will go hand-in-hand with hostility towards minorities.

8 | *The Wealth Paradox Explained*

As argued in the previous chapter, SIT enables us to move beyond accounts that explain harsh attitudes by focusing solely on dissatisfaction with material living conditions and realistic conflict. Rather, a social identity perspective enables us to recognise that deprivation can, *under some conditions*, fuel outgroup hostility, and that *under some conditions* prosperity can harden outgroup attitudes – a counterintuitive pattern that we call 'the wealth paradox'. To understand these conditions and associated outcomes, we need to first acknowledge that the psychological consequences of economic performance and wealth do not emerge in a vacuum, but in particular social contexts that shape attitudes towards others. Rather than asking whether it is economic decline *or* economic prosperity, and whether it is poverty *or* wealth that is associated with enhanced hostility and prejudice (Hypotheses 1a–2b), we need to focus instead on *when* it is that poverty or wealth predicts such outcomes.

In this chapter, we will systematically examine how the effects of poverty and economic decline, as well as the effects of wealth and economic prosperity, can be explained through the lens of social identity theorising. We start with a classic SIT analysis of how poverty and economic decline shape intergroup attitudes, and we will subsequently turn to wealth and economic prosperity. In short, we argue that just as much as responses to deprivation are shaped by perceptions of the broader socio-structural context, so are responses to gratification a direct response of those perceptions.

Permeability of Group Boundaries: 'Everyone Can Make It If They Try'

As discussed in previous chapters, in times of economic decline and for those living in poverty, a sense of relative deprivation will prevail. Put

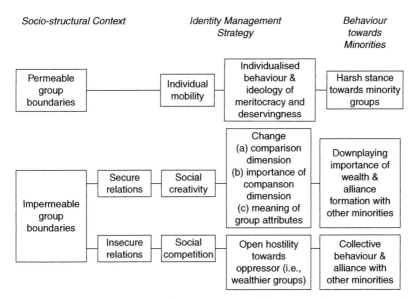

Figure 8.1. Relation between the socio-structural context and strategies used by the poor. Adapted and expanded from Haslam, 2004.

differently, in such times or for such groups, there is a discrepancy between what one would like to have and what one actually has in terms of income, assets and financial wealth.

People facing such circumstances are first and foremost interested in coping with or trying to rid themselves of low-status, poverty or relative deprivation. To do so, they can either engage in behaviour to improve their own individual position within the hierarchy (so-called individual mobility), or band together with others who are in a similar low-status position (either because they are also poor or face other type of disadvantage) and aim to improve the status position of the collective (so-called collective mobility strategies; see Figure 8.1).

According to SIT, whether people in low-status positions gravitate towards individual or more collective identity management strategies in their quest to improve their low-status position depends first and foremost on whether boundaries between groups are permeable (Ellemers, 1993; Tajfel & Turner, 1979), allowing individuals to cross group boundaries and join higher status groups (see Figure 8.1). In particular, individual mobility is more likely to be the dominant response when group boundaries are permeable and when exit to a more desirable group is possible (Ellemers & van Rijswijk, 1997; Ellemers, van Knippenberg, & Wilke, 1990; Lalonde & Silverman, 1994; Wright, Taylor, & Moghaddam, 1990).

Permeability of boundaries may on the one hand be a blessing for societies. After all, in this setting everyone can engage in upward mobility, and attempts to climb the ladder may well be successful. Indeed, in such societies, there may be a strong belief in meritocracy and a strong endorsement of the idea that 'the sky is the limit', including for those born into poverty (see Figure 8.1).

However, there is also a dark side to collectively held beliefs that 'everyone can make it if they tried'. Belief in meritocracy also means that those who are not upwardly mobile are perceived as deserving their disadvantage (Sidanius & Pratto, 1999). The more poor and deprived individuals endorse beliefs that the world is fair and meritocratic, the more they will believe that their own low wealth position is their own fault, and that 'things would have been different' for them if only they had exerted themselves more. An important side effect of belief in meritocracy is reduced compassion for those who struggle to get by. In other words, even among the poor, the belief in meritocracy and permeability of boundaries fuels the perceptions that everyone can control their own destiny (Weiner, 1985), and this paves the way for harsh attitudes towards those in need.

Permeability of Group Boundaries: The High-status Group's Perspective

Even though the social identity approach was developed to explain responses by those without status, power and wealth in society (Tajfel & Turner, 1979), it is increasingly recognised that SIT also helps in understanding the responses of those high in status, power and wealth (Haslam, 2004). Importantly, Haslam (2004) argued that responses by high-status groups are guided by the same socio-structural factors as for low-status groups – permeability and security of intergroup relations (see Figure 8.2). Here, we will redeploy Haslam's framework and apply it to the context of wealth and affluence.

How, then, would permeability of boundaries affect responses by the wealthy? There are two responses in particular that we are interested in. First, if boundaries are permeable, and if there is widespread belief

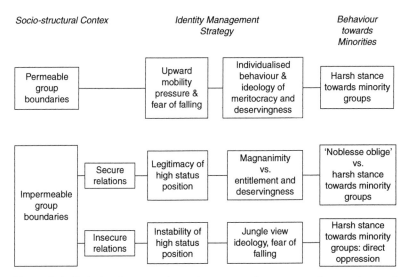

Figure 8.2. Relation between the socio-structural context and strategies used by the wealthy when responding to minorities. Adapted with permission from Haslam, 2004.

that everyone can 'make it', this leads to a greater need to 'keep up with the Joneses'. This is a problem in and of itself because consumption and materialism lead people to live beyond their means. Credit card debt and 'conspicuous consumption' (Veblen, 1899/1994) are likely to increase under such conditions. What is more, the aspiration to become accepted by wealthy people as 'one of us' (upward social mobility) creates additional pressure to climb the financial ladder. This weights more heavily on those higher up in the hierarchy than on those at the bottom.

Second, even though those who are affluent may themselves have benefitted from greater permeability of boundaries between groups over recent decades, such permeability is anxiety provoking because it feeds fears that one can also fall. In the words of Adam Smith:

Riches leave a man always as much and sometimes more exposed than before to anxiety, to fear and to sorrow. (Adam Smith, 1776)

From this we learn that those who are wealthy and affluent are not exempt from anxiety, fear and sorrow. In fact, as Smith argued, such emotions may particularly be found among the wealthy. When one's wealth position is not guaranteed or fixed by birth, and lower-class citizens appear able to climb the ladder and engage successfully in upward mobility (when boundaries are permeable), it is the people with a lot who have a lot to lose. Although the arrival of 'nouveaux riches' may not have a negative effect on the actual wealth of those who were already wealthy, what can nonetheless arouse anxiety is a decreasing gap between 'old money' and the 'nouveau riche', and a sense that newcomers are joining the ranks and diluting the group's exclusivity (see Chapter 6, this volume; Jetten, Chu, & Mols, 2016). It is therefore in times of economic decline or economic instability that fear of falling will be experienced, and the ones most likely to experience such fears are those who have acquired wealth in the recent past. The wealthy can respond to this threat in different ways. For example, they may respond by denigrating the nouveau riche by portraying them as having lots of cash, but lacking culture and sophistication. As an example, during the mining boom in Australia, the derogatory term 'cashed up bogans' was coined to disparage wealthy working-class citizens benefitting from the mining boom, suddenly able to afford luxury mansions and lifestyles. Anger and hostility may also be directed towards immigrants who seek to rebuild their lives in the host society. The more successful these newcomers are, and the more they make use of the permeability of boundaries to climb the ladder, the more they risk becoming regarded as a threat.

In sum, when boundaries are permeable, those who are wealthy are likely to become dissatisfied with the wealth they have and feel pressured to acquire even more, so as to maintain the distance between themselves and those below them who are climbing the social ladder (upward mobility threat). Likewise, they may become obsessed with worries that, one day, they may lose their wealth. All of this will lead them to pursue their narrow self-interest more ruthlessly, thereby justifying decreasing concern and empathy for those less well off (Jetten, Mols, Healy, & Spears, 2017; Postmes & Smith, 2009). Interestingly, these processes are the same processes as those described in Table 7.1 on why we find that relative gratification can be associated with harsh attitudes. Here, however, by illuminating the role of permeability of group boundaries, we are in a better position to understand what is driving these processes. More specifically, it is because the wealthy perceive that group boundaries are permeable that they (a) experience status anxiety because they are not climbing the ladder fast enough (or faster than other groups), and (b) fear for downward mobility whereby they fear losing their wealth (i.e. Explanations 1 and 3 from Table 7.1).

The Problem of the Belief in Individual Mobility at a Societal Level

The perception of permeability of boundaries not only triggers specific behaviours from the poor and the wealthy, it may also affect society as a whole. Among all strata of society, there is evidence for the notion that the rise of the ideology of meritocracy, and the greater perception that individual mobility is possible (because boundaries between groups are permeable), has also led to a decline of sympathy for and empathy with those in need (e.g. de Wachter, 2012; Stokkom, 2010). For instance, in his 1958 book *The Rise of Meritocracy* the British author Michael Young observed that:

Today all persons, however humble, know they have had every chance ... If they have been labelled 'dunce' repeatedly they cannot any longer pretend ... Are they not bound to recognize that they have inferior status, not as in the past because they were denied opportunity, but because they are inferior. (Young, 1958, p. 97)

There are other indicators that perceived scope for upward mobility (i.e. perceived permeability of boundaries between wealth groups; see Figures 8.1 and 8.2) and harshness go hand-in-hand. For example, governments eager to crack down on welfare dependency will typically portray boundaries between groups as permeable. The reasoning goes that when society offers plenty of opportunity to get ahead and when there are no structural barriers to do so, those willing to exert themselves will be rewarded (even when unemployment is high). When one believes that wealth and economic success boil down to making use of the permeability of boundaries, it follows logically that an inability to climb the ladder is seen as being due to the individual's own failings. It is therefore not the system that is to blame, but the failing individual. This stance was embraced by British Prime Minister Margaret Thatcher, and it is this belief in permeable group boundaries that justified her government's harsh stance on welfare and welfare recipients. As Thatcher famously said:

I think we've been through a period where too many people have been given to understand that if they have a problem, it's the government's job to cope with it. 'I have a problem, I'll get a grant.' 'I'm homeless, the government must house me.' They're casting their problem on society. And you know, there is no such thing as society. There are individual men and women, and there are families. And no government can do anything except through people, and people must look to themselves first. It's our duty to look after ourselves and then, also, to look after our neighbour. People have got the entitlements too much in mind, without the obligations. There's no such thing as entitlement, unless someone has first met an obligation. (Margaret Thatcher, Interview, 23 September 1987 with Douglas Keay, Women's Own)

Although Thatcher's portrayal of society as a mere collection of competing individuals would send shivers down the backs of social democrats committed to the welfare state, her interpretation of society would gradually gain ground, and provide governments with a rationale to reduce welfare provision. Not surprisingly, this exercise in 'rolling back the frontiers of the state' (justified on the grounds that boundaries between wealth groups are permeable) did go hand-in-hand with a gradual hardening of attitudes, both in government circles and among the public at large. Indeed, one does not have to search for very long to come across more recent (post-GFC) newspaper headers warning that we have entered an era dominated by individualism and selfishness, in which people are first and foremost interested in their own welfare. For instance, a newspaper article in the Dutch *Volkskrant* (24 January 2014) observes that 'the tendency to see poverty as one's own fault is back'.[1] In the article, Rutger Bregman outlines how in times of economic crisis, when the average citizen is struggling, empathy for the poor as well as willingness to pay social welfare declines.

Similar sentiments were expressed in Australia, with political commentator Bruce Haigh noting in a contribution on 24 April 2015 in *The Drum* that 'We have become a nation of individuals with a sense of entitlement, and are prone to narcissism, jingoism and chauvinism'. He states:

Brace yourselves: things are not going to get better in Australia, at least not for some time. It is to do with our collective moral fibre – or lack of it – as exhibited by our politicians, public servants, captains of business and

[1] www.volkskrant.nl/opinie/-de-neiging-armoede-als-eigen-schuld-te-beschouwen-is-terug-van-weggeweest~a3583110/

industry, senior military officers and the media. And the reason is selfishness, greed and immaturity. (Haigh, April 24, 2015)

Another Australian commentator, in a contribution for *The Conversation*, notes:

Ironically, our ability to identify with others because of our essential similarities leads to a singular lack of empathy by the advantaged. Because the disadvantaged look like us, despite very real differences, we conclude that their disadvantage is their own fault. We believe that the disadvantaged would succeed, just like us, if only they would work harder. We conclude, in effect, that they have freely chosen not to succeed. This is, for the most part, untrue. (Mitchell, 8 December 2014)

We argue that growing endorsement of the ideology that 'everyone can make it if they try' (which rests on the meritocratic assumption that there are no structural reasons why the poor should remain poor) has led to a change in zeitgeist (or 'spirit of the time'). The hallmark of this change is the gradual erosion of tolerance for those at the bottom of society.

Impermeability of Group Boundaries: The Perspective of the Poor

Let us turn our attention to how the poor or deprived respond when boundaries between groups are impermeable. Based on classic social identity theorising, we predict that, when individual mobility is not an option (e.g. it is impossible within a society to become part of more affluent groups), poor and deprived people are likely to consider more collective responses to achieve a positive identity (see Figure 8.1). Which strategy they choose depends very much on the security of the existing status relations – i.e. the perceived legitimacy and stability of their wealth position.

When groups perceive that their status is not legitimate and/or when status relations are unstable, members of low-status groups in particular are likely to deploy more direct strategies aimed at improving the status position of the group as a whole (i.e. social mobility; Tajfel & Turner, 1979). This can take the form of civil unrest, political protest and, in more extreme cases, revolution (as reviewed in Chapter 2). In such conditions, the poor are likely to form alliances with other groups in society, in particular groups perceived as equally oppressed by the wealthy. As a result, and despite the strong sense of relative deprivation, attitudes of the poor towards other minorities may be relatively favourable because they are seen as suffering the same fate at the hands of the high-status group in society. This can lead to contexts where deprivation among the poor and limited opportunities to improve their situation may go hand-in-hand with greater compassion for immigrants and other minorities – a shared fate may bring these victim groups closer together.

When mainstream society or dominant groups perceive poverty as relatively legitimate and when the poor perceive that the status quo is unlikely to change (i.e. secure intergroup relations), those facing poverty may engage in so-called social creativity strategies. These are rather indirect identity management strategies to cope with low-status and lack of wealth (see Figure 8.1). Unlike social change strategies, social creativity does not involve attempts to change the social structure; rather, it involves subtle ways to bolster the identity of low-status groups (Ellemers, 2003; Tajfel & Turner, 1979). For example, those who are relatively poor may change the dimension of comparison on which they compare themselves with wealthier groups. Instead of comparing themselves unfavourably with other groups in terms of financial assets and wealth, they may choose a more favourable comparator for their group (e.g. distinguishing themselves from wealthy people, they may emphasise that their group is the most compassionate, generous and kind). As a result, the poor may not

Your health is your real wealth
- Mahatma Gandhi

Figure 8.3. Social media meme as social creativity strategy downplaying the importance of money as a source of happiness and self-esteem.

only be able to maintain a positive sense of self and their group, they may also feel particularly compelled to be generous and help those in society who are even worse off than themselves.

Another known social creativity strategy involves changing the *importance* of the comparison dimension. For example, the poor may downplay the importance of wealth (e.g. by arguing that life is too short to worry about money). Instead of pursuing wealth, they may instead adopt alternative lifestyles and ideologies, denouncing mainstream society as materialist, narrow-minded and 'bourgeois'. By talking down the importance of money and wealth, the own group compares well (e.g. as wiser and as superior) and this allows group members to achieve a positive identity and self-esteem (see Figure 8.3).

Finally, social creativity strategies can be aimed at changing the attributes of a group so that the comparison with other groups is no longer negative (see Figure 8.1). For example, low-status groups such as the poor may embrace features that set them apart from the wealthy (e.g. happiness, morality and compassion for others) and adopt these as identity defining. Also, to the extent that such social creativity ideologies emerge among the poor, it may protect positive identity and it may result in more generosity towards others that are also facing a daily struggle for survival and recognition – e.g. minorities such as immigrants and asylum seekers.

This reasoning can help to explain the mixed support for H1a and H2a – the notion that relative deprivation (economic downturn or poverty) is associated with harsh attitudes towards others. Specifically, for those groups experiencing relative deprivation, it depends on perceptions of permeability of group boundaries, the perceived legitimacy of the low-status position and the perceived stability of the wealth position whether low-status groups respond to their fate with increased hostility towards other groups (Hypothesis 2a and 2b), or whether they adopt a warmer, more caring stance. Relative deprivation is thus most likely to be related to harsh attitudes towards minorities when there are plenty of opportunities (perceived or real) for upward mobility for the own group or for the individual. In contrast, when poverty is perceived as 'locked in' and unlikely to change, and when the poor perceive (to some extent, at least) that they deserve their inferior wealth position, attitudes towards minorities should be more favourable. Ironically, then, it may be when the situation for those living in poverty looks most dire (in the sense that it is unlikely that their fate will change) that the poor will be most generous towards others who, *like them*, face a daily struggle to 'make ends meet' and to become recognised as worthy citizens.

Impermeability of Group Boundaries: The Perspective of the Wealthy

How, then, do wealthy groups in society respond to the notion that boundaries between groups are impermeable, whereby it is largely impossible for the poor to become wealthy and for the wealthy to become poor? The simple response to this question is that, just as for low-status groups such as the poor, for the wealthy too the perception that boundaries are impermeable may lead to a myriad of responses. Key here too is whether impermeability of boundaries goes hand-in-hand with secure status relations or with insecure status relations (see Figure 8.2).

Secure Wealth: Entitlement and Deservingness

In societies where upward mobility is limited and where status relations are secure (i.e. unlikely to change), it is likely that high status, power or wealth will be associated with 'noblesse oblige' – the notion that the wealthy behave and conduct themselves in a noble and honourable way towards others who are less well off. When members of the high-status group feel secure in their high status and when they feel comfortable at the top of the hierarchy, they may show greater generosity towards members of lower-status groups, in particular on those aspects of the status comparison that are irrelevant to the key comparison dimension (Sachdev & Bourhis, 1985; Vanbeselaere, Boen, van Avermaet, & Buelens, 2006). For example, research has revealed that members of high-status groups show ingroup bias on the status-defining dimensions, but no bias or even bias in favour of another group with less status on status-irrelevant dimensions (Bettencourt, Dorr, Charlton, & Hume, 2001; Mullen et al., 1992; Turner & Brown, 1978).

Researchers have also found that members of high-status groups, who have already secured a positive social identity, may be relatively relaxed about relations between classes, and, as a result, be tolerant and generous (see Doosje, Ellemers, & Spears, 1995; Spears, Doosje, & Ellemers, 1997). Harvey and Bourhis (2011) recently provided experimental evidence for this. In a study, participants were allocated randomly to a poor or wealthy group. The findings showed that those in a wealthy group (those who were made to feel powerful) were most likely to share their resources equally with subordinate poor group members.

Research has also shown that relative gratification can be associated with a greater motivation to correct poverty and oppression (Beaton & Deveau, 2005) and a push for the implementation of affirmative action programmes in organisations to address inequality (Tougas & Veilleux, 1990). This is rather similar to an observation by Moscatelli and colleagues (2014) that wealthy group members may feel guilty because they have an advantaged position. However, it is also clear from their research that such guilt can trigger a harsher stance towards those who are less well off, this because the wealthy fear revenge by the poor and therefore feel entitled to strike first (see Table 7.1). The finding that guilt does not lead to a genuine attempt to achieve greater equality may explain the observation in Chapter 5 that noblesse oblige behaviours typically involve rather small donations and generosities, and rarely contribute to a substantial change in the status quo.

The idea of a link between status security and more relaxed attitudes makes intuitive sense. However, there is also a dark side to the security of high status or wealth. Because such high-status groups perceive that their advantage and affluence is the result of real (or natural) differences between groups, such high-status groups may show considerable favouritism for the own group and hostility towards other groups, manifesting in elitist attitudes and belief that 'we' are better than 'them' (e.g. Mullen et al., 1992; Turner & Brown, 1978).

Although such views may be considered politically incorrect, reflecting potentially dangerous world views (e.g. Social Darwinism), they may be entertained nonetheless, and explain findings showing that members of high-status groups do display more favouritism of the own group than members of low-status groups (e.g. Brewer, 1979; Ellemers et al., 1992; Sachdev & Bourhis, 1985; 1987; 1991; Turner & Brown, 1978). These findings are important too in that they demonstrate that certain privileged groups have no qualms about claiming that 'we are better than them' (e.g. Rothgerber, 1997). What is more, the sense of entitlement that goes with such a position of privilege may lead to high-status group members feeling justified in excluding those who are less well off. For example, Haslam (2004) argues that under such conditions, high-status group behaviour is 'likely to take a more sinister form and be reflected in ideologies (racism and sexism for example) that attempt to justify and rationalise the ingroup's superiority and the outgroup's inferiority' (p. 27).

LeBlanc and colleagues (2015) showed this in a study in which they examined the role of legitimacy of privilege. In their study, Canadian undergraduate participants were presented with a fictitious government report on the employment rate of graduates from their alma mater (Université de Moncton) and another (English-speaking) university situated in the same province (University of New Brunswick). They were presented with a graph showing that employment opportunities for students at both universities were currently rather similar, but that employment for students from the participants' university would progressively improve over time (see Figure 8.4).

Participants were asked to first study this graph, and then to indicate to what extent they felt relatively satisfied (gratified) by answering two

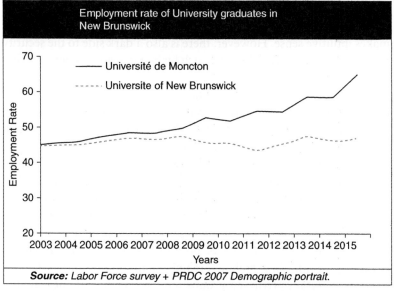

Figure 8.4. Graph presented to participants in a study by LeBlanc et al. (2015) in order to manipulate perceived employment opportunities for graduates at their own and another rival university. Reprinted with permission.

questions: 'I feel that the fate of graduates from the Université de Moncton is improving relative to that of graduates from the University of New Brunswick', and 'In the next few years, graduates from the Université de Moncton will have much better job opportunities than graduates from the University of New Brunswick.' Participants were then presented with one of two explanations for the difference in employment opportunities. One group of participants were told that the differences between the two groups were legitimate. In particular, they were provided with information that 'experts explain that because graduates students from the Université de Moncton have a better grasp of both French and English languages, they are better prepared to face the demands of a global economy'. Another group was presented with an explanation suggesting that the difference was illegitimate: 'Experts explain that Université de Moncton alumni give hiring preference to those who have graduated from their alma mater, irrespective of the competence and experience of the graduate from the Université de Moncton.' A third and final control group received no explanation about what caused the difference between the groups. After this, racism towards Aboriginal people in Canada was measured by asking participants to indicate their agreement with items such as 'I wouldn't like any member of my family to marry an Aboriginal person'.

The results of this study showed that participants' perceptions of the relative gratification that their group experienced was more strongly related to racism for those participants who were provided with the explanation that group differences were legitimate. For participants who were informed that the difference between the two groups was based on illegitimate grounds, there was no relationship between perceptions of relative gratification and racism. What this suggests is that when advantaged group members perceive that their greater wealth, status and opportunities are obtained by legitimate means, that they are less inclined to feel guilty about their advantaged status. As LeBlanc and colleagues note 'Legitimacy endows them with *carte blanche* on the means used to promote their relative advantage' (2015, p. 152).

There are other laboratory studies showing similar results. For example, Bettencourt and Bartholow (1998) conducted an experiment in which participants were allocated randomly to groups with legitimate or illegitimate high status. They found (in particular when these groups were also numerically in a minority) that ingroup bias was higher when high status was framed as 'legitimate' rather than 'illegitimate'.

Similarly, Harvey and Bourhis (2013) allocated participants randomly to one of two groups and informed them that the two groups differed in wealth – one being a poor group and the other group the wealthy group. They then made group members believe that the stratification was either based on chance (i.e. the toss of a coin had determined which group would be poor and which group would be wealthy) or that the wealth difference was based on merit (i.e. the wealthy group had performed better on a mathematical test than the poor group). Participants in both groups were subsequently asked to allocate money to both their own group and the other group.

The findings of this experiment also shed interesting new light on the relationship between the perceived legitimacy of privilege and generosity. First, those in the wealthy group felt that the stratification was more legitimate when their wealth was based on merit than when it was based on chance. There was also evidence that the wealthy were more likely to give some of their money to the poor when wealth inequalities were caused by good luck than when wealth stratification was the result of merit. This chimes well with the finding that those who have acquired wealth by chance or through illegitimate means may feel insecure and worry about being an impostor (Hornsey & Jetten, 2011). People facing this predicament will feel anxious about their wealth and not feel the same sense of entitlement as those who have acquired wealth legitimately.

In sum, among wealthy people, when wealth is fixed because group boundaries are impermeable and when their position of affluence is secure and legitimate, the own wealth position will be associated with deservingness and entitlement (see Figure 8.2). The sense of superiority that comes with such a secure high-status position may at times lead to 'noblesse oblige' compassion, whereby the wealthy feel they have to take care of those less well-off. However, at other times, and in particular when the poor and deprived are challenging the status quo, wealthy groups may strike hard to protect their privileged position. In those times, the negative treatment of those who are less well-off may not even be regarded by the wealthy as 'harshness' because it is seen as reflecting a 'natural order', a social reality in which the ingroup happens to be superior.

As we saw in Chapter 7, from the 1970s onwards researchers have examined these relative gratification processes. More specifically, as we showed in Table 7.1, researchers have explained the relationship between relative gratification and harsh attitudes as due to (a) the present value of the past, where high-status groups perceive a sense of entitlement because of the heavy investments they made in the past (Grofman & Muller, 1973) and (b) a cultivation of system justification beliefs and legitimising ideologies (Jost, Banaji, & Nosek, 2004; Sidanius & Pratto, 1999). Here, we show that these two processes are most likely to emerge in response to relative gratification when the wealthy perceive that their high-status position is fixed and secure, thereby legitimising a harsh stance towards minorities and other vulnerable groups.

Insecure Wealth: Economic Instability

How, then, do members of higher status groups respond when their status position is not secure? There is a growing body of work showing that those who are privileged, powerful and wealthy are most likely to react in a hostile manner when their high status is not stable. Research has revealed that high-status group members whose status is threatened or insecure might engage in status protection, or even oppression, to avoid losing their higher status. Consistent with this, Scheepers, Ellemers and Sintemaartensdijk (2009) showed experimentally that only high-status groups who feared losing their status in the future displayed a physiological stress response, as measured by higher systolic blood pressure and pulse pressure. Those lower in status and higher-status group members who perceived their status as relatively stable showed less of a physiological stress response (see also Scheepers & Ellemers, 2005). More generally, sociologists have argued that high-status groups perceive threats to their status position when they feel that they might lose concrete privileges to lower-status groups (e.g. Blumer, 1958; Bobo, 1988). As outlined in Figure 8.2, this can be expected to increase open hostility towards others who are perceived as threatening the status quo.

These effects of instability are important when considering that insecurity and instability has increased dramatically over recent decades. We live in a world of profound, unprecedented and irreversible change and this affects people's sense of security. In particular, with the entire world now in the grip of the GFC, it is clear that one can no longer rely on old certainties, either as an individual or as a society as a whole. The 2008 GFC not only led to dramatic increases in unemployment, the sudden devaluation of assets and the collapse of the housing market in many Western countries, it also changed people's perceptions about the stability of the world they live in. What the GFC revealed was that financial stability cannot be taken for granted and that looks can be deceiving: stable economies turned out to be bubble economies and 'triple A rated' investments, deemed super-safe assets, lost their value overnight and became dangerous 'toxic' liabilities. The GFC not only rocked people's business confidence and belief that the world is predictable and controllable, it also heightened more general concerns about the future vitality of modern-day society.

As a result, and in particular among the more wealthy segments in society, concerns have grown that one's own wealth and achievements could all turn out to be a bubble, a bubble that can burst any time. In such a society, 'jungle view' ideologies will thrive (Duckitt, 1992/1994) and this will, particularly in meritocratic societies and among the middle classes, enhance 'status anxiety' (de Botton, 2004) and 'fear of falling' (Ehrenreich, 1990). This reasoning is consistent with SIT and its core tenet that an insecure high-status position will enhance status protection behaviour and enhance the motivation to justify the current status quo (Tajfel & Turner, 1979).

We conducted two studies to examine the question of *who* is most likely to be sensitive to financial instability resulting from the collapse of an economic bubble – the wealthy or the poor? An argument can be made for either of these groups. On the one hand, one can argue that people living in poverty are harder hit by economic recessions compared to those who are more prosperous precisely because they have fewer resources to fall back on (Riek, Mania, & Gaertner, 2006; Walker & Smith, 2001). On the other hand, however, one can argue that economic bubbles that threaten to burst are particularly threatening for those with greater wealth in society. More specifically, and consistent with research examining the effect of instability among high-status groups (e.g. Scheepers et al., 2009), we reasoned that being confronted with a bubble economy is more consequential for 'the haves' than 'the have-nots'. After all, it is the wealthy who have a lot, and therefore who have a lot to lose when financial markets collapse.

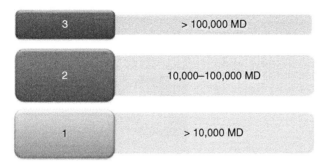

Figure 8.5. The three wealth groups in the hypothetical society of Mambiza.

We conducted two studies testing these predictions, using a stratified 'virtual reality' society named Mambiza, which participants 'entered' using a computer laboratory workstation (Jetten et al., 2017). Participants were informed that, as in most societies, in Mambiza there are rich and poor groups of people, and participants were randomly assigned to either a poor (1), moderately wealthy (2), or wealthy (3) income group (see Figure 8.5).

Next, we informed participants that, to start their new life, they would have to shop for essential items such as a house, a car and a phone. As in the studies discussed in Chapter 6 where we followed similar procedures, participants were presented with a range of choices but they could only 'buy' a house, car or phone that fell within their income group.

We then provided participants with information about the state of the economy in Mambiza. Half of our participants were provided with a fictitious article outlining Mambiza's economy as stable (see Figure 8.6, left-hand article) and the other half received a news article stating that the Mambiza's economy was unstable (i.e. a bubble and likely to burst any moment; see Figure 8.6, right-hand article).

Participants were then asked to what extent they agreed with statements that assessed the extent to which they feared for the future of their income group. For example, they were presented with statements such as 'I am worried about the future vitality of my income group' and 'I feel anxious about the future of my income group'.

Analyses of responses showed that fear for the future not only differed according to the income group participants were allocated

Figure 8.6. The economy in the hypothetical society of Mambiza is portrayed as stable (left-hand) or as unstable (right-hand).

to, but also depended on which newspaper article they had read. When reading the article stating that the economy of Mambiza was stable, not surprisingly, it was the participants in the wealthy income group and those in the moderately wealthy income groups who were less fearful of the future of their income group compared to those who were allocated to the poor income group. However, this situation changed when the economy in Mambiza was presented as a bubble about to burst. Even though all participants who had read this article were more fearful of the future than those who had read the article that the economy was stable, fear arose particularly for participants in the wealthiest income group (see Figure 8.7). Put differently, it was only for participants in the moderate and wealthy income groups that the economic situation mattered – we found that they expressed a higher fear for the future of their income group when the economic situation was unstable compared to when it was stable. In contrast, those in the poor group were fearful of the future of their income group *regardless* of the state of the economy.

Interestingly, in this study, the moderately wealthy responded in rather similar ways to instability of the economy than those who were at the top of the wealth pyramid. This is consistent with classic theorising that being 'stuck in the middle' is a particularly unfortunate and uncomfortable position to be in – one that is associated with high anxiety and fear of falling in and of itself. This because people in such groups perceive they are perhaps better off than other groups (e.g. immigrant groups, working classes), but they also know that their

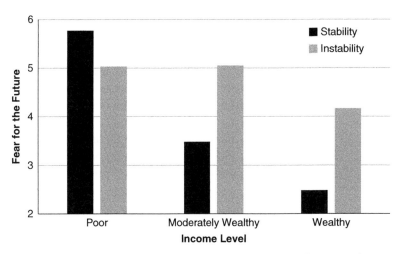

Figure 8.7. Fear for the future of one's income group as a function of income level and stability of the economy.
Source: Reprinted from Jetten et al. (2017) with permission

status is not as high and secure as it is for some other groups (e.g. upper classes). This is often the fate of lower middle classes (or 'petite bourgeoisie', to use Karl Marx's terminology).

These findings shed interesting new light on the question we had asked ourselves: *who* is most likely to be sensitive to financial instability resulting from the collapse of an economic bubble – the wealthy or the poor? Well, it appears that the poor are chronically fearful of the future, and their anxiety and fear levels clearly trump those of the moderately wealthy and the wealthy, regardless of the economic context in which they find themselves (see also Mullainathan & Shafir, 2013). However, those who are wealthier may rapidly *become* more fearful when they perceive that the economic context becomes unpredictable and unstable. In fact, fear may be particularly difficult to cope with when fear is not a chronic state, but one that is out of the ordinary and not expected.

Consistent with this, it has been argued that the wealthy are more scared of poverty than the poor are. Greve (2009) makes this point in a newspaper article in which he seeks to explain why, relatively speaking, poor people are more generous than their wealthier counterparts (see also Chapter 5). He cites Herbert Smith (31 years old), a Seventh-day Adventist who tithed his $1,010 monthly disability check – giving away 10% of it to others who were even less well off. When asked, Smith argues that poor people give more because, in some ways, they worry less about not having any money and because they are more resourceful than wealthy people when they do not have any money. As Smith puts it: 'we're not scared of poverty the way rich people are. We know how to get the lights back on when we can't pay the electric bill.'

We might be inclined to dismiss such stories as flimsy anecdotal evidence. However, we were able to establish experimentally that the affluent do indeed worry disproportionately about losing their wealth and about slipping into poverty when the economic situation is unstable. One would therefore expect the affluent to be more or less permanently 'on the lookout' for forces that could threaten their future wealth, such as the potential arrival of a relatively large group of needy newcomers who need financial assistance.

We conducted a second study to examine this prediction. Our second study involved an online study among Australian undergraduate students. The procedure of the study was identical to the first one except that, after participants had learned about the state of society (stable for half of the participants and unstable for the other half), they were told that a new group would be joining Mambiza. Participants were informed that these newcomers might need help from the other income groups in order to be able to start their new lives. Participants were then asked to complete measures that assessed their attitudes towards immigration.

When we analysed participants' responses, we found that opposition to immigration not only differed according to the income group participants were allocated to, but also depended on which newspaper article they had read. As we had observed in the first study when examining fear for the future of the income group responses, the poor opposed immigration by the newcomers regardless of the stability of the economy. However, participants in the wealthy group were quite sensitive to the stability of the economy. Whereas opposition to immigration was relatively low when the economy was presented as stable, those in the wealthy income group were more opposed to the arrival of the newcomers when the economy was presented as vulnerable and unstable – as a bubble about to burst (see Figure 8.8).

LeBlanc, Beaton and Walker (2015) found similar results in a study among undergraduate students at a prestigious Canadian university.

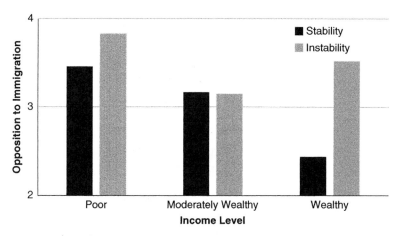

Figure 8.8. Opposition to immigration as a function of income level and stability of the economy.
Source: Reprinted from Jetten et al. (2017) with permission

The purpose of the study was to ascertain whether a perceived decline in advantage would engender prejudice towards minorities. Decline in advantage was induced by exposure to a pessimistic message about declining future employment prospects for the students of the university in question, relative to that of students from a lower-status competitor university (whose employment prospects were portrayed as consistently strong and stable). The findings showed that prejudice increased significantly among participants who were made to feel as though they were losing advantage. This confirmed the authors' prediction that when there is a decline in the students' advantaged status vis-à-vis students from another university (i.e. in terms of future employment rates, the advantaged group learns that employment rates for members of the own university drop while they remain promising for students from another university that is more disadvantaged), perceived relative gratification positively predicts prejudice towards a minority group (in this case, Aboriginals in Canada).

In sum, we live in uncertain times, in a time in which countries across the globe are desperately seeking to overcome the GFC and its ramifications, with few economic and financial certainties. The above-mentioned studies focused on those who are prosperous and have most to lose when the 'bubble is about to burst' (see also Jetten et al., 2015) or when the status of the ingroup becomes precarious (LeBlanc et al., 2015). Both lines of work show that instability resulting from economic uncertainty enhances anxiety among the affluent. To overcome enhanced anxiety associated with instability, the wealthy may engage in status protection, manifesting in enhanced anti-immigrant sentiments and prejudice.

Taking Stock

Taken together, the picture looks rather dire. Now that we have discussed the responses of wealthy groups to the socio-structural context that they may find themselves in (Figure 8.2), it becomes clear that members of these groups are more likely to lash out against minority groups (either openly or more subtly) than that they are propelled to be generous and tolerant. However, this conclusion would be premature. Clearly, and as we have pointed out in this book, there are instances when wealth goes together with generosity and kindness towards minority groups.

We would argue though that there are two developments in particular that will discourage the wealthy from becoming more generous and welcoming in the years to come. These are (a) growing societal inequality (manifesting in a small class of super-wealthy individuals, the so-called 1%) and (b) the emergence of a harsh normative climate (or 'zeitgeist'), in which harshness towards vulnerable minorities is condoned or even promoted. When considering these two trends, it becomes plausible to predict that, now and in the future, we are more likely to find evidence for a wealth paradox than for a wealth–generosity link. Let us unpack these predictions in greater detail.

Societal Inequality and Its Effect on Prejudice

There is growing concern about the widening income gap between those at the bottom of society and those at the top (Wilkinson & Pickett, 2009). Growing societal inequality not only lowers levels of trust and cohesion, it also leads to perceived loss of control (Marmot, 2006), it renders societies harsher and more violent (Wilkinson & Pickett, 2009), and it undermines faith in the long-term viability of society itself. Indeed, when the gap between those at the bottom of the hierarchy and those at the top becomes too large, the system as a whole may become dangerously unstable.

We asked ourselves whether it is those who live in poverty or those who are more affluent in society who are most affected by inequality. On the one hand, one can predict that inequality is particularly 'hard to swallow' for those at the bottom of the wealth hierarchy. This is because the gulf between the 'haves' and the 'have-nots' will be particularly visible for those at the bottom of society, and this is known to be associated with resentment and dissatisfaction. This, in turn, enhances competition with others at the bottom of society and may explain lashing out to others who are also struggling economically (e.g. minorities or immigrants), and especially those who are competing for the same scarce resources.

However, the opposite prediction appears true too. Precisely because inequality brings instability, it may be the 'haves' who are more likely to be concerned about their financial future than the 'have-nots'. Indeed, inequality may evoke anxiety, fear and sorrow among those who are relatively gratified because in an unequal society, the wealthy may not only face increased envy, but also enhanced self-awareness that one can fall quite low when wealth evaporates. Furthermore, inequality fuels desires to have more, and in particular the wealthy will be prone to such desires (Frank, 1999). Indeed, in unequal societies 'the sky may well be the limit', but this knowledge can be expected to lead to restlessness and a more or less constant desire to increase one's wealth (due to more or less constant upward mobility threat).

We conducted a study examining these opposing predictions (Jetten et al., 2015) using yet another 'new life' experiment. In this study, 153 mostly North American participants were recruited via the online platform MTurk. The participants in this study were informed that they would become part of a hypothetical virtual-reality society, Bimboola. After the participants had been randomly assigned to one of three wealth groups in a five income-group society, they were asked to purchase items that would help them to get started in their new life in Bimboola. After receiving their instructions, participants were provided with either a growing or a declining inequality manipulation. In the declining inequality condition, participants were told (growing income inequality condition in brackets):

Imagine that over the next 20 years, Bimboola is affected by a change in economy. As a result, the wealth gap in Bimboolean society has decreased (increased). Status differences have decreased (increased): the poor have become richer (poorer), the moderately wealthy earn about the same, and the rich have lost some of the wealth and become poorer (gained more wealth and become richer).

After this, participants were presented with a corresponding graphical representation of this change (see Figure 8.9). Importantly, in the graph, the wealth of their own income group was presented as unaffected over time and this was emphasised in an accompanying note.

The results showed that *all* wealth groups became more opposed to immigrants when inequality was growing rather than declining. This finding is interesting and suggests that growing inequality is equally threatening for those at the bottom, middle or top of a wealth hierarchy. The finding is consistent with observations by political scientists and sociologists that growing inequality leads to greater status competition whereby *everyone* experiences greater status instability and status anxiety, regardless of one's class, status or income. Indeed, this finding also speaks to Wilkinson and Pickett's (2009) observation that inequality is a threat to everyone in society – the poor as well as the wealthy.

Consistent with our social identity analysis, it appears that inequality increases people's tendencies to see the world through a lens of wealth. Unpacking this, growing inequality enhances the likelihood that income and wealth differences become more visible. As Wilkinson and Pickett (2009) argue:

If inequalities are bigger ... where each one of us is placed becomes more important. Greater inequality is likely to be accompanied by increased status competition and increased status anxiety. It is not simply that where the stakes are higher each of us worries more about where he or she comes. It is also that we are likely to pay more attention to social status in how we assess each other. (p. 44)

In other words, with increasing levels of inequality, wealth becomes a fitting basis for categorising self and others in society (Turner et al., 1987). As a result of this, and consistent with the notions in Table 7.1 that link harsh attitudes to stronger intergroup dynamics (Dambrun et al., 2006), we predict that 'us' versus 'them' perceptions become more salient when inequality grows. Over time, this will lead to deteriorating relations between different wealth groups, as will be evident from greater intergroup competition. Ultimately, this will lead to other negative outcomes than harsh attitudes towards minorities: for

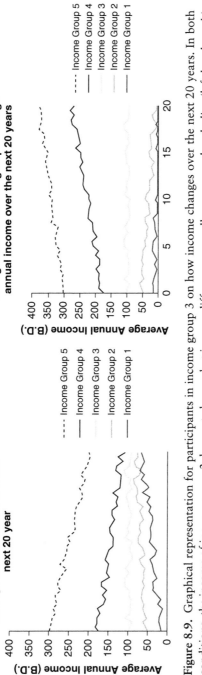

Figure 8.9. Graphical representation for participants in income group 3 on how income changes over the next 20 years. In both conditions, the income of income group 3 does not change, but income differences overall are expected to decline (left-hand graph) or increase (right-hand graph).

example, a splintering of society into subgroups, the withdrawal of individuals from society at large, lower social cohesion and lower levels of identification with society.

The Broader Normative Climate Promotes Harsh Attitudes

There is a second reason why we suspect that it will be likely that the link between wealth and harsh attitudes will be observed more often in the future – i.e., that the wealth paradox becomes stronger. In many countries, there are growing concerns about societies becoming less tolerant and caring, and about individualism being rife (Stokkom, 2010). Put differently, an era of sympathy for the needy and 'noblesse oblige' appears to have given way to a new zeitgeist, whereby concerns for those less well-off have been replaced with a sense that wealth comes with entitlements and greater deservingness. Consistent with the process described in Table 7.1, in such normative climates, self-definitions emerge that the own group is competent but cold, justifying hostility towards other groups that are less well off.

Linking this to our current analysis, we predict that status anxiety, entitlement and deservingness effects should be amplified in contexts where the broader normative climate promotes a harsh stance towards minorities and vulnerable groups. Postmes and Smith (2009) present empirical evidence in support of this reasoning. In a first study, they presented British participants (undergraduate students at the University of Exeter) with one of two types of information to manipulate the perceived normative climate. Under the guise that the study was examining politics in Britain and differences between rich and poor, participants were given fictional feedback about 'affluent people, with influence and advantage over others'. They were told that these affluent people either do (or do not) 'use their wealth and status as a way of helping those less fortunate than themselves'. After this, participants in both conditions were provided with a number of examples to back up these claims.

A second manipulation in this study involved a manipulation of future prospects of University of Exeter students compared to students of another university. In a relative gratification condition, participants were presented with information that, 'A recent survey ... has found that students graduating from Exeter University now have the same job prospects as Oxbridge graduates'. Participants were also asked to examine a graph showing the projected income of Exeter graduates overtaking that of Oxbridge graduates (traditionally higher status) and rising significantly above that of graduates from lower-status universities. In the control condition, no such feedback was provided. After this, participants were asked to indicate their agreement with items assessing their support for calls to adopt stricter anti-immigrant policies in Britain (e.g. 'The British are entitled to have priority over immigrants in receiving social security benefits').

Consistent with Postmes and Smith's hypotheses, it was found that support for anti-immigrant policies was higher only when gratified participants were led to believe that the normative climate in Britain is one where wealthy people are selfish (i.e. hostile norm condition). When the norm was benevolent, there was no difference between participants in the gratified condition and those in the control condition. Postmes and Smith (2009) replicated this finding in a second study in which they manipulated the perceived normative context in a slightly different way. Now, the content of the feedback about the privileged

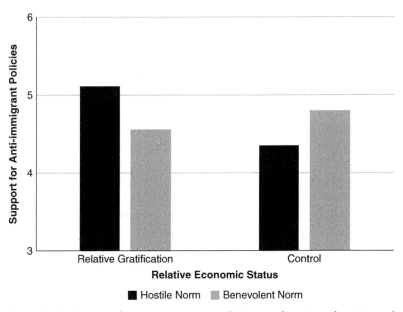

Figure 8.10. Support for anti-immigrant policies as a function of anticipated relative economic status (gratification versus control) and perceived normative climate in Britain. Adapted from Postmes and Smith (2009) with permission.

group's attitudes was specific to immigrants. For example, participants received fictional feedback that a 'Recent survey by the government body *National Statistics*, regarding attitudes towards immigration' found significantly higher levels of concern about immigration among those who were on higher salaries. Participants in the control condition were not provided with feedback about the norm.

This study too showed that those participants who anticipated relative gratification in the future were only more supportive of anti-immigrant policies when the normative climate was hostile towards immigrants (not when the normative climate was portrayed as benevolent). Again, the normative climate did not affect attitudes of participants differently in a control condition where no feedback was provided about the normative climate.

This study can be regarded as a stark reminder that there is no automatic link between relative gratification and hostility towards immigrants and other minorities (or between relative deprivation and outgroup hostility), and that such perceptions and accompanying sentiment will only translate into greater hostility if this can be reconciled within the overarching normative climate and prevailing narratives in society.

There is also anecdotal evidence for the point that relative gratification is more likely to trigger hostility towards minorities when the normative climate promotes a harsh stance. We know that societies that were once renowned for their hospitality and tolerance have become harsher in their attitudes towards minorities, those living on welfare, and immigrants. As an example of how extreme some of these changes can be, consider the two posters in Figure 8.11. These posters, produced by the Australian Department of Immigration for potential immigrants, have changed dramatically, from being extremely welcoming (left-hand poster from circa 1948) to messages that immigrants (in particular refugees who aim to reach Australia by sea) should not have any illusions about making Australia their home (right-hand poster from 2014).

What makes the contrast all the more interesting is that the Australian economy was booming during both these times (i.e. Australian people were relatively gratified). The 1940s/1950s would become remembered as a time of unprecedented growth and prosperity, achieved through various nation-building projects. The 2000s/2010s would bring another boom, driven by Chinese construction and demand for Australian natural resources, which enabled the

Figure 8.11. Posters from the Australian Department of Immigration welcoming (left hand) versus warning potential immigrants (right-hand).

country to survive the GFC relatively unscathed, and to become the envy of economists around the globe.

Consistent with reasoning by Postmes and Smith (2009), when the normative climate turns negative, and when there is greater acceptance of the exclusion of minorities and the restriction of minorities' rights, oppression will become normalised. In such normative climates, perceptions of minorities as a threat dominate public discourse and perception (or 'Zeitgeist'), justifying and condoning harsh attitudes, racism and prejudice.

Finally, whereas we focused predominantly on norms promoting harsh attitudes and intolerance, it should be kept in mind that norms can also prescribe groups (including wealthy groups) to become more tolerant towards minorities. Consider, for example, groups or societies for whom philanthropy and generosity are normative. For members of such groups, internalising such norms into their self-concepts would lead them to behave in ways that are consistent with the local group norm, even if that goes against broader societal norms. A case in point here are philanthropic organisations such as Rotary International, which tend to attract wealthy citizens and business leaders eager to promote peace, fund education and secure greater prosperity for the poor.

In Conclusion

In this chapter, we turned the spotlight on the conditions under which we are likely to witness the wealth paradox – hardening attitudes (e.g. vis-à-vis immigrants and asylum seekers) among the wealthy and in times of economic prosperity. Unlike low-status groups, high-status groups by definition already compare favourably on the central status-defining dimension, imparting a positive identity. As a result, superior status (e.g. wealth) confers both psychological and material rewards. It is thus not surprising that members of advantaged groups are first and foremost interested in maintaining and protecting their dominant position (e.g. Branscombe & Ellemers, 1998; Kobrynowicz & Branscombe, 1997). Also here, though, the way in which high-status group members protect their high-status position depends on the broader contexts and, in particular, on the security of their high-status position. According to SIT, it is also here that permeability of boundaries, stability of wealth and legitimacy of the wealth position play a key role, but in different ways as they do for the poor or in times of economic decline. Interestingly too, in our analysis of the way that socio-structural factors determine identity management strategies by wealthy groups, we developed reasoning that maps very well onto the seven processes that have been put forward in previous research to explain why relative gratification can be associated with harsh attitudes towards minorities (see Table 7.1).

Having reviewed the literature and relevant work, we conclude that we are most likely to find that poverty leads to harsh attitudes when permeability of boundaries between groups (and the accompanying sense of meritocracy) leads to individualised behaviour whereby people gradually internalise the belief that they have to look after themselves first and foremost. Such focus on one's narrow self-interests is amplified when the economy is declining, further justifying decisions to look after one's own interests rather than helping more vulnerable groups in society.

We also found that due attention for classic social identity factors is essential when trying to explain the relationship between wealth and attitudes towards minorities. We found evidence that affluence and wealth is most likely to be related to harsh attitudes when (a) those who are wealthy perceive that boundaries between groups are permeable, enhancing 'pressure for individual mobility' and 'fear of encroachment', (b) when wealth, because it is perceived as having been acquired legitimately, goes hand-in-hand with a sense of entitlement justifying the exclusion of those less well-off and (c) when the affluent worry that their wealth could dissipate in a short timespan (instability of wealth due to economic instability or fear that the economy might collapse overnight).

The latter two processes are interesting and suggest that, given the impermeability of boundaries between wealth groups, it depends on other features of the broader socio-structural context how the affluent respond to minority groups. Specifically, status and wealth protection might result from one of two processes: it results from entitlement and deservingness (because status relations are secure and legitimate) or from status anxiety (because status relations are insecure and unstable). While the outcome of the two processes may be the same (more negative attitudes towards minorities), the processes are different in that the former is driven by the security of wealth and the anticipated need to justify one's affluence and/or lavish lifestyle whereas the latter is driven by the insecurity of the wealth position and a fear of 'slipping back'. We also predicted that these effects should be amplified when society reaches unprecedented levels of inequality and when the normative climate in a society condones or even encourages harshness towards the vulnerable.

In summary, having abandoned the notion that there should be straightforward relationships between wealth and attitudes towards minorities, in this chapter we examined the *conditions under which* poverty and wealth, as well as economic decline and economic prosperity, are associated with harsher attitudes. In order to shed light on this, we turned to classic social identity reasoning and used it to examine the different kinds of anxieties and worries those at the top and those at the bottom of the social ladder might have about their current and future position in society.

Now that we unpacked the underpinnings of the wealth paradox, it is time to turn our attention to the ways in which crafty politicians with an anti-immigrant agenda harness some of these sentiments, and how they persuade relatively gratified voters that it is time to curb immigration and reduce support for vulnerable minorities.

9 | *The Missing Link: Crafty Politicians Galvanising Latent Sentiments*

Populist Right-Wing Parties (PRWPs) are typically assumed to be most successful in times of economic struggle as this provides an ideal platform to create fear-based narratives (Arzheimer & Carter, 2006; Betz, 1993; Golder, 2003; Jackman & Volpert, 1996; Jenks & Lauck, 1912). However, as we saw in Chapter 4, when considering election results it becomes clear that such parties have often done surprisingly well in times of economic prosperity. But how can we explain the popularity of populist anti-immigrant parties when the economy is booming? That is, flourishing economies would appear to constrain the viability of realistic threat arguments and this should make it harder for parties with an anti-immigration or an anti-minority agenda to make their case. This is because it should be less plausible to present immigrants and refugees as a realistic threat (e.g. as responsible for unemployment) when the economy is flourishing and unemployment is not a concern. To answer this question, let us first consider a large body of research that has examined factors that predict when people are most likely to be drawn to populist movements and far-right parties.

Current Approaches Explaining the Appeal of Populist Political Parties

The literature has focused on explaining the popularity of PRWPs by pointing to personality and individual differences in value orientation, such as Right Wing Authoritarianism and Social Dominance Orientation (Adorno et al., 1950; Altemeyer, 1981; Sidanius & Pratto, 1999). Others have pointed to triggering conditions, and have argued that such parties thrive when society is in a state of anomie (Parsons, 1942), when progressive movements become regarded as having too much influence (Ignazi, 1992), when citizens experience a sense of powerlessness (Arendt, 1951), when there is realistic conflict between different groups in society (Coser, 1956; LeVine & Campbell, 1965; Sherif, 1966; Sherif & Sherif, 1953), when citizens experience a gap between expectations and achievements (Davies, 1962) or when relative deprivation perceptions are widespread (Gurr, 1970). Still others have pointed to ideologies that promote scapegoating (Dollard et al., 1939), political opportunity structures affording the rise of such movements (Koopmans, 1996), strategic spatial party-positioning (Bale, 2003) and symbolic threat perceptions (Esses, Haddock, & Zanna, 1993; Kinder & Sears, 1981; Stephan, Ybarra, & Bachman, 1999). Thanks to this vast literature, we now know a lot about the kinds of fears and sentiments that enhance the appeal of far-right parties and movements.

However, as Rydgren (2007, p. 247) explains, the explanations on offer in this literature are 'almost all based on grievance theory, [focusing on] objective – mostly macro-structurally shaped – conditions that have increased grievances and discontent among the people' (see also De Witte & Klandermans, 2000; Koopmans et al., 2005). In other words, it is typically assumed in these contributions that far-right support is fuelled more or less automatically by frustration with (real or perceived) *deteriorating* socio-economic conditions for one's group or social class. In this perspective, the role of leaders is conceived as merely voicing popular discontent, rather than as arousing and shaping discontent.

Not surprisingly, researchers have therefore tended to focus on what far-right leaders have to say during economic downturns. What they found – and this should not come as a surprise – is that, in times of economic decline, leaders of PRWPs with an anti-immigrant agenda do indeed construct narratives based on perceived competition between citizens and immigrants (Betz, 1993). Specifically, the narratives deployed in such times blame immigrants for taking jobs and for further burdening the already-stretched public purse. It therefore appears that these narratives serve the function of inducing unfavourable comparisons, competition and fear, all of which result in support for such parties (Betz, 1993). While this can explain the type of arguments that such leaders put forward in times of economic downturn, it does not help us to understand what leaders with an anti-immigrant agenda say when the economy is flourishing. This is an important question because, as we saw in Chapter 4, there is now compelling evidence that such leaders are at times particularly popular with the electorate when the economy is booming. In other words, what do these leaders say when the economy is not a cause for concern, and how do they argue their anti-immigration case when there are enough resources to go around?

Three Narratives That Dominate in Times of Economic Prosperity

In this chapter, we explore the missing link between economic prosperity and harsh attitudes by focusing on the role of leaders in *shaping perceptions*. We focus in particular on leaders of populist far-right parties, and the ways in which these leaders argue their case when the economy is not a cause for concern. We start from the observation that successful leaders are crafty 'identity entrepreneurs' who position themselves strategically (Mols & Jetten, 2015). This also means that the way that they hope to garner support for their message is tailored to the context whereby they speak to the fears and anxieties that dominate public discourse at a particular moment in time. Indeed, there is now greater recognition that, as Reicher and Hopkins (2001) have shown, career politicians behave like chameleons, constantly modifying their message so it fits the interests and concerns of the audience being addressed.

We propose that in times of economic prosperity, populist leaders will use, and at times alternate between, three threat narratives: (a) acknowledging that the economy is healthy but argue that society is nonetheless at the brink of collapse due to other subversive forces, (b) question official statistics to cast doubts on the premise that the economy is not a cause for concern, or (c) remain silent about the state of the economy but raise suspicions about the fairness of wealth distribution by arguing that immigrants receive more than their fair share of the cake. To be sure, a clear exception to this rule is times in which countries with prospering economies face large-scale refugee crises (e.g. the European refugee crisis in the wake of the breakup of Yugoslavia in the 1990s, or the current mass influx of refugees from Syria and Iraq). In such times, far-right parties have been found to seek to seize the obvious opportunity to cultivate symbolic threat, by pointing to differences in culture and values between the newcomers and the host society. However, as we will see next, successful far-right leaders are remarkably creative, so much so that they do not need an economic crisis or a refugee crisis to make their case that immigration should be curbed.

(A) *The Economy May Be Healthy, but We Are Nonetheless About to Fall*

Intuitively, one would expect that populist leaders would simply remain silent on the economy when the economy is prospering because the state of the economy constrains the strengths of arguments that immigration should be curbed to protect the material interests of the native population. However, this is not what we observed in our research (Mols & Jetten, 2015). Rather, we found that in such economic contexts, populist leaders acknowledge the healthy state of the economy, but complement this statement with reasoning that other forces are at play – forces that pose a real threat to the health and strength of society.

To illustrate this, let us have a closer look at Pim Fortuyn, the leader of the LPF party in the Netherlands – a party with an outspoken anti-immigrant and anti-Islam agenda. Fortuyn was assassinated on 6 May 2002, nine days before the national elections, in which the LPF secured 26 seats in Parliament (17% of the vote). What makes this landslide victory so paradoxical and fascinating is the fact that it occurred at a time of prolonged economic growth and prosperity. This is also evident from the fact that in the same year *The Economist* ran a special issue showcasing the remarkable successes of the Dutch economic model, the so-called Polder Model. How, then, did Fortuyn make a case that immigrants pose a threat to the economy and the health of the Dutch society more generally?

As the following extract from his 2001 acceptance speech illustrates, Fortuyn explicitly acknowledged the booming Dutch economy, but also argued that the country was in the grip of other forces that would bring the country down – namely secrecy, collusion and nepotism within the country's public administration:

Most of my colleagues believe politics is about the economy, but that is precisely what politics is not about. Had I been PM … then the Queen's address to Parliament would have started with thanking … employers, their employees, but also the Unions, for eight consecutive years of economic growth. After all, it is employers and their employees who run the economy'.

We should thank [Finance] Minister Zalm for bringing national debt back under control. The problem, though, is that he got weak knees, the last 18 months, but that is to be expected if you're in a cabinet with subsidizing socialists … But then comes what politics is really about: the public sector.

And if we then look back at the last eight years, then I become saddened. (Fortuyn, 25 November 2001).

As the following extract from his 2002 book *De Puinhopen van Acht Jaar Paars* illustrates, by downplaying the importance of a booming economy, Fortuyn paves the way for a much gloomier alternative analysis of the country's current state and future viability, one that portrays the country as on the brink of collapse:

[We now have] an elite democracy which mostly plays out behind the scenes, away from the public eye, with most negotiations being 'pre-cooked' and taking place in back- rooms ... The Dutch political and administrative elite does not care about the ordinary citizen. (Fortuyn, 2002, p. 11)

[The public sector] is an incestuous network, consisting of self-nominating, reciprocating political and administrative elite. (Fortuyn, 2002, p. 136)

The 2002 election result can be seen as evidence that Fortuyn had been able to persuade a significant proportion of the electorate that Dutch public administration was 'rotten to the core'. Looking more closely at his reasoning and arguments, it becomes clear that in this particular instance Fortuyn deployed a rather unique indirect strategy to argue the case for less immigration, one that targeted not immigrants or asylum seekers as such, but the 'flawed' system and its corrupt administrators.

Anti-immigrant narratives often focus on immigrants as an economic threat as well as a symbolic and existential threat (Riek, Mania, & Gaertner, 2006). Even though realistic conflict and symbolic threat narratives are not incompatible and often go hand-in-hand, it is often the case that one of the two narratives dominates at a particular moment in time. For example, in the Netherlands, the populist right-wing leader Geert Wilders has focused on both. That is, at times he presents immigrants and refugees as a realistic threat (i.e. immigrants are portrayed as a burden to ordinary hard-working Dutch tax-payers), and at other times he represents them as a symbolic threat – depicting Islam as an existential threat to national values and as an incompatible alien influence (e.g. the 'Islamisation' of Dutch culture; see González, Verkuyten, Weesie, & Poppe, 2008).

While realistic threat narratives may be compelling in times of economic downturn because they speak to the fears and anxieties that dominate public discourse at a particular moment in time, this discourse is less powerful (and is therefore less likely to be used) in times of economic prosperity. In such contexts, narratives that focus on immigrants as other types of threat will dominate – for example, narratives that immigrants are a threat to culture (symbolic threat). We can find some evidence for this in other speeches by Fortuyn. Indeed, rather than arguing that immigrants pose a realistic threat, he argued that they are a symbolic threat to Dutch society. More specifically, he portrays Islam as a threat to Western values and Dutch culture in particular. An example of this can be found in his 2002 book:

[Here in the Netherlands] we now have separation of State and Church. It took us many centuries, and rivers of blood. It made us the beacon of light in the world in terms of individual freedoms and human rights. Many Islamic countries, on the other hand, have horrendous oppression in all sorts of domains, including constant breaches in human rights. A backward desert culture, based on an equally backward, oppressive and imperialist religion and belief system. Those who do not believe will be forced to swallow, dead or alive. (Fortuyn, 2002, p. 89)

I am an optimist, and I certainly do not want to scaremonger or incite hatred towards foreigners. On the contrary, I just want to warn. It is not too late. Let us use our time wisely. Continuing on the road we followed for decades is no longer an option. A rigorous U-turn in asylum and immigration policy is needed urgently in order to repel the looming dangers described above. (Fortuyn, 2002, p. 160)

In sum, what sets Fortuyn apart from other populist leaders is his explicit acknowledgement that the economy is thriving. However, he directs the electorate's attention to two other – in his eyes – more serious threats: a complacent and untrustworthy public administration that fails to recognise that the county's future is at risk, and immigration and asylum seekers as a symbolic threat (see also Jetten, Ryan, & Mols, in press).

(B) We Are Being Told the Economy Is Sound, but Is It Really?

Another way in which populist leaders can appraise a healthy economy is by casting doubt on official statistics. For example, they may argue that there are hidden problems and pitfalls that are not reflected in those economic indicators, masking the real state of the economy. At other times, they may point to the importance of other indicators (according to which the economy is not performing that well) or even go as far as accusing government officials of spreading false information about the 'real' state of the economy.

An example of a populist leader casting doubt on official reports about the economy is Pauline Hanson, the leader of Australia's One Nation, a party with a strong anti-immigrant and anti-indigenous agenda. Hanson, a former member of the Liberal Party of Australia (LPA), founded One Nation in 1997, at a time in which Australia had experienced four consecutive years of GDP per capita growth (from US$17,661 in 1993 to US$ 23,526 in 1997) and a falling unemployment rate (from 10.6% in 1993 to 8.3% in 1997). Although the country would experience something of a slowdown from 1997 onwards, on the whole Australia's economy was in a very good condition at the time Hanson became popular.

Unlike Fortuyn, who acknowledged outright that the country's economy was not at all a cause for concern, Hanson's strategy was more indirect and involved merely casting doubt on whether the country's economy was in actual fact in a good state. As the following extract from Hanson's 1996 maiden speech (delivered in the national parliament in Canberra as a member of the LPA) shows, she does so by pointing to the country's national debt, by describing it as a heavy burden, by questioning the meaning and validity of official national unemployment statistics, and by arguing that the country's economy was in fact extremely fragile.

This country of ours has the richest mineral deposits in the world and vast rich lands for agriculture and is surrounded by oceans that provide a wealth of seafood, yet we are $190 billion in debt with an interest bill that is strangling us.

Youth unemployment between the ages of 15 to 24 runs at 25 per cent and is even higher in my electorate of Oxley. Statisticians, by cooking the books, say that Australia's unemployment is at 8.6 per cent, or just under one million people. If we disregard that one-hour's work a week classifies a person as employed, then the figure is really between 1.5 million and 1.9 million unemployed.

This is a crisis that recent governments have ignored because of a lack of will. We are regarded as a Third World country with First World living conditions. We have one of the highest interest rates in the world, and we owe more money per capita than any other country. All we need is a nail hole in the bottom of the boat and we're sunk. (Hanson, 10 September 1996)

As the following extract from a speech delivered at One Nation's party launch in 1997 illustrates, Hanson portrayed Australia as a country that is slipping backwards, and as falling behind rapidly.

Jobs are going to countries like Indonesia, where pay is 39 cents an hour. The government's enthusiastic removal of tariff protection has forced manufacturers overseas. No wonder Asia boasts their 'Tiger Economics': they manufacture our goods, to their benefit, and at the cost of our jobs. In the seventies Australia accounted for 4% of world trade, in the nineties it is down to 1%, and still falling. We are simply not keeping up with rest of the world. (Hanson, 11 April 1997)

As the following extract shows, Hanson not only casts doubt on whether Australia's economy is as healthy as people believed it to be; in her speeches, she also goes to considerable lengths to persuade voters that Australia's culture, norms and values are at risk:

I believe we are in danger of being swamped by Asians. Between 1984 and 1995, 40 per cent of all migrants coming into this country were of Asian origin. They have their own culture and religion, form ghettos and do not assimilate. Of course, I will be called racist but, if I can invite whom I want into my home, then I should have the right to have a say in who comes into my country. A truly multicultural country can never be strong or united. (Hanson, 10 September 1996)

[Immigrants] should have a knowledge of how to speak English. They must know how to assimilate. They must respect our laws, our flag and what Australia stands for. . . . We have a country that so many people want to come and live in. Yet we seem to be bending over backwards to change our ways, our values and what we believe in to accommodate these people. (Hanson, 3 September 1997) [1]

Populist leaders may also seize the opportunity to point to a negative economic trend in reports that is otherwise optimistic

---

[1] Electoral support for Pauline Hanson declined significantly between 1998 and 2012. However, Hanson made a remarkable comeback in the federal elections, held on 2 July 2016, when she was elected into the Australian Senate as the (One Nation) member for Oxley. Her maiden Senate speech, delivered on 14 September 2016, drew considerable media attention, this because she reused a memorable sentence from her 1996 maiden speech, which she adapted to contemporary circumstances. More specifically, whereas in her 1996 maiden speech Hanson observed 'I believe we are in danger of being swamped by Asians', this time, two decades later, she warned 'Now we are in danger of being swamped by Muslims, who bear a culture and ideology that is incompatible with our own'.

about the country's overall economic state and outlook. For example, a populist leader may point to a small seasonal increase in unemployment and interpret this in an alarmist way, as a sign the economy is about to stall.

A fitting example of such a strategy can be found in Austria. Austria is not only ranked 12th in Forbes' list of the world's richest countries in 2015, the country has a long legacy of prosperity. For example, Austria experienced ten consecutive years of economic growth between 1985 and 1995, followed by two years of moderate slowdown and decline in levels of GDP per capita (1996–1997). During this entire period, unemployment remained below 5%, and although, at the time, economists may have been concerned about contracting GDP per capita figures, the overall picture was not alarming, and Austria remained one of the wealthier countries in the world. Yet, as the following speech extract shows, Jörg Haider, the leader of the right-wing and anti-immigrant Freiheitliche Partei Österreich (FPÖ), portrayed his country's economy as a serious cause for concern, requiring a strong hand and decisive action:

Ladies and Gentlemen, it is time, in this country, to take a different course. We have to find the path to the future. We have to pay more attention to the economic situation, and the dangers to our jobs. And it's not enough to placate people, and claim to be the strong hand for jobs, as the socialists do. Where is this strong hand? Where is it?

Well then, where are those measures, the measures that made this country competitive? That too matters. That we open opportunities for our people. That we give our people renewed confidence. But all that happens is taxes. Thanks to Brussels we now have to accept a new tax regime being dropped on our economy, which is already in the biggest possible downward spiral. And ordinary citizens are of course in the firing line; the hardworking citizen will see their income reduced as a result of higher tax rates. (Haider, 10 October 1996)

As the following extracts show, at times Haider uses realistic threat narratives by describing immigrants and ordinary hard-working Austrians as competitors in an already tense housing market.

I am always annoyed when [the Mayor of Vienna] says, there are no foreigners in the council's buildings. For goodness sake, how dumb does he think Austrians are? … Everyone knows that it is his very own politics, to welcome foreigners, to grant them citizenship. On average they have more children than Austrians, and that's why they get moved up to the top of the waiting lists, and that's why they get a council home quicker than Austrians, who have been waiting for years. (Haider, 10 October 1996)

However, he too uses symbolic threat narratives simultaneously, framing immigrants as a group with alien values that threaten 'our way of life'. As the following extract from a speech delivered in 1990 shows, there have been times at which Haider was quite outspoken about alien influences representing symbolic threat, and undermining Austrian/Western norms, values and culture:

The social order of Islam is opposed to our Western values. Human rights and democracy are as incompatible with the religious Muslim doctrine as is the equality of women. In Islam, the individual and his free will count for nothing, faith and religious struggle – Jihad, the holy war – for everything. (Haider, early 1990, cited in Merkl & Weinberger, 2003, p. 80)

A final example of a populist leader casting doubts about the health of the economy is Jean-Marie Le Pen. France, like most European countries, went through a more difficult economic phase between 1996 and 2001, when GDP per capita fell from approximately 'US$ 25,000 to US$ 20,000 and unemployment reached 12.6% in 1997. However, in 1999, unemployment started to decline, and from 2001 onwards, GDP per capita started to grow; this trend continued until 2008, when the GFC hit. As the following extracts show, these positive trends are not mentioned in Le Pen's speeches, who instead offers a narrative of an unprecedented slide into economic misery.

And what about this radiant future, which we were promised 50 years ago, when the Common Market was launched? The EU could have been a success if it had been well conceived, but it hasn't. Open borders, the single currency, have had catastrophic consequences for our wallets.

Just consider the following statistics. While the average economic growth rate stood at 3% during the 30 post war glory years [referred to in France as 'les Trentes Glorieuses'], the figure was barely 1.7% between 1990 and 2007, compared with 2.8% on average in other OECD countries. (Jean-Marie Le Pen, 25 March 2007)

In a speech delivered earlier that same year, Le Pen offers a similar analysis, with an even starker conclusion about the state of the French economy at the time:

It must have taken extraordinary incompetence to take France from thirty glory years, to thirty pitiful, shameful years, in which we have plunged since the mid-1970s. (Jean-Marie Le Pen, 11 March 2007).

And, once again, this narrative stands in contrast with the official statistics which show that, between 2001 and 2006, France experienced five consecutive years of GDP per capita growth, which, from 2005 onwards, started to translate into modest decreases in unemployment levels. And here too, negative appraisals of the economy went hand-in-hand with realistic and symbolic threat narratives, according to which immigrants from different cultural background are not only a drain on France's economy, but also a threat to Western/French norms and values:

War has arrived back on the old continent ... In 1991, President George Bush declared we entered a new era, a new enlightened and peaceful new world order, marked by reconciliation. The end of conflict between East and West, a triumph of people's right to self-determination, a victory for democracy, the individual, free markets ... principles the USA would stand for. Communism may be dead, but let's not forget belief systems that come from outside the West, like Islam, which is dynamic and takes over everything in one go: religion, politics, and society. (Jean-Marie Le Pen, 22 October 2006)

Who has institutionalised Islam in France? Who wants to help with the construction and financing of Mosques, including ones that are as big as Cathedrals, like the one here in Marseille? ... Who abolished the double penalty, weakening our system that once deterred foreigners from committing crimes? (Jean-Marie Le Pen, 3 March 2007)

In sum, what the above extracts show is that it is not so much the actual state of the economy that matters, but the way in which populist leaders appraise the economy, and the way this appraisal is subsequently used to create an alarmist climate in which radical proposals become regarded as desirable or even inevitable. Indeed, it appears that the following comment by Jenks and Lauk from the United States Immigration Commission in 1912 is as true now as it was then:

Many persons who have spoken and written in favor of restriction of immigration, have laid great stress upon the evils to society arising from immigration. They have claimed that disease, pauperism, crime and vice have been greatly increased through the incoming of the immigrants. Perhaps no other phase of the question has aroused so keen feeling, and yet perhaps on no other phase of the question has there been so little accurate information. (Jenks & Lauk, 1912)

Even though it may be the case that arguments put forward by leaders of populist parties may not be based on accurate information, it is nevertheless true that many leaders of these parties are able to convince a significant proportion of the electorate that immigration needs to be curbed.

(C) *The Economy May Be Healthy, but Who Is Reaping the Benefits?*

Another strategy populist leaders use in times of economic prosperity is to remain silent on the economy itself – thereby accepting the general idea that the economy is not a cause for concern tacitly – but to raise suspicions about the way in which wealth is being distributed. For example, Pauline Hanson focuses on the way the electorate has been left in the cold and has not benefitted from economic growth and prosperity. Although she stops short of using the word 'conspiracy', the language she uses nonetheless conveys the message of secret deals between transnational corporations and Australia's leftist elite, who have betrayed ordinary hard-working Australians by embracing the idea of free markets and open borders.

Your town is a steel town. For you, the making of steel has been a tradition that has been passed down from father to son, and fed local families for generations. Steel is in your blood. How betrayed you must feel as your lives are rusted away by the dollars demanded by shareholders with no regard for the workers who made BHP what it is today.

The Australian worker usually turns to their union leaders for help, but many of these people are the same ones who have financially and physically sponsored the Labor Party who is actively pursued policies that have broken the back of Australian manufacturing, and opened our country to plundering by multinationals.

Now they say we must become part of Asia, yet according to the World Bank Australia is the wealthiest country in the world. You might ask if we are so wealthy, where is all the money going? And if we are to be Asianised, who is it that stands to gain, us or them? (Hanson, Newcastle, 30 May 1997)

Although Hanson does not use the word 'freeriding' as such, the message she conveys is that the leftist elite are actively engaged in

initiatives and projects that enable immigrants and newcomers to
enter the country and to take advantage of ordinary hard-working
Australian tax-payers. Hanson's choice to single out the *leftist* elite
as the group responsible for helping to bring about free-market
reforms, and for creating precarious working-class conditions, is of
course rather curious if we consider that, on the whole, right-wing
parties have tended to be more favourable towards free-market
reforms than their left-wing counterparts. However, Hanson uses it
nonetheless to drive a wedge between the political left and its traditional support base, and to portray the political left as a parasite
feeding off the efforts of ordinary hard-working Australian tax-
payers.

This is consistent with research that has shown that populist leaders
tend to portray society as the realm of a standoff between the virtuous
people ('us') and the malicious elite ('them'), requiring a strong leader
to protect the virtuous people from the elite's vices (Mudde, 2004;
Vossen, 2010). At first glance, Hanson's narrative may appear to fit
this description. However, as the following extract shows, the way in
which she portrays society involves not two, but three groups: the
virtuous people, the malicious elite and needy minorities. What is
more, the latter are being portrayed as protected and empowered by
the elite, who in turn are portrayed as consistently overlooking the
needs of ordinary hard-working Australians.

As it stands, the future is one where the majority of Australians will
become second-class citizens in their own country, under a government
who panders to minority interests and denies the majority their right of
decision. (Hanson, 11 April 1997)

As the following extracts show, Hanson's more specific argument is
that assistance programmes are merely a means for the self-serving
malicious elite to advance and enrich themselves, while ordinary hard-
working tax-payers are made to pay for the elite's wealth and generosity towards needy minorities.

We now have a situation where a type of reverse racism is applied to mainstream Australians ... by those who promote political correctness and those
who control the various taxpayer funded 'industries' that flourish in our
society servicing Aboriginals, multiculturalists and a host of other minority
groups. (Hanson, 10 September 1996)

In response to my call for equality for all Australians, the noisiest criticism came from the fat cats, bureaucrats and the do-gooders. They screamed the loudest because they stand to lose the most – their power, money and position, all funded by ordinary Australian tax-payers. (Hanson, 10 September 1996)

As Rapley (1998) points out, Hanson's success can in part be attributed to her ability to portray herself as an ordinary hard-working Australian representing other ordinary hard-working Australians. This may have put her in the best possible position to argue for a covert alliance between the malicious elite and needy minorities.

As the following extracts show, Jean-Marie Le Pen used a very similar narrative to arouse suspicions about wealth distribution in 2006 and 2007 (when France's economy was not a cause for concern):

It is the illegitimate elite who betrayed the nation, its people, and the Republic ... It is them who, through selfish politics or naïve beliefs, surrendered us to foreign powers, and exposed us to mass-immigration and globalization. What a reversal. How dare they? ... We, who have fought for France, have every right to be in this sacred place. (Jean-Marie Le Pen, 20 September 2006)

I thank those who helped to inform fellow citizens about what is at stake, and our plan to stop the country being led into disaster by politician on the left and right, who belong to the system. (Jean-Marie Le Pen, 19 April 2007)

Here too, we see society being portrayed as the realm of not two, but three competing groups, and ordinary hard-working tax-payers as the victims of elite-led programmes. These programmes are supposed to help everyone (international organisations, transnational corporations, needy minorities and, above all, themselves), except ordinary, hard-working French people who are 'left behind in the cold'.

Populist leaders have also been found to level more direct accusations at more mainstream politicians, and in particular left-wing politicians – for example, by accusing them of profligacy at the expense of ordinary hard-working tax-payers. For instance, Jörg Haider accused Prime Minister Franz Vranitzky of the Socialist Democratic Party of Austria (SPÖ) of wasting taxpayer's money, arguing that this was yet another piece of evidence showing that socialists cannot be trusted with the economy:

And then there is Vranitzky, who travelled to China a couple of days ago for a formal visit. And of course, not in a normal airliner, but in an Airbus 310 which has been specially rebuilt for him. In a plane with 260 empty seats, just so he can go and walk around a bit ... When he flies from Vienna to Salzburg, he sends his chauffeur ahead of him to collect him from the airport ... If this is not wasting tax-payers' money, then what is? They cannot be trusted with our money. And that's the problem, that's what we have to teach them on the 13th, this cannot go on. Socialists cannot run the economy. (Jörg Haider, 10 October 1996)

And here too, accusations are levelled at the 'leftist elite' (in this case Prime Minister Vranitzky and President Heinz Fisher) for lending a helping hand to needy groups at the expense of ordinary Austrian tax-payers:

[And as for foreign policy] you are being told that there is no money for schools, for learning places, five thousand students have not found a learning place. We have no money for that anymore. And at the same time we are opening our borders, letting in hundred and fifty-three children, youths, mothers, women, family-members, who in turn also will need housing, learning places and family assistance. And you will all end up paying for this! (Jörg Haider, 10 October 1996)

It should be clear from the above that there are definite similarities in the way in which populist leaders raise suspicion about wealth distribution. More specifically, in all cases 'the elite' (typically the *leftist* elite) is framed as lending needy groups such as immigrants and asylum seekers a helping hand at the taxpayer's expense, and not out of altruistic intentions, but as a covert means to secure greater wealth and status for themselves. The image that is thus created can be likened with a cuckoo (the malicious elite) who secretly lays its eggs (needy minority groups) in a stranger's nest, hoping the host bird (the virtuous people) will unwittingly work hard to protect and hatch the eggs of a stranger.

This 'cuckoo nest' narrative enables those who are relatively gratified (relatively well-to-do voters) to feel as though they are exploited and relatively deprived. As the following extract from Fortuyn's 2002 book shows, once this message is conveyed, the ground has been prepared for the argument that immigrants and asylum seekers have had it too easy, and that they should be treated more harshly:

We have to get rid of this pity syndrome which still dominates the asylum debate, we have to let the facts speak for themselves … without all this wallowing and pitying by the Left Church and its many business managers who earn a handsome income managing the asylum industry. (Fortuyn, 2002, p. 165)

Note also the term 'Left Church', which Fortuyn coined to capture the idea of a leftist self-serving elite that helps minorities to serve their own interests. Our research revealed that Fortuyn was not the only one to characterise the relationship between the elite and needy minorities as 'clientelistic'. For example, Pauline Hanson used the term 'Indigenous Industries' to portray the elite's generosity towards minorities as self-serving (Mols & Jetten, 2015). What is more, far-right leaders do not have to abandon convoluted conspiracy theories immediately when an economic crisis eventually hits. A case in point here is Marine Le Pen, leader of Front National since 2011, who at times uses the term 'patrons négriers' (slave traders) to describe the political left. For example, she used the term in a speech in Six-Fours on 12 March 2011, when she proposed once more that the self-serving leftist elite are rolling out the red carpet for transnational corporations and European integration. They do this, so she argues, to enrich themselves and climb the ladder, thereby weakening the position of ordinary French people, who are forced down the ladder.

Spontaneous Worries or Leadership Influence?

What all three narratives have in common is that they show that leaders do more than read public sentiments. Indeed, they actively seek to *induce* fears, by pointing to other factors threatening the country, by challenging statistics about the state of the economy, by presenting the country's welfare distribution as flawed and unfair and by persuading voters that the country's elite has 'rigged' the economy and wealth distribution to enrich itself and needy groups at the expense of ordinary, hard-working, law-abiding natives.

This narrative of a malicious ruling elite at the helm of a rigged economy and flawed wealth distribution system is powerful because it enables populist leaders to unite strange bedfellows. More specifically, this narrative will arouse fear and anxiety among both blue-collar workers and the self-employed, two groups typically overrepresented in the support base of these parties even though they have opposing economic interests (Evans, 2005; Ivarsflaten, 2005). The former will be sensitive to the portrayal of immigrants as 'queue jumpers' who receive a helping hand from those in powerful positions. The latter will be sensitive to the idea of their hard-earned taxes being spent on projects servicing immigrants and benefitting the already-rich elite. That is, by presenting society as the realm of a standoff between 'us hardworking natives' versus 'those needy non-natives and their powerful allies', populist leaders are able to cast the net much wider, to appeal to yet other groups in society, and to promote a sense of outcry about (what is presented as) the malicious self-serving elite and its clientele feeding of the efforts of ordinary hard-working natives.[2]

Such strategic positioning also suggests that populist leaders will be sensitive to changes to the economic contexts. Indeed, there is evidence that realistic threat narratives reappear once the economy declines. For example, as the following extract from a public statement by Dutch PVV leader Geert Wilders shows, more conventional realistic threat narratives will reappear once a country faces an actual economic crisis:

I have been to the Romanian embassy and made it clear that Dutch people want their border to remain closed. [Deputy Prime Minister] Asscher has to return from the EU summit and announce we changed our mind . . . that the border will remain closed . . . Romanians and Bulgarians are not welcome in the Netherlands after January 1st. The Dutch are more than concerned. Almost three quarters of the population fear an increase in crime and fear being squeezed out of the job market (Wilders, quoted in De Telegraaf, 9 September 2013)

A 'Winning Formula'?

One conclusion to draw from this is that populist right-wing leaders are not all that concerned about the actual state of the economy. This observation is consistent with research into the content of populist party-programmes. From the mid-1990s onwards, neoliberal free-

---

[2] Since the 2008 GFC, the appeal of populist parties appears to have increased significantly among disgruntled liberal/left-wing voters, who feel malicious pre-GFC banking practices have been rewarded rather than punished (via bank bailouts and banker bonuses), while ordinary hard-working citizens have been forced to foot the bill for these bailouts (via austerity measures, asset value losses and declining superannuation savings).

market ideology became regarded as a defining feature of PRWPs, and as one of the two key ingredients (alongside authoritarianism) of what became known as Kitschelt's 'winning formula' (Betz, 1994; Kitschelt, 1995). However, this view was later rejected when analysis of a wider range of parties and party programmes revealed that populist parties tend to be ambivalent about free-market reforms and state control (Alaluf, 1998; Bastow, 1997; Eatwell, 2006; Govaert, 1998; Mudde, 2004; Roy, 1998; Spruyt, 1995; cf. De Lange, 2007), and that they are more concerned about what can be described as 'welfare chauvinism': ensuring the native population gets its fair share (Mudde, 2007).

As Mudde (2007, p. 135) points out in a book chapter entitled 'It's not the economy stupid', populist far-right parties tend to offer a somewhat schizophrenic socio-economic agenda, using both neoliberal and welfare chauvinistic rhetoric. Managing the economy is typically regarded as one of the main tasks of government, and the absence of a coherent agenda for economic governance would thus be a serious, if not fatal, handicap for parties aspiring to office. However, populist parties are typically semi-permanently in opposition, and they can thus overpromise, knowing the odds of holding/sharing office are negligible. What is more, an ambivalent program provides more freedom to interpret the economy in a creative and ad-hoc manner, depending on events of the day, and the audience being addressed. As Minkenberg (2000, pp. 173–174) explains:

[M]arket-liberalism was never a key component of right-wing ideology. [Rather] it was a tactical tool for populist right-wing parties [in the 1980s], to be abandoned as soon as the political winds changed and protection and welfare chauvinism seemed more promising.

The winds did indeed change in the 1990s, when Europe entered an era of unprecedented growth and prosperity, and when it thus became necessary to adapt the narrative to the new context. Consistent with our analysis, when it is not about the economy, 'identity entrepreneurs' might develop the argument that appears most compelling on the day. In doing so, they are more likely to creatively 'use' the economy, rather than engage with it.

While researchers may have rejected the idea of neoliberal programmes being one of the two key ingredients of a 'winning formula', the search for key factors 'driving' support for populist parties continues unabatedly. The question, though, is whether it is possible to single out and rank the relative weight of driving factors, or whether we should focus on understanding the dynamics between the various factors. As several authors have noted (Koopmans, 1996; Mudde, 2010; Rydgren, 2007; van Kessel, 2013), the vast majority of research focuses on voter characteristics and voter preferences, and this has helped to advance our understanding of so-called demand-side factors. However, to date there has been limited research into these supply-side factors (i.e. what populist parties and party leaders do to actively enhance the appeal of their party) – this despite growing awareness that voter preferences are highly context-dependent, and thus not generalisable across time and jurisdictions (Lubbers & Scheepers, 2000; Lubbers, Gijsberts, & Scheepers, 2002).

Our own research, reported in this book and elsewhere (Mols & Jetten, 2014; 2015), straddles both areas. In our view the challenge for research into right-wing populism will be to synthesise insights using multi-method approaches. As it stands, the literature on far-right voting is highly specialised, with authors focusing on particular aspects, such as voter characteristics (e.g. gender, educational attainment, and social class), contextual factors (e.g. relative deprivation), leadership influence (e.g. realistic and symbolic threat narratives) or strategic party positioning (mainstream parties seeking to minimise voter exit). In our view, the challenge facing us is to step up efforts to join-up insights from various research strands, to focus on *constellations* of factors rendering humans and societies vulnerable to radicalisation, and to examine the interplay between different factors in a coherent and theoretically informed way. We hope that the theoretical framework we presented in Chapter 8 will help to achieve this.

Final Word

In the first chapter, we argued that we (researchers and other commentators) have jumped a little too quickly to conclusions. We have interpreted violent protests, hostility towards minorities and support for populist leaders and parties all too readily as the product of economic downturn, deprivation and grievances among poor working-class citizens. This thinking is consistent with classic theorising such as Karl Marx's influential work on revolutions and working class uprisings, in which material conditions take centre stage. Although Marx's views were challenged, in particular by those following in the footsteps of Emile Durkheim who saw uprisings as manifestation of societal breakdown rather than class solidarity, Marx's work would nonetheless become the main 'compass' for subsequent generations of researchers and commentators interested in radical social movements and contentious politics.

Although there is clear evidence that deprivation and grievances *can* produce intergroup hostility, the unintended consequence of this sustained 'Marxian' focus on deprivation and grievances as factors fuelling intergroup hostility is that we have developed a blind spot, and have ignored the possibility that affluence can *also* fuel intergroup hostility.[1] Indeed, in our view the most compelling evidence for this blind-spot argument is the fact that (as a simple Google Scholar search will confirm) there are many more papers examining 'relative deprivation' (40,600) than papers examining 'relative gratification' (409). What is more, we are exposed to regular news broadcasts about violent

---

[1] At the time of finalising this book the 2016 US presidential election campaign was in full swing, and media commentators tended to explain Donald Trump's popularity in the exact same way: as disgruntled uneducated working class uprising in so-called rust-belt states. We expressed our concern about this in our view misleading one-sided rust-belt narrative in several radio interviews with SBS Radio, arguing that there was a risk of underestimating appeal of Donald Trump's message among more affluent sections of the population.

protests, and more often than not these reports go to considerable lengths to inform us about the material challenges facing the group in question. Such news stories perpetuate existing understandings of intergroup conflict whereby we inadvertently overlook the possibility of protests being fuelled by other causes and forces (e.g. the fear that recent gains could be lost, or the fear that others might be 'encroaching' and climbing the social ladder faster than us). Thus, according to conventional wisdom, the ideal breeding ground for far-right move- ments would be an economic crisis and a surge in immigration or asylum seeking. However, the fact that such parties have performed exceptionally well in times of economic prosperity suggests that it is time for a new approach, one that takes into account relative realistic and symbolic threat, demand- and supply-side factors and, last but not least, relative deprivation and relative gratification.

We hope that this book, with its focus on relative gratification, will pave the way for a revival in research into the psychological conse- quences of wealth and wealth acquisition. A deeper understanding of the link between prosperity and intergroup hostility will not only enable us to shed new light on past events (e.g. support for the NSDAP in Weimar Germany), but also to avoid complacency. For example, governments may be inclined to downplay intergroup ten- sions when the economy is booming, or expect relatively prosperous groups to be too busy or too civilised to engage in contentious politics. Hence, they may be ill-prepared when intergroup violence erupts despite a sound economy, or when relatively prosperous groups turn violent. Indeed, when considering the evidence, it becomes clear that governments eager to ensure domestic peace and stability should be vigilant at all times, regardless of economic conditions. They would be well advised to avoid a narrow focus on poor, urban, working-class citizens as the most likely group to become harsh and prejudiced (treating them as 'the usual suspects'), and understand that there is more to conflict prevention than conflict over scarce resources.

In this book we focused on an intriguing, counterintuitive trend: evidence of hardening attitudes in times of economic prosperity, and among relatively affluent groups. We termed this phenomena 'the wealth paradox'. Rather than rejecting the intuitive notion that 'harsh times produce harsh attitudes', we set out to (a) demonstrate that wealth and prosperity (relative gratification) can *also* harden attitudes, and (b) examine the psychological processes underlying relative gratification. The conclusion that economic hardship *and* economic prosperity and that poverty *and* wealth and affluence may *all* relate to harsh attitudes towards minorities may not be one that will satisfy everyone. We agree that theories can derive strength from parsimoniousness. However, a theory can also be too parsimonious and only capture a particular dimension of the phenomenon being examined. In our view this applies to the literature on intergroup hostility, with its heavy focus on deprivation and scant attention for relative gratification.

We are aware that our task (explaining the wealth paradox) is far from over, and that much more work needs to be done to tease out how prosperity affects outgroup attitudes. This book is therefore best regarded not as the end, but as the beginning of what hopefully will become an interesting and exciting new line of research. We presented a social identity analysis of the wealth paradox, one that enabled us to capture its more specific underlying aspects, such as 'perceived stability', 'permeability of group boundaries' and 'legitimately of wealth'. Equipped with these concepts, we were able to shed new light on the wealth paradox, and to render this apparent paradox a little less paradoxical.

Finally, it is worth noting the relevance of wealth paradox research for policy-makers facing real-world challenges. Rather than asking whether governments can afford to take an interest, the question we should be asking is whether governments can afford not to take an interest in the wealth paradox. After all, failure to engage with this question would mean governments and government advisers continue to operate on the basis of out-dated received wisdoms, and this, in turn, would expose governments to the risk of being caught off-guard, too late to defuse tensions, using the wrong instruments, and losing the public's trust along the way. To conclude, if anything, it would seem to be in governments' self-interest to address this blind spot, and to help researchers in their collective endeavour to explain what we have described as 'the wealth paradox'.

References

Aaker, J., & Akutsu, S. (2009). *Why do people give? The role of identity in giving*. Research Paper 2027, Stanford Graduate School of Business Research Paper Series, May 2009.

Adorno, T. W., Fenkel-Brunswik, E., Levinson, D. J., & Stanford, R. N. (1950). *The authoritarian personality*. New York: Harper.

Alaluf, M. (1998). L'émergence du Front national en Belgique est plus redevable aux circonstances qu'à son programme. In P. Delwit, J. M. De Waele, & A. Rea (Eds), *L'extrême droite en France et en Belgique*. Brussels: Éditions Complexe.

Altemeyer, R. (1981). *Right-wing authoritarianism*. Winnipeg: University of Manitoba Press.

Andreoni, J. (2001). The economics of philanthropy. In N. J. Smelser & P.B. Baltes (Eds), *International encyclopedia of the social and behavioral sciences* (pp. 11369–11376). Oxford: Elsevier.

Arendt, H. (1951). *The origins of totalitarianism*. New York: Harcourt Brace.

Arzheimer, K. (2009). Contextual factors and the extreme right vote in Western Europe 1980–2002. *American Journal of Political Research*, 53(2), 259–275.

Arzheimer, K., & Carter, E. (2006). Political opportunity structures and right-wing extremist party success. *European Journal of Political Research*, 45, 419–443.

Aunel, R. K., & Basil, M. D. (1994). A relational obligation approach to the foot-in-the-mouth effect. *Journal of Applied Social Psychology*, 24(6), 546–556.

Bale, T. (2003). Cinderella and her ugly sisters: The mainstream and the extreme right in Europe's bipolarising party systems. *West European Politics*, 26(3), 67–90.

Barder, O. M., Clarke, J., Lépissier, A., Reynolds, L. E., & Roodman, D. (2012). Europe beyond aid: Assessing Europe's commitment to development. *Centre for Global Development Working Paper* (313).

Basil, D. Z., Ridgeway, N., & Basil, M. D. (2006). Guilt appeals: The mediating effect of responsibility. *Psychology & Marketing*, 23(12), 1035–1054.

Bastow, S. (1997). Front National economic policy: From neo-liberalism to protectionism. *Modern & Contemporary France*, 5(1), 61–72.

Beaton, A. M., & Deveau, M. (2005). Helping the less fortunate: A predictive model of collective action. *Journal of Applied Social Psychology*, 35, 1609–1629.

Beck, E. M., & Tolnay, S. E. (1990). The killing fields of the deep south: The market for cotton and the lynching of blacks, 1882–1930. *American Sociological Review*, 55(4), 526–539.

Bekkers, R. (2006). Traditional and health related philanthropy: The role of resources and personality. Social Psychology Quarterly, 68, 349–366.

Bekkers, R., & Schuyt, T. (2008). And who is your neighbor? Explaining denominational differences in charitable giving and volunteering in the Netherlands. *Review of Religious Research*, 50(1), 74–96.

Bekkers, R. H. F. P., & Wiepking, P. (2011). A literature review of empirical studies of philanthropy: Eight mechanisms that drive charitable giving. *Nonprofit and Voluntary Sector Quarterly*, 40(5), 924–973.

Bettencourt, B. A., & Bartholow, B. D. (1998). The importance of status legitimacy for intergroup attitudes among numerical minorities. *Journal of Social Issues*, 54, 759–775.

Bettencourt, B. A., Dorr, N., Charlton, K., & Hume, D. L. (2001). Status differences and in-group bias: A meta-analytic examination of the effects of status stability, status legitimacy, and group permeability. *Psychological Bulletin*, 127, 520–542.

Betz, H.-G. (1993). The new politics of resentment: Radical right-wing populist parties in Western Europe. *Comparative Politics*, 25(4), 413–427.

Betz, H.-G. (1994). *Radical right-wing populism in Western Europe*. New York: St Martin's Press.

Betz, H.-G. (2009). Xenophobia, identity politics and exclusionary populism in Western Europe. *Socialist Register*, 39(39), 193–210.

Billig, M. (1973). Normative communication in a minimal intergroup situation. *European Journal of Social Psychology*, 3, 339–343.

Billig, M. (1976). *Social psychology and intergroup relations*. London: Academic Press.

Billig, M., & Tajfel, H. (1973). Social categorization and similarity in intergroup behaviour. *European Journal of Social Psychology*, 3, 27–52.

Blumer, H. (1958). Race prejudice as a sense of group position. *Pacific Sociological Review*, 1, 3–7.

Bobo, L. D. (1988). Group conflict, prejudice, and the paradox of contemporary racial attitudes. In P. A. Katz & D. A. Taylor (Eds), *Eliminating racism: Profiles in controversy* (pp. 85–114). New York: Plenum Press.

Bouclier, T. (2006). *Les années Poujade: Une histoire du poujadisme (1953–1958)*. Paris: Éditions Rémi Perrin.

Branscombe, N. R., & Ellemers, N. (1998). Coping with group-based discrimination: Individualistic versus group-level strategies. In J. K. Swim & C. Stangor (Eds), *Prejudice: The target's perspective*. New York: Academic Press.

Brewer, M. B. (1979). In-group bias in the minimal intergroup situation: A cognitive-motivational analysis. *Psychological Bulletin, 86*, 307–324.

Brewer, M. B., & Kramer, R. M. (1985). The psychology of intergroup attitudes and behaviour. *Annual Review of Psychology, 36*, 219–243.

Brooks, A. C. (2006). *Who really cares: The surprising truth about compassionate conservatism*. New York: Basic Books.

Brooks, A. C. (2008). The poor give more. *Condé Nast Portfolio*, March 2008. Retrieved from: www.aei.org/publication/the-poor-give-more/

Brown, R. (1988). *Group processes: Dynamics within and between groups*. Oxford: Blackwell.

Cai, H., Kwan, V. S. Y., & Sedikides, C. (2012). A socio-cultural approach to narcissism: The case of modern China. *European Journal of Personality, 26*, 529–535.

Campbell, D. T. (1965). *Ethnocentric and other altruistic motives*. Lincoln: University of Nebraska Press.

Carlsmith, J. M., & Gross, A. E. (1969). Some effects of guilt on compliance. *Journal of Personality and Social Psychology, 11*, 232–239.

Ceobanu, A. M., & Escandell, X. (2010). Comparative analyses of public attitudes toward immigrants and immigration using multinational survey data: A review of theories and research. *Annual Review of Sociology, 36*, 309–328.

Coenders, M. T. A., & Scheepers, P. (2008). Changes in resistance to the social integration of foreigners in Germany 1980–2000. *Journal of Ethnic and Migration Studies, 34*(1), 1–26.

Coenders, M. T. A., Gijsberts, M. I. L., & Scheepers, P. L. H. (2004). Resistance to the presence of immigrants and refugees in 22 countries. In M. I. L. Gijsberts, A. J. M. W. Hagendoorn, & P. L. H. Scheepers (Eds), *Nationalism and exclusion of migrants: Cross-national comparisons* (pp. 97–120). Aldershot: Ashgate Publishers.

Coenders, M. T. A., Lubbers, M., Scheepers, P., & Verkuyten, M. J. A. M. (2008). More than two decades of changing ethnic attitudes in the Netherlands. *Journal of Social Issues, 64*(2), 269–285.

Coser, L. (1956). *The functions of social conflict*. New York: The Free Press.

Cuddy, A. J. C., Fiske, S. T., & Glick, P. (2007). The BIAS map: Behaviors from intergroup affect and stereotypes. *Journal of Personality and Social Psychology, 92*(4), 631–648.

Cuddy, A. J. C., Fiske, S. T., & Glick, P. (2008). Warmth and competence as universal dimensions of social perception: The stereotype content model and the BIAS map. *Advances in Experimental Social Psychology, 40*, 61–149. doi:10.1016/S0065-2601(07)00002-0

Dambrun, M. Taylor, D. M., McDonald, D. A., Crush, J., & Méot, A. (2006). The relative deprivation-gratification continuum and the attitudes of South Africans toward immigrants: A test of the V-curve hypothesis. *Journal of Personality and Social Psychology, 91*, 1032–1044.

Darwin, C. (1859/1975). *The origin of species.* London; Totowa: Dent.

Davies, J. C. (1962). Toward a theory of revolution. *American Sociological Review, 27*(1), 5–19.

De Botton, A. (2004). *Status anxiety.* New York: Penguin.

De Lange, S. L. (2007). From pariah to power broker: The radical right and government in Western Europe. In P. Delwit, & P. Poirier (Eds), *Extreme droite et pouvoir en Europe.* Brussels: Éditions de l'Universite de Bruxelles.

De Tocqueville, A. (1835/2000). *Democracy in America.* Chicago: University of Chicago.

De Wachter, D. (2012). *Borderline times: Het einde van de normaliteit.* Leuven, Belgium: Lamnoo Campus.

De Witte, H., & Klandermans, B. (2000). Political racism in Flanders and the Netherlands: Explaining differences in the electoral success of extreme right-wing parties. *Journal of Ethnic and Migration Studies, 26*(4), 699–717.

Dekker, P., & Ester, P. (1987). Working-class authoritarianism: A re-examination of the Lipset thesis. *European Journal of Political Research, 15*(4), 395–415.

Diehl, M. (1990). The minimal group paradigm: Theoretical explanations and empirical findings. In W. Stroebe & M. Hewstone (Eds.), *European Review of Social Psychology* (Vol. 1, pp. 263–292). Chichester: Wiley.

Dixon, J. C., & Rosenbaum, M.S. (2004). Nice to know you? Testing contact, cultural, and group threat theories of anti-black and anti-Hispanic stereotypes. *Social Science Quarterly, 85*(2), 257–280.

Doise, W. (1978). *Groups and individuals. Explanations in social psychology.* Cambridge: Cambridge University Press.

Dollard, J., Doob, L. W., Miller, N. E., Mowrer, O. H., & Sears, R. R. (1939). *Frustration and aggression.* New Haven: Yale University Press.

Donnelly, F. K. (2008). The Scottish rising of 1820: A reinterpretation. *International Review of Scottish Studies, 6*, 27–37.

Doosje, B., Ellemers, N., & Spears, R. (1995). Perceived intragroup variability as a function of group status and identification. *Journal of Experimental and Social Psychology, 31*, 410–436.

Dorling, D. (2016) The decision of a divided country. *British Medical Journal*, 354, i3697.

Duckitt, J. (1992/1994). *The social psychology of prejudice*. New York: Praeger Publishers.

Eatwell, R. (2006). The concept and theory of charismatic leadership. *Totalitarian movements and political religions*, 7(2), 141–156.

Ehrenreich, B. (1990). *Fear of falling: The inner life of the middle class*. New York: Harper Perennial.

Ellemers, N. (1993). The influence of socio-structural variables on identity enhancement strategies. *European Review of Social Psychology*, 4, 27–57.

Ellemers, N. (2003). Identity, culture, and change in organizations: A social identity analysis and three illustrative cases. In Haslam, A., Van Knippenberg, D., Platow, M., & Ellemers, N. (Eds), *Social identity at work: Developing theory for organizational practice* (pp. 191–204). Hove, UK: Psychology Press.

Ellemers, N., & Van Rijswijk, W. (1997). Identity needs versus social opportunities: The use of group-level and individual-level identity management strategies. *Social Psychology Quarterly*, 60, 52–65.

Ellemers, N., Doosje, B., van Knippenberg, A., & Wilke, H. (1992). Status protection in high status minority groups. *European Journal of Social Psychology*, 22, 123–140.

Ellemers, N., van Knippenberg, A., & Wilke, H. (1990). The influence of permeability of group boundaries and stability of group status on strategies of individual mobility and social change. *British Journal of Social Psychology*, 29(3), 233–246.

Esses, V. M., Haddock, G., & Zanna, M. P. (1993). Values, stereotypes and emotions as determinants of intergroup attitudes. In D. M. Mackie & D. L. Hamilton (Eds), *Affect, cognition and stereotyping: Interactive processes in group perception* (pp. 137–166). Orlando: Academic Press.

Evans, J. A. J. (2005). The dynamic of social change in radical right-wing populist party support. *Comparative European Politics*, 3(1), 76–101.

Falter J. W., & Klein, M. (1994). *Wehr wählt rechts? Die Whäler und Anhänger des rechtsextremisticher Parteien im vereinigten Deutschland*. Munich: Verlag C.H. Beck.

Ford, R., & Goodwin, M. J. (2014). *Revolt on the right: Explaining support for the radical right in Britain*. London: Routledge.

Fortuyn, P. (2002). *De puinhopen van acht jaar Paars*. Uithoorn: Karakter.

Frank, R. H. (1999). Luxury fever: Why money fails to satisfy in an era of excess. New York: Free Press, Princeton University.

Geary, R. (2002). *Hitler and Nazism*. London: Routledge.

Giving USA (2013). *The annual report on philanthropy for the year 2012.* Lilly Family, School of Philanthropy. Indiana University.

Golder, M. (2003). Explaining variation in the success of extreme right parties in Western Europe. *Comparative Political Studies, 36*(4), 432–466.

González, K. V., Verkuyten, M., & Poppe, E. (2008). Prejudice towards Muslim in the Netherlands: Testing integrated threat theory. *British Journal of Social Psychology, 47*(4), 667–685.

Govaert, S. (1998). Le programme economique du Vlaams Blok. In P. Delwit, J. M. De Waele, & A. Rea (Eds), *L'extreme droite en France et en Belgique.* Brussels: Éditions Complexe, 119–131.

Graham, R. (1977). Loaves and liberty: Women in the French Revolution. In R. Bridenthal, & C. Koonz (Eds), *Becoming visible: Women in European history* (pp. 236–254). Boston: Houghton Mifflin.

Green, D. P., Glaser, J., & Rich, A. (1998). From lynching to gay bashing: The elusive connection between economic conditions and hate crime. *Journal of Personality and Social Psychology, 75*(1), 82–92.

Greve, F. (2009, May 19). America's poor are its most generous. *McClatchy Newspapers.* Retrieved from www.mcclatchydc.com/news/politics-government/article24538864.html

Grofman, B. N., & Muller, E. N. (1973). The strange case of relative gratification and potential for political violence: The V-curve hypothesis. *American Political Science Review, 67,* 514–539.

Guimond, S., & Dambrun, M. (2002). When prosperity breeds intergroup hostility: The effects of relative deprivation and relative gratification on prejudice. *Personality and Social Psychology Bulletin, 28,* 900–912.

Gurr, T. R. (1970). *Why men rebel.* Princeton: Princeton University Press.

Habermas, J. (1981). New social movements. *Telos, 1981*(49), 33–37.

Haigh, B. (2015, April 24). *If we were ever the lucky country, we aren't now* [Blog post]. Retrieved from www.abc.net.au/news/2015–04-24/haigh-if-we-were-ever-the-lucky-country-we-arent-now/6411240

Hamilton, R. F. (1984). Braunschweig 1932: Further evidence on the support for National Socialism. *Central European History, 17*(1), 3–36.

Hamilton, W. D. (1963) The evolution of altruistic behavior. *American Naturalist, 97*(896), 354–356.

Hanson, F. (2011). Australia and the world: Public opinion and foreign policy. *Lowy Institute for International Policy.*

Harsin, J. (2002). *Barricades: The war of the streets of revolutionary Paris, 1830–1848.* New York: Palgrave.

Harvey, S. P., & Bourhis, R. Y. (2011). Discrimination in wealth and power structures. *Group Processes & Intergroup Relations, 15,* 21–38.

Harvey, S. P., & Bourhis, R. Y. (2013). Discrimination between the rich and the poor under contrasting conditions of wealth stratification. *Journal of Applied Social Psychology, 43,* 351–366.

Haslam, S. A. (2004). *Psychology in organisations: The social identity approach* (2nd edn). London: Sage.

Haslam, S. A., & Reicher, S. D. (2007). Beyond the banality of evil: Three dynamics of an interactionist social psychology of tyranny. *Personality and Social Psychology Bulletin, 33,* 615–622.

Henrich, J., Boyd, R. Bowles, S., Camerer, C. Fehr, E., Gintis, H., & McElreath, R. (2001). In search of homo economicus: Behavioral experiments in 15 small-scale societies. *American Economic Review, 91,* 73–78.

Henry, J. (2013). De sociale staat van Nederland 2013. Social en Cultureel Planbureau. Den Haag, December 2013. www.scribd.com/doc/1908760 96/De-Sociale-Staat-Van-Nederland-2013

Henson, S., Lindstrom, J., Haddad, L., & Mulmi, R. (2010). Public perceptions of international development and support for aid in the UK: Results of a qualitative enquiry. *IDS Working Papers, 2010*(353), 1–67.

Hepworth, J. T., & West, S. G. (1988). Lynchings and the economy: A time-series reanalysis of Hovland and Sears (1940). *Journal of Personality and Social Psychology, 55,* 239–247.

Heywood, C. (1995). *The development of the French economy, 1750–1945.* Cambridge: Cambridge University Press.

Hirschman, A. O., & Rothschild, M. (1973). The changing tolerance for income inequality in the course of economic development. *The Quarterly Journal of Economics, 87,* 544–566.

Hood, M., & Morris, I. (1997). 'Amigo o Enemigo': Context, attitudes, and Anglo public opinion toward immigration. *Social Science Quarterly, 78,* 309–323.

Hornsey, M. J., & Jetten, J. (2011). Impostors within groups: The psychology of claiming to be something you are not. In J. Jetten & M. J. Hornsey (Eds), *Rebels in groups: Dissent, deviance, difference, and defiance* (pp. 158–178). Chichester: Wiley-Blackwell.

Hovland, C. J., & Sears, R. R. (1940). Minor studies in aggression: VI correlation of lynchings with economic indices. *The Journal of Psychology: Interdisciplinary and Applied, 9,* 301–310.

Hufton, O. (1971). Women in revolution 1789–1796. *Past and Present, 53,* 90–108.

Ignazi, P. (1992). The silent counter-revolution: Hypotheses on the emergence of extreme right-wing parties in Europe. *European Journal of Political Research, 22,* 3–34.

Independent Sector (2002). *Giving and volunteering in the United States* (pp. 28–29). Washington DC: Independent Sector.

Irvine, W.D. (1988). French Royalists and Boulangism. *French Historical Studies, 15*(3), 395–406.

Ivarsflaten, E. (2005). The vulnerable populist right parties: No economic realignment fuelling their electoral success. *European Journal of Political Research, 44*(3), 465–492.

Jackman, R. W., & Volpert, K. (1996). Conditions favouring parties of the extreme right in Western Europe. *British Journal of Political Science, 26*(4), 501–521.

James, R. N., & Sharpe, D. L. (2007) The nature and causes of the U-shaped charitable giving profile. *Nonprofit and Voluntary Sector Quarterly, 36*, 218–238.

Jefferson, P. N., & Pryor, F. L. (1999). On the geography of hate. *Economics Letters, 65*(3), 389–395.

Jenks, J. W., & Lauck, W. J. (1912). *The immigration problem.* New York: Funk & Wagnalis.

Jetten, J., & Mols, F. (2014). 50:50 hindsight: Appreciating anew the contributions of Milgram's obedience experiments. *Journal of Social Issues, 70*(3), 587–602.

Jetten, J., Chu, A., & Mols, F. (2017). *Wealth and the fear of being overtaken.* Manuscript in preparation. University of Queensland.

Jetten, J., Mols, F., Healy, N., & Spears, R. (2017). Fear of falling: Economic instability enhances collective angst among societies' wealthy. *Journal of Social Issues.*

Jetten, J., Mols, F., & Postmes, T. (2015). Relative deprivation and relative wealth enhances anti-immigrant sentiments: The v-curve re-examined. *PLoS ONE,* 10(10): e0139156.

Jetten, J., Ryan, R., & Mols, F. (in press). Stepping in the shoes of leaders of populist right-wing parties: Promoting anti-immigrant views in times of economic prosperity. *Social Psychology.*

Jetten, J., Spears, R., & Manstead, A. S. R. (1997). Strength of identification and intergroup differentiation: The influence of group norms. *European Journal of Social Psychology, 27*, 603–609.

Jonas, E., Schimel, J., Greenberg, J., & Pyszczynski, T. (2002). The scrooge effect: Evidence that mortality salience increases pro-social attitudes and behaviour. *Personality and Social Psychology Bulletin, 28*(10), 1342–1353.

Jones, O. (2012). *Chavs: The demonization of the working class.* London: Verso Books.

Jost, J. T., Banaji, M. R., & Nosek, B. (2004). A decade of system justification theory: Accumulated evidence of conscious and unconscious bolstering of the status quo. *Political Psychology, 25*, 881–920.

Kearney, H. (1997). Contested Ideas of Nationhood 1800–1995. *The Irish Review*, 20(1), 1–22.

Kim, M. (2012). Unfairly disadvantaged? Asian Americans and unemployment during and after the Great Recession (2007–10). *Issue Brief #323*, 5 April 2012.

Kinder, D. R., & Sears, D. O. (1981). Prejudice and politics: Symbolic racism versus racial threats to the good life. *Journal of Personality and Social Psychology*, 40(3), 414–431.

Kitschelt, H. (1995). *The radical right in Western Europe: A comparative analysis*. Ann Arbor: The University of Michigan Press.

Kobrynowicz, D., & Branscombe, N. R. (1997). Who considers themselves victims of discrimination? Individual difference predictors of perceived gender discrimination in women and men. *Psychology of Women Quarterly*, 21, 347–363.

Kolinsky, E. (1992). A future for right extremism in Germany? In P. Hainsworth (Ed), *The extreme right in Europe and the USA* (pp. 61–94). New York: St Martin's Press.

Koopmans, R. (1996). Explaining the rise of racist and extreme right violence in Western Europe: Grievances or opportunities? *European Journal of Political Research*, 30, 185–216.

Koopmans, R., Statham, P., Giugni M., & Passy, F. (2005). *Contested citizenship: Immigration and cultural diversity in Europe*. Minneapolis: University of Minneapolis Press.

Kraus, M. W., & Keltner, D. (2009). Signs of socioeconomic status: A thin-slicing approach. *Psychological Science*, 20, 99–106.

Krueger, A., & Pischke, J. (1997). A statistical analysis of crime against foreigners in unified Germany. *Journal of Human Resources*, 32, 182–209.

Lalonde, R. N., & Silverman, R. A. (1994). Behavioral preference in response to social injustice: The effects of group permeability and social identity salience. *Journal of Personality and Social Psychology*, 66, 78–85.

Le Bon, G. (1896). *The crowd: A study of the popular mind*. New York: Macmillan.

LeBlanc, J., Beaton, A. M., & Walker, I. (2015). The downside of being up: A new look at group relative gratification and traditional prejudice. *Social Justice Research*, 28, 143–167.

Lerner, M. J., & Miller, D. T. (1978). Just world research and the attribution process: Looking back and ahead. *Psychological Bulletin*, 85, 1030–1051.

LeVine, R. A., & Campbell, D. T. (1972). *Ethnocentrism: Theories of conflict, ethnic attitudes, and group behavior*. New York: John Wiley and Sons.

Lipset, S. M., & Raab, E. (1978). *The politics of unreason: Right-wing extremism in America, 1790–1977* (2nd edn). Chicago: University of Chicago Press.

Lloyd, T. (2004). *Why rich people give.* London: ACF.

Lombroso, C. (1876) *L'uomo delinquent studiato in rapport all'antropologia, alla medicina legale e alle discipline carcerarie.* Milan: Hoepli.

Lubbers, M., & Scheepers, P. (2000). Individual and contextual characteristics of the German extreme right-wing vote in the 1990s: A test of complementary theories. *European Journal of Political Research, 41,* 345–378.

Lubbers, M., Gijsberts, M., & Scheepers, P. (2002). Extreme right-wing voting in Western Europe. *European Journal of Political Research, 41,* 345–378.

Lucassen, G., & Lubbers, M. (2012). Who fears what? Explaining far-right-wing preference in Europe by distinguishing perceived cultural and economic ethnic threat. *Comparative Political Studies, 45(5),* 547–574.

Lusher, D., & Haslam, N. (2007). *Yearning to breathe free: Seeking asylum in Australia.* Annandale: The Federation Press.

Marmot, M. (2006). *Status syndrome: How your social standing directly affects your health and life expectancy.* London: Bloomsbury.

Mayda, A. M. (2006). Why are people more pro-trade than pro-migration? *Economics Letters, Elsevier, 101(3),* 160–163.

Merkl, P. H., & Weinberg, L. (2003). *Right-wing extremism in the twenty-first century.* New York: Psychology Press.

Merriman, J. (1996) *A history of modern Europe: From the French Revolution to the present.* New York: WW Norton.

Messick, D. M., & Mackie, D. M. (1989). Intergroup relations. *Annual Review of Psychology, 40,* 45–81.

Meuleman, B., Bavidov, E., & Biliet, J. (2009). Changing attitudes toward immigration in Europe, 2002–2007: A dynamic group conflict theory approach. *Social Science Research, 38(2),* 352–365.

Middendorp, C. P., & Meloen, J. D. (1990). The authoritarianism of the working class revisited. *European Journal of Political Research, 18(2),* 257–267.

Middendorp, C. P., & Meloen, J. D. (1990). The authoritarianism of the working class revisited. *European Journal of Political Research, 18(2),* 257–267.

Milgram, S. (1974). *Obedience to authority: An experimental view.* New York: Harper and Row.

Minkenberg, M. (2000). The renewal of the radical right: Between modernity and anti-modernity. *Government and Opposition, 2,* 170–188.

Mintz, A. (1946). A re-examination of correlations between lynchings and economic indices. *The Journal of Abnormal and Social Psychology, 41*(2), 154–160. doi:10.1037/h0056837

Mischel, W. (1968). *Personality and assessment.* New York: John Wiley.

Mitchell, L. (2014, December 8). The wealthy suffer from an 'empathy gap' with the poor that is feeding a rise in inequality [Blog post]. Retrieved from https://theconversation.com/the-wealthy-suffer-from-an-empathy-gap-with-the-poor-that-is-feeding-a-rise-in-inequality-34226

Mols, F., & Jetten, J. (2014). No guts, no glory: How framing the collective past paves the way for anti-immigrant sentiments. *International Journal of Intercultural Relations, 43,* 74–86.

Mols, F. & Jetten, J. (2015). Explaining the appeal of populist right-wing parties in times of economic prosperity. *Political Psychology, 37,* 275–292. doi: 10.1111/pops.12258.

Mols, F., & Jetten, J. (2016b). Why Brexit and Trump are NOT Working Class Revolts. *ABC Religion and Ethics.* Retrieved from: http://www.abc.net.au/religion/articles/2016/11/15/4575585.htm

Mols, F., & Weber, M. (2013) Laying sound foundations for SIT inspired EU attitude research: Beyond attachment and deeply rooted identities. *Journal of Common Market Studies, 51*(3), 505–521.

Moscatelli, S., Albarello, F., Prati, F., & Rubini, M. (2014). Badly off or better off than them? The impact of relative deprivation and relative gratification on intergroup discrimination. *Journal of Personality and Social Psychology, 107,* 248–262.

Mudde, C. (2004). The populist zeitgeist. *Government and Opposition, 39*(4), 542–563.

Mudde, C. (2007). *Populist radical right parties in Europe.* Cambridge: Cambridge University Press.

Mudde, C. (2010). The populist radical right: A pathological normalcy. *West European Politics, 33*(6), 1167–1186.

Mullainathan, S., & Shafir, E. (2013). *Scarcity: Why having too little means so much.* New York: Times Books.

Mullen, B., Brown, R., & Smith, C. (1992). Ingroup bias as a function of salience, relevance, and status: An integration. *European Journal of Social Psychology, 22,* 103–122.

Ng, S. H. (1981). Equity theory and the allocations of rewards between groups. *European Journal of Social Psychology, 11,* 439–443.

O'Loughlin, J., Flint, C., & Shin, M. (1995). Regions and milieux in Weimar Germany: The Nazi Party vote of 1930 in geographic perspective. *Erdkunde, 49*(4), 305–314.

Olzak, S. (1990). The political context of competition: Lynching and urban racial violence, 1882–1914. *Social Forces, 69,* 395–421.

Otten, S., Mummendey, A., & Blanz, M. (1996). Intergroup discrimination in positive and negative outcome allocations: Impact of stimulus valence, relative group status, and relative group size. *Personality and Social Psychology Bulletin, 22*, 568–581.

Oyserman, D., & Lee, S. W. S. (2008). Does culture influence what and how we think? Effects of priming individualism and collectivism. *Psychological Bulletin, 134*(2), 311–342.

Parsons, T. (1942). Review of dimensions of society: A quantitative systematics for the social sciences by Stuart Carter Dodd. *American Sociological Review, 7*(5), 709–714.

Parssinen, T. M. (1973). Association, convention and anti-parliament in British radical politics, 1771–1848. *The English Historical Review, 88*(348), 504–533.

Pentland, G. (2015). *The spirit of the union: Popular politics in Scotland.* London: Routledge.

Perroulaz, G., Fioroni, C., & Carbonnier, G. (2010). Trends and issues in international development cooperation. *International Development Policy, 1*, 143–160.

Piff, P. K. (2014). Wealth and the inflated self: Class, entitlement, and narcissism. *Personality and Social Psychology Bulletin, 40*, 34–43.

Piff, P. K., Kraus, M. W., Côté, S., Cheng, B. H., & Keltner, D. (2010). Having less, giving more: The influence of social class on prosocial behavior. *Journal of Personality and Social Psychology, 99*(5), 771–784.

Piff, P. K., Stancato, D. M., Côté, S., Mendoza-Denton, R., & Keltner, D. (2012). Higher social class predicts increased unethical behaviour. *Proceedings of the National Academy of Sciences, 109*, 4086–4091.

Postmes, T., & Smith, L. G. E. (2009). Why do the privileged resort to oppression: A look at some intragroup factors. *Journal of Social Issues, 65*(4), 769–790.

Postmes, T., & Branscombe, N. R. (Eds). (2010). *Rediscovering social identity.* New York: Psychology Press.

Pratt, T. C., & Cullen, F. T. (2005). Assessing macro-level predictors and theories of crime: A meta-analysis. In M. Tony (Ed.), *Crime and justice: A review of research* (Vol. 32) (pp. 373–450). Chicago: University of Chicago Press.

Pratto, F., Sidanius, J., Stallworth, L. M., & Malle, B. F. (1994). Social dominance orientation: A personality variable predicting social and political attitudes. *Journal of Personality and Social Psychology, 67*(4), 741–776.

Quillian, L. (1995). Prejudice as a response to perceived group threat: Population composition and anti-immigrant and racial prejudice in Europe. *American Sociological Review, 60*, 586–611.

Quillian, L. (2006). New approaches to understanding racial prejudice and discrimination. *Annual Review of Sociology, 32,* 299–328.

Rabbie, J. M., & Horowitz, M. (1969). Arousal of ingroup-outgroup bias by a chance win or loss. *Journal of Personality and Social Psychology, 13,* 269–277.

Rapley, M. (1998). 'Just an ordinary Australian': Self-categorization and the discursive construction of facticity in 'new racist' political rhetoric. *British Journal of Social Psychology, 37*(3), 325–344.

Reed, J. S., Doss, G. E., & Hulbert, J. S. (1987). Too good to be false: An essay in the folklore of social science. *Sociological Inquiry, 57,* 1–11.

Reicher, S. D., & Haslam, S. A. (2011). After shock? Towards a social identity explanation of the Milgram 'obedience' studies. *British Journal of Social Psychology, 50,* 163–169.

Reicher, S., & Hopkins, N. (2001). *Self and nation.* London: Sage.

Renneville, M. (2012). Lombroso in France: A paradoxical reception. In P. Knepper & P. J. Ystehede (Eds), *The Cesare Lombroso handbook.* London: Routledge.

Riek, B. M., Mania, E. W., & Gaertner, S. L. (2006). Intergroup threat and outgroup attitudes: A meta-analytic review. *Personality and Social Psychology Review, 10,* 336–353.

Roberts, G. (2005). Cooperation through interdependence. *Animal Behavior, 70,* 901–908.

Rokeach, M. (1960). *The open and closed mind.* New York: Basic Books.

Roodman, D. (2008, October 14). History says financial crisis will suppress aid. *Global Development: Views from the Center.*

Rooney, P. M., & Frederick, H. K. (2007). *Portraits of donors: Bank of America study of high net-worth philanthropy.* Centre on Philanthropy, Bloomington: Indiana University.

Rothgerber, H. (1997). External intergroup threat as an antecedent to perceptions of ingroup and outgroup homogeneity. *Journal of Personality and Social psychology, 73,* 1206–1212.

Rothwell, J. T., & Diego-Rosell, P. (2016) Explaining nationalist views: The case of Donald Trump, SSRN Draft Working Paper, available on-line at: https://papers.ssrn.com/sol3/Papers.cfm?abstract_id=2822059

Roux, C., Goldsmith, K., & Bonezzi, A. (2012). *On the consequences of a scarcity mindset: Why thoughts of having less can lead to taking (and giving) more.* Available online at SSRN 2147919.

Roy, J. P. (1998). Le programme economique et social du Front national en France. In P. Delwit, J. M. De Waele, & A. Rea (Eds), *L'extreme droite en France et en Belgique* (pp. 85–100). Brussels: Éditions Complexe.

Rubin, M., & Hewstone, M. (2004). Social identity, system justification, and social dominance: Commentary on Reicher, Jost et al., and Sidanius et al. *Political Psychology*, *25*, 823–844.

Rudé, G. (1964). *The crowd in history: A study of popular disturbances in France and England, 1930–1848.* New York: Wiley.

Runciman, W. C. (1966). *Relative deprivation and social justice.* London: Routledge and Kegan Paul.

Rydgren, J. (2005). Is extreme-right populism contagious? Explaining the emergence of a new party family. *European Journal of Political Research*, *44*, 413–437.

Rydgren, J. (2007). The sociology of the radical right. *Annual Review of Sociology*, *33*, 241–262.

Sachdev, I., & Bourhis, R. Y. (1985). Social categorization and power differentials in group relations. *European Journal of Social Psychology*, *15*, 415–434.

Sachdev, I., & Bourhis, R. Y. (1987). Status differentials and intergroup behaviour. *European Journal of Social Psychology*, *17*, 277–293.

Sachdev, I., & Bourhis, R. Y. (1991). Power and status differentials in minority and majority group relations. *European Journal of Social Psychology*, *21*, 1–24.

Savelkoul, M., Scheepers, P., Tolsma, J., & Hagendoorn, L. (2011). Anti-Muslim attitudes in the Netherlands: Tests of contradictory hypotheses derived from ethnic competition theory and intergroup contact theory. *European Sociological Review*, *27*(6), 741–758.

Scheepers, D. T., & Ellemers, N. (2005). When the pressure is up: The assessment of social identity threat in low and high status groups. *Journal of Experimental Social Psychology*, *41*(2), 192–200.

Scheepers, D. T., Ellemers, N., & Sintemaartensdijk, N. (2009). Suffering from the possibility of status loss: Physiological responses to social identity threat in high status groups. *European Journal of Social Psychology*, *39*(6), 1075–1092.

Scheepers, P., Gijsberts, M., & Coenders, M. (2002). Ethnic exclusionism in European countries: Public opposition to civil rights for legal migrants as a response to perceived ethnic threat. *European Sociological Review*, *18*, 17–34.

Schervish P. G., & Havens, J. J. (2002). The Boston area diary study and the moral citizenship of care. *Voluntas*, *13*(1), 47–71.

Schissel, B., Wanner, R., & Frideres, J.S. (1989). Social and economic context and attitudes toward immigrants in Canadian cities. *The International Migration Review*, *23*(2), 289–308.

Semyonov, M., Raijman, R., & Gorodzeisky, A. (2006). The rise in anti-foreigner sentiment in European societies, 1988–2000. *American Sociological Review, 71*, 426–449.

Sherif, M. (1966). *In common predicament: Social psychology of intergroup conflict and cooperation.* New York: Houghton Mifflin.

Sherif, M., & Sherif, C. W. (1953). *Groups in harmony and tension: An integration of studies of intergroup relations.* Oxford: Harper & Brothers.

Sherif, M., Harvey, O. J., White, B. J., Hood, W. R., & Sherif, C. W. (1961). *Intergroup cooperation and competition: The Robbers' Cave experiment.* Norman: University Book Exchange.

Sidanius, J., & Pratto, F. (1999) *Social dominance: An intergoup theory of social hierarchy and oppression.* New York: Cambridge University Press.

Sighele, S. (1891). *La folla delinquent.* Turin: Bocca.

Small, D. A., & Simonsohn, U. (2008). Friends of victims: Personal experience and pro-social behaviour. *Journal of Consumer Research, 35*(3), 532–542.

Smith, A. (1776). *The wealth of nations.* London: Strahan & Cadell.

Smith, H., & Pettigrew, T. F. (2015). Advances in relative deprivation theory and research. *Social Justice Research, 28*, 1–6.

Smith, H., Pettigrew, T. F., Pippin, G., & Bialosiewicz, S. (2012). Relative deprivation: A theoretical and meta-analytic critique. *Personality and Social Psychology Review, 16*(3), 203–232.

Snibbe, A. C., & Markus, H. R. (2005). You can't always get what you want: Educational attainment, agency, and choice. *Journal of Personality and Social Psychology, 88*, 703–720.

Spears, R., Doosje, B., & Ellemers, N. (1997). Ingroup stereotyping in the face of threats to group status and distinctiveness: The role of group identification. *Personality and Social Psychology Bulletin, 23*, 538–553.

Spruyt, M. (1995). *Grove borstels: Stel dat het Vlaams Blok morgen zijn programma realiseert, hoe zou Vlaanderen er dan uitzien?* Leuven: Van Halewyck.

St. Claire, L., & Turner, J. C. (1982). The role of demand characteristics in the social categorization paradigm. *European Journal of Social Psychology, 12*, 307–314.

Stephan, W. G., Ybarra, O., & Bachman, G. (1999). Prejudice toward immigrants. *Journal of Applied Social Psychology, 29*(11), 2221–2237.

Stipek, D. J., & Ryan, R. H. (1997). Economically disadvantaged pre-schoolers: Ready to learn but further to go. *Developmental Psychology, 33*, 711–723.

Stokkom, B. (2010). *Wat een hufter! Ergernis, lichtgeraaktheid en maatschappelijke verruwing.* Amsterdam: Boom.

Stöss, R. (1991). *Politics against democracy: Right-wing extremism in West Germany*. New York: St Martin's Press.

Stouffer, S. A., Suchman, E. A., De Vinney, L. C., Star, S. A., & Williams, R. M., Jr. (1949). *The American soldier: Adjustment during army life, Volume I*. Princeton Princeton University Press.

Tajfel, H. (1970). Experiments in intergroup discrimination. *Scientific American, 223*, 96–102.

Tajfel, H. (1978). Interindividual behaviour and intergroup behaviour. In H. Tajfel (Ed.), *Differentiation between social groups: Studies in the social psychology of intergroup relations* (pp. 27–60). London: Academic Press.

Tajfel, H. (1982). Social psychology of intergroup relations. *Annual Review of Psychology, 33*, 1–39.

Tajfel, H., & Billig, M. (1974). Familiarity and categorization in intergroup behaviour. *Journal of Experimental Social Psychology, 10*, 159–170.

Tajfel, H., & Turner J. C. (1979). An integrative theory of intergroup conflict. In W. G. Austin & S. Worchel (Eds), *The social psychology of intergroup relations* (pp. 33–48). Monterey: Brooks/Cole.

Tajfel, H., & Turner J. C. (1986). The social identity theory of intergroup behavior. In S. Worchel & W. G Austin (Eds), *Psychology of intergroup relations* (pp. 7–24). Chicago: Nelson Hall.

Tajfel, H., & Wilkes, A. L. (1963). Classification and quantitative judgement. *British Journal of Psychology, 54*, 101–114.

Tajfel, H., Billig, M. G., Bundy, R. P., & Flament, C. (1971). Social categorization and intergroup behavior. *European Journal of Social Psychology, 1*, 149–178.

Tarde, G. (1885). Le type criminel. *Revue Philosophique, 19*, 593–627.

Taylor, F. W. (1911). *Principles of scientific management*. New York: Harper.

Taylor, P., Kochhar, R., Fry, R., Velasco, G., & Motel, S. (2011). *Wealth gap rise to record highs between Whites, Blacks and Hispanics* (Vol. 26). Washington, DC: Pew Research Centre, July.

Tienhaara, N. (1974). *Canadian views on immigration and population: An analysis of post-war Gallup polls*. Ottawa: Department of Manpower and Immigration.

Tilly, C., Tilly, L., & Tilly, R. (1975). *The rebellious century: 1830–1930*. Cambridge, MA: Harvard University Press.

Tougas, F., & Veilleux, F. (1990). The response of men to affirmative action strategies for women: The study of a predictive model. *Canadian Journal of Behavioural Science, 22*, 424–432.

Traugott, M. (2010). *The insurgent barricade*. Oakland: University of California Press.

Turner, J. C. (1975). Social comparison and social identity. *European Journal of Social Psychology, 5*, 5–34.

Turner, J. C. (1981). The experimental social psychology of intergroup behaviour. In J. C. Turner & H. Giles (Eds), *Intergroup behaviour* (pp. 66–101). Oxford: Blackwell.

Turner. J. C., & Brown, R. (1978). Social status, cognitive alternatives, and intergroup relations. In H. Tajfel (Ed), *Differentiation between social groups: Studies in the social psychology of intergroup relations* (pp. 202–234). New York: Academic Press.

Turner, J. C., Hogg, M. A., Oakes, P. J., Reicher, S. D., & Wetherell, M. S. (1987). *Rediscovering the social group: A self-categorization theory.* Oxford: Basil Blackwell.

UK House of Commons (2009). *Aid under pressure: Support for development assistance in a global economic downturn.* Fourth report, International Development Committee.

Utz, S. (2004). Self-construal and cooperation: Is the interdependent self more cooperative than the independent self? *Self and Identity, 3*, 177–190.

Van Kessel, S. (2013). A matter of supply and demand: The electoral performance of populist parties in three European countries. *Government and Opposition, 48*(2), 175–199.

Van Rossem (2010). *De puinhopen van Paars.* Historisch Nieuwsblad, 2/2010.

Vanbeselaere, N., Boen, F., van Avermaet, E., & Buelens, H. (2006). The Janus face of power in intergroup contexts: A further exploration of the noblesse oblige effect. *The Journal of Social Psychology, 146*, 685–699.

Vanneman, R. D., & Pettigrew, T. F. (1972). Race and relative deprivation in the urban United States. *Race, 13*, 461–486.

Veblen, T. (1994/1899). *The theory of the leisure class: An economic study of institutions.* New York: Penguin Books.

Vossen, K. (2010). Populism in the Netherlands after Fortuyn: Rita Verdonk and Geert Wilders compared. *Perspectives on European Politics and Society, 11*(1), 22–38.

Walker, I., & Smith, H.J. (2001). *Relative deprivation: Specification, development, and integration.* Cambridge: Cambridge University Press.

Wear, R. (2008). Permanent populism: The Howard government 1996–2007. *Australian Journal of Political Science, 43*(4), 617–634.

Weiner, B. (1985). An attributional theory of achievement motivation and emotion. *Journal of Personality and Social Psychology, 92*, 548–573.

Wiepking, P., & Breeze, B. (2012). Feeling poor, acting stingy: The effect of money perceptions on charitable giving. *International Journal of Nonprofit and Voluntary Sector Marketing, 17*, 13–24.

Wilkinson, R. G., & Pickett, K. (2009). *The spirit level: Why more equal societies almost always do better*. London: Allen Lane.

Wilson, R., & Hainsworth, P. (2012). *Far-right parties and discourse in Europe: A challenge for our times*. European Network Against Racism, ENAR March 2012.

Wong, R. Y., & Hong, Y. (2005). Dynamic influences of culture on cooperation in the prisoner's dilemma. *Psychological Science, 16*, 429–434.

Wright, S. C., Taylor, D. M., & Moghaddam, F. M. (1990). Responding to membership in a disadvantaged group: From acceptance to collective protest. *Journal of Personality and Social Psychology, 58*, 994–1003.

Young, M. (1958). *The rise of the meritocracy*. London: Thames & Hudson.

Index

Aaker, J., 99
Adorno, Theodor, 38n.9
affluence. *See also* prosperity
  boundary impermeability perspective and, 148
  boundary permeability and, 140–143
  charitable giving and, 94–99
  European countries support for anti-immigration parties and, 72–73
  fear of poverty with, 157–160
  hostility towards minorities and, 84–85
  individual charitable giving and, 97–99
  national differences in, 86–92
  social identity theory and, 136–137
  V-curve hypothesis and shadow-side of, 109–115
affluence, tolerance and permissiveness linked to (Hypothesis 1b)
  absence of research on, 16, 43–44
  anti-immigrant attitudes and, 53–55
  basic assumptions in, 7–10, 21
  focus of, 123–124
  geographic variations and, 63–64
  key indicators for, 56–58
  limitations of, 58–59
  national, regional, and local trends in, 67–73
  research concerning, 13–16, 55–58
  support for, 124–125
African Americans, effects of recession for, 3–6
Age of Revolutions, Tilly's theory of, 36
aggression
  criminologist's pathologization of, 33–35
  economic triggers for, 37–40
  frustration-aggression research on, 44–46

social identity theory and, 130–132
Aid Under Pressure: Support for Development Assistance in a Global Economic Downturn, 91–92
Akutsu, S., 99
allocation matrix, in minimal group studies, 132–134
Altemeyer, R., 39n.10
American Revolutionary War, 24n.1
Annual Gross Income (AGI), charitable giving as percentage of, 94–99
anti-foreigner sentiment index, mean values for European countries, 51–55
anti-immigration attitudes. *See also* populist anti-immigrant parties
  in Bimboola study, 111–115
  class politics and education levels and, 55–58
  competition and, 50–55
  distribution of benefits narrative and, 181–185
  economic conditions, xiii–xiv, 3–6
  economic crises and absence of, 11–13
  electoral success of anti-immigrant parties and, 65–66
  geographic variations in, 63–64
  hostile norms and, 164–167
  income levels and, 111–115, 117–119, 158
  key predictors of, 56–58
  limits of hypotheses on, 58–59
  national differences, in European countries, 56–58
  poverty and, 6–7
  prosperity and surge in, 10–16
  relative gratification theory and, 107–109

210